The Boy With
the Topknot

*A Memoir of Love, Secrets and
Lies in Wolverhampton*

SATHNAM SANGHERA

PENGUIN BOOKS

PENGUIN BOOKS
THE BOY WITH THE TOPKNOT

'This is not just another misery memoir, or provincial coming-of-age story. It is a meditation on mental illness and cultural difference, told with enormous compassion and the most unexpected dry wit. The climax had me on the edge of my seat. What a painful and joyous voyage of discovery Sathnam Sanghera has been on in the last few years, and how perfectly he recreates it for us!' Jonathan Coe

'As charming as it is wrenching, as funny as it is haunting, this book is wonderfully unlike any other' Andrea Ashworth

'Gripping and entertaining, horrifying and tender . . . The bravery with which the author relates events that most other families would seek to hide means that his book throbs with honesty, frustration and pathos' Hardeep Singh Kohli, *The Times*

'As the facts emerge, Sanghera's speedy wit gives way to bursts of anger and anguish . . . It is testament to the emotional connection he forges with the reader that we end up caring deeply' Meg Rosoff, *Guardian*

'An absorbing, ongoing drama, played out on the page . . . full of gentle, hyperbolic wit . . . Could not be more enjoyable, engaging or moving' Kate Kellaway, *Observer*

'Funny and revealing . . . warm, witty, neurotic, self-deprecating . . . In bearing witness to his family's experience, Sanghera has brought to us rare news of working-class life, of living with mental illness and of overwhelming filial love . . . How far he's come, you think, against such odds, and you want to punch the air and cry at the same time' Lynsey Hanley, *Sunday Times*

'A touching, revealing account of two worlds – Sikh and English, and the Midlands of the Eighties – as well as an intimate portrait of life lived with mental illness' Andrew O'Neill, *Daily Express*

'Instead of simply telling his parents' story, Sanghera charts the various emotional processes involved in its telling. It digs into some dark areas, but this is a hugely enjoyable book' Natasha Tripney, *New Statesman*

'A rigorous and thoroughly intelligent rebooting of the misery memoir that recalls Dave Eggers' *A Heartbreaking Work of Staggering Genius* and deserves to do as well' *Time Out*

'Witty, poignant and affectionately rude about inner-city Wolverhampton, this book confronts some of the key issues about multicultural Britain while acting as a painful and touching family memoir'
Martin Warrilow, *Birmingham Post*

'An incredibly moving memoir and a compelling read . . . This funny, heartfelt memoir reveals the distressing history of Sanghera's family while celebrating the love that kept them together' *Marie Claire*

'Sanghera must be a time lord – or, at the very least, a time tailor – so seamlessly does he weave together disparate strands of his life from different decades . . . There is no shred of misery or self-pity in this story, rather an endearing and intelligent humour which provokes honest laughter and absolute respect' Imran Ahmad, *Daily Mail*

'Holding up his own human failings, Sanghera strives to overcome the chasm between his urban, modern life and the cloistered, uneducated life of his parents. His warm, largely happy memories of sibling fun, George Michael posters and first kisses shine through, while his witty take on Wolverhampton from 1970 to today is priceless' Zena Alkayat, *Metro*

'The most moving debut we've read in ages' *Elle*

'Marvellous' Jackie Wullschlager, *Financial Times*

'Like some of the very best books, it defies easy categorization . . . I'd recommend it to absolutely anybody – it's charming and illuminating'
Alice O'Keeffe, *The Bookseller*

ABOUT THE AUTHOR

Born in the West Midlands in 1976, Sathnam Sanghera attended Wolverhampton Grammar School and graduated from Christ's College, Cambridge with a first class degree in English Literature. He joined the *Financial Times* in 1998, and worked as its chief feature writer and a weekly columnist, before moving to *The Times* in 2007. Published in hardback as *If You Don't Know Me By Now*, *The Boy With the Topknot* was shortlisted for the Costa Biography Award 2008. He lives in London.

For my family

'Out of darkness cometh light'

Wolverhampton motto

Contents

Author's note: This is a true story, but I have altered some names and other details to protect the privacy and conceal the identities of certain individuals.

1. Life of Surprises

Drinking alone needn't necessarily be a lowering experience. If you're in the right place, say Paris or New York, in the right bar, somewhere with pavement tables or window seats, and in the right frame of mind – having just made a couple of billion from shorting the US dollar, for instance – I imagine it could be quite pleasant kicking back with a whisky sour, watching those less fortunate than yourself (i.e. everyone) shuffle past as you sit snug and smug in your tailored Gucci suit.

But sipping neat vodka smuggled into your mum's house in a promotional Fitness First rucksack, dressed in a lumberjack shirt that cost £7.99 fifteen years ago, and peering out at a double-glazed view of Wolverhampton, a town which was once the beating heart of Britain's Industrial Revolution but whose only claim to fame now is that it is home to the headquarters of Poundland, 'the UK's largest £1 retailer', isn't so cheerful.

This isn't where I pictured myself as a thirty-year-old. But then very little of what has happened recently was planned, and I certainly didn't expect to do what I'm going to do next. You see, after a few more weeks behind this Argos flatpack desk, and a few more bottles of this Asda own-brand vodka, I'm going to type up a letter I've been drafting, in one way or another, for half a lifetime. When I'm done, I'm going to send it to someone in India who, for an almost unethically small fee, will translate it into a language I can speak and understand but cannot read or write, and when he is done, I'm going to get him to read it out over the phone. Finally, if satisfied with the diction and the tone, I will hand it over to the person I love more than any other and let the contents break her heart . . .

Perhaps the biggest surprise in all of this is the sense of resolution. I always thought that when it came to the crunch, at the moment of assassination, I would, as I always seem to at critical moments, consider the consequences and flounder. But while there is a powerful urge to run away, there is a stronger determination not to let yet another opportunity for a better life drift by. And, unless I'm very much mistaken, this shortness of breath, this tightness in my chest, isn't due just to anxiety, but to excitement also. Excitement borne from the knowledge that this is necessary and I am right.

★

Things were very different six years ago, when I was twenty-four. I worked for a newspaper then, a job in the media, writing about the media; I had a girlfriend – let's call her Laura, and let's say she was a TV producer – and I didn't split my time between London and my parents' home in Wolverhampton as I do now. In those days, coming to the West Midlands was a monthly, sometimes fortnightly occurrence. And the weekend it all began, I was due to come to see my parents after a guilty gap of nine weeks.

If memory serves, on the Friday night before I set off there was a dinner party at Laura's flat in north London. All the guests, like us, worked in the media, the menu consisted of recipes from Jamie Oliver's *The Naked Chef*, and discussion ranged from complaints about Tony Blair's religiosity, to complaints about the celebrities we'd respectively met, to extended moaning about how we wanted to quit our lousy highly paid jobs, which allowed us to meet our heroes, wangle backstage tickets and hold the high and mighty to account, in favour of less stressful, more meaningful lives as bricklayers in the Outer Hebrides.

Throughout, I stayed true to three fundamental tenets of middle-class London life: never confess to religiosity (you may as well confess to paedophilia); never admit to being impressed by a celebrity you've met (you may as well confess to paedophilia); and always moan about your job (it seems the price of a flash job in your twenties is self-loathing). In practice this meant suppressing the fact that there was once a time when I prayed for an hour every day, concealing the fact that I'd entered the number of every celebrity I'd ever interviewed into my mobile phone, and ignoring the voice of the Indian immigrant in my head which, during the Hebridean bricklaying fantasies, kept on muttering: *there's a lot to be said for an office job and an opportunity to contribute to a money purchase pension scheme.*

The evening ended with a spilt glass of red, a group rendition of Elton John's 'Rocket Man' and the embittered charity worker living upstairs asking whether we knew what time it was. It was 3 a.m. Laura and I were in bed soon afterwards. And, five hours later, I was reaching blindly for her Jacob Jensen alarm clock, dragging myself out of her John Lewis bed and brushing the cobwebs from my teeth with her Paul Smith toothbrush.

I fixed myself a breakfast of muesli and unconcentrated orange juice and, on hearing deathly murmurings drifting from the bedroom, went in to say goodbye.

'You okay?' She had a sweet way of sleeping curled up in the middle of mattresses.

'Feel. Sick.'

'You drank two bottles of wine.'

'Two?' I kissed her on her forehead and passed the Evian from her bedside cabinet. 'Why didn't you stop me?' She pressed the plastic bottle against the side of her face, as if trying to ease bruising.

'I've got to go.'

'Eugh.'

'Drink lots of water.'

'What if I die?'

'Drink lots of water.'

'How come you're okay?'

'Water, my dear.'

She put a pillow over her head and groaned: 'Could you leave a bucket next to the bed?'

Leaving the flat, I headed off to what I called, with the compulsory irony of my trade, 'the Paki shop', where I picked up an edition of the national newspaper I worked on, to check whether they had run an interview I'd conducted with a prominent media personality. This being London, I made no attempt at small talk with the newsagent as I did so, and he knew better than to attempt banter in return, and on the way to the Tube station I proceeded not to give the time of day to: the embittered charity worker from upstairs, who was walking down the street in Birkenstocks, having most likely spent the morning washing lepers or helping violent lunatics reintegrate into the local community; the spaced-out German banker whom I'd never spoken to and who lived below Laura; the teenager whom I'd never spoken to and who lived with the Spanish architects next door to Laura; and the postman I had down as a madman because he was forever smiling and trying to wish people a 'good morning'.

I fell asleep on the Tube halfway through my own article, woke up at Euston, and caught an overland train, on which I surrendered to my delayed hangover, waking up two hours later to the sight of rusty corrugated roofs and polluted land dissected by lines of poisoned, trolley-strewn canalways. Wolverhampton. I disembarked feeling even worse than Laura had looked, and felt worse still as I approached the taxi rank and remembered I was related to at least a third of the cabbies in Wolverhampton.

This may not, on the face of it, sound like a problem. But it plays havoc with Punjabi etiquette: the cabbie, on seeing you are a relative, will feel honour-bound not to charge you; but you, knowing the cabbie will have been queuing for some time for a lucrative fare, will feel honour-bound to insist he takes payment. Like so many social interactions in the Sikh community, the encounter will end in a kind of wrestling match, with one person trying to thrust money on the other, the other refusing to accept, and both people ending up offended and possibly physically bruised by the other's persistence.

That afternoon, with my head throbbing, I didn't have the stamina for such a showdown so ended up hovering around the taxi rank, variously pretending I was waiting for someone, pretending I was taking vital phone calls, and trying to catch glimpses of drivers' faces without actually catching their eye, until I was certain my driver wasn't an uncle or a brother-in-law. He was, however, inevitably, a member of the world's fifth largest organized religion. Couldn't have been any more Sikh, in fact: pictures of all ten gurus sellotaped on to the dashboard; incense sticks dangling out of air vents; a pair of miniature boxing gloves bearing the Sikh *khanda* hanging from the driving mirror. Moreover, his turban was Khalistan orange, suggesting militancy. And if he was anything like my militant Sikh relatives who also drove taxis for a living, there was a possibility he was carrying a 'ceremonial' sword under his seat for protection, though I tried not to think about this as we pulled away, instead just tried to wallow in the happy fact that he barely grunted in acknowledgement when I announced my destination. Sweet silence . . .

. . . until the Ring Road, when he was suddenly overwhelmed by the loneliness of the short distance cab driver and the intercom sign flickered into life.

'SO WHERE YOU FROM THEN?'

I dread this question in London cabs because it usually means me replying: 'Wolverhampton' . . . and the London cabbie responding with: 'Ha. I mean, where are you from *originally*?'

I will then say: 'I'm *originally* from Wolverhampton.'

The cabbie will say: '—'

I will then say: 'You want to know which country *my parents* are from?'

The cabbie (usually pretty uninterested by now) will say: 'Yeah.'

'They are from the Punjab, in north India.'

'When did they come here?'

'Erm . . . dunno.'

'Why did they come here?'

'Dunno.'

The remainder of the journey invariably passing in awkward silence.

While the categories and vocabulary differ in Wolverhampton,

I dread the conversation for the same reason: because the cabbie's aim is to pigeonhole and classify.

'I'M FROM LONDON,' I shouted back in bad Punjabi.

'*Ki?*'

I repeated myself, louder, more slowly, but in English.

'You don't speak Punjabi then?' he asked in Punjabi.

'*Hahnji*, I do,' I said in bad Punjabi. 'Just out of practice.'

The rear-view mirror framed only one eye, but I could tell his glare was one of disdain. 'So where you from originally?' he continued in Punjabi, regardless.

'I'm originally from Wolverhampton,' I said in bad Punjabi.

'I mean . . . which *pind*? Your father's village?'

I really should have known the answer to the question. The nature of Sikh migration from the Punjab into Britain – some villages were transposed, complete with their broiling caste strife, en masse – means I grew up hearing names of villages being bandied about. I even spent a fortnight at my father's home in India during one of my university holidays. But so intense was my boredom during this trip – my extended family's interest in me limited to asking how much I might earn on graduation, when I was going to get married and, in the case of my male cousins, whether English girls were easy – that I'd developed a mental block on the name.

'Can't remember,' I admitted eventually, in bad Punjabi.

The cabbie rolled his eyes. At least, he rolled the one eye I could see.

'I think my father's village is somewhere near Jalandhar,' I added, realizing as soon as I'd uttered the words that they were as helpful as saying a town was 'somewhere in the vicinity of London'.

The end of the cabbie's moustache twitched. I knew what he was thinking: *idiot* bilayati*, doesn't know anything about his own culture*. I glowered back in a way that intended to convey: *you're in England now, make some kind of effort to learn the language of your new home* – before developing a sudden and keen interest in the view from the window. We were travelling down from the town centre to my parents' suburb in the south of the town via the

6

Dudley Road, a corridor lined with Indian doctors' surgeries, Indian sweet shops, two Sikh temples – one for the Jat (farmer) caste I belong to, the other for those of the Chamar caste – Indian supermarkets, Indian barber shops, Indian insurance brokers and Indian jewellery shops. You could, if you lived here, never deal with anyone who wasn't Indian. And my parents rarely do.

Eventually, having driven past an uncle's house, around the corner from my parents', and an aunt's house, just up the road from my parents', we pulled up outside the semi-detached I spent my teens in. The fare came to £5.90 and I passed a tenner through the passenger window: 'Make that £6.50, mate.'

He repeated the amount back to me in Punjabi, in an incredulous tone. *'Sade chhe pornd?'*

For a moment I couldn't figure out why he was scowling. Was it that I was addressing him in English? Or had the unnecessary and admittedly moronic 'mate' proved grating? It's not a word I normally use, but it springs from nowhere when I talk to men from lower socio-economic groups. Plumbers, builders, all C2DEs get it, which is ironic as I hardly have any mates in these professions at all. But eventually the penny dropped. He was cross because he thought I was asking for £6.50 *in change*. I'd forgotten people don't tip in the West Midlands.

'Nai, nai,' I said, cringing. 'I mean *take* £6.50. I'm giving you a sixty pence tip. You know . . .' For some reason I had switched back to English, albeit with an Indian accent '. . . EXTRA. BONUS. THANK YOU.'

What seemed reasonable in a mental calculation sounded derisory uttered out loud. He took the money, flipped the change back in my direction without taking the tip, and screeched off with the closest thing you can get to wheelspin in a 2.4-litre diesel-engined TXII.

★

In the hallway, there was the familiar aroma of chopped onion and cardamom and an unfamiliar hush. I've got used to it recently, but the quietness would often take me by surprise in those days. A part of me expected it to be like it was when I was a teenager: my brother playing R. Kelly in his room; my two sisters squabbling in their bedroom; Mum crashing pans in the kitchen; Dad watching TV in the living room. But standing there, my eyes gradually becoming accustomed to the light, all I could hear was a tape recorder murmuring prayers in the kitchen, and four plastic fish bopping around epileptically in the made-in-China twenty-inch-tall aqua lamp placed on the phone stand. Opposite the lamp – probably a present from one of my market-trading relatives – hung a framed and flashing picture of the Golden Temple, and at my feet lay a set of bathroom weighing scales and two ancient brown suitcases, a reminder of the reason for this particular visit home: my parents were heading off on one of their biennial trips to India.

Needless to say, this was no impulse trip. Like most Punjabis, my parents don't really do spontaneity. Even a picnic in the park requires several hours' preparation: an hour to make the necessary dal and samosas; half an hour to pack the necessary dal and samosas into Tupperware boxes; and an additional hour or so for complaining about ailments (my mother's favourite pastime) and watching *BBC Parliament* (my father's favourite). For them, the relationship between the distance due to be travelled and the preparation required is exponentially proportional – a return journey to the Subcontinent being planned with the kind of precision and detail that NASA usually reserves for launching a space shuttle, the intention to travel to India being announced at least twelve months before anyone gets near a plane. The brown suitcases had been half-packed when I'd last visited.

I swayed on the spot, psyching myself up for what was to come: the switch from West to East, South to North, English to Punjabi, rationality to superstition, smoked almonds to salted peanuts . . .

'Mum?' I said it with a slight Indian accent. 'Dedi? *Main aa gaya.*'

Dad appeared first. Slouched and barefoot, he walked up to

me slowly, shook my hand, patted me on the back and returned soundlessly to his armchair in the living room. Next, Mum came out of the kitchen smiling, looking broad in a *chuni*, a scarf and a shawl, and gave me a suffocating hug. She then took me to a sideboard in the kitchen, where she had laid out, waiting for me, a large cauldron full of birdseed, a tin of spinach, a packet of kidney beans, and a tin of plum tomatoes. First, I was instructed to wash my hands and run them through the birdseed. Then I was told to touch, in specific order, the packaged foodstuffs. Finally, she fetched a single large red chilli from the larder, squeezed it between her fingers, and, after circling it around my head five times, set it alight on the gas stove.

Centuries of superstition have probably gone into each element of this ritual, none of which I understand fully, but the birdseed would subsequently be scattered in the local park, an act of inter-species charity designed to bring luck; the spinach, kidney beans and plum tomatoes would be donated to the temple – again, to bring luck; while the burning of the chilli was meant to get rid of '*nazar*', a concept loosely translating as 'evil eye', which you can supposedly contract if you are admired in any way. Other Indians choose to ward it off by hanging fresh green chillies over doorways or wearing anti-evil-eye bracelets.

While the chilli snapped and crackled, my mother, contrary to her nature, didn't utter a single word, and as she stood with her hands held up in prayer, I padded off to the living room. The wall dividing the two downstairs rooms has now been knocked through, and the main room is wide and airy and filled with large sofas. But then it was cramped, with a line of chairs bought in an office clearance sale against one wall and a short settee opposite the TV, which itself stood next to a large set of double-glazed patio doors offering a view of the expansive lawn. Dad was dozing on the settee behind a curtain drawn to protect him from the midday sun. I sat down next to him, removed the remote from his hand, and flicked away from the Welsh Assembly coverage he had been watching until I found a music programme.

Before I'd even had time to begin despairing at the state of modern pop, Mum had produced a lunch consisting of aubergine curry, lentil curry, mango pickle, chapattis, Indian salad, concentrated orange juice, and a Penguin bar. She watched as I began to eat and halfway through the first chapatti asked how many more I would like. I said one, knowing she would give me at least two more than I asked for, and she went into the kitchen and came back with three, knowing that I would have asked for two fewer than I actually wanted. As I ate, she attempted to increase the number of chapattis that ended up in my belly ('You're fading away!') by taking some away while I was part-way through them ('That one's gone cold,' 'Oh dear, forgot to smear butter on that one') – until the sum of the fractions amounted to seven chapattis.

Thus weakened, and unable to move from the pink sofa because of the bolus dilating my intestine, I listened as Mum began listing her latest maladies (a new crick in her neck, a throb in her knee), bringing me up to date with what she had been up to (a combination of visits to the temple and looking after the adored grandchildren), handing over the day's mail for translation into Punjabi (a letter from the dentist, a leaflet from the Jehovah's Witnesses), and asking whether I'd called or liked any of the nice Sikh girls whose telephone numbers had been sent to me in recent months.

On receiving the inevitable 'Not really,' she sighed long-sufferingly, stated once again that any girl would do, as long as she was the right religion, right caste, right age, right skin colour, right height, right profession and displayed the traditional skills of cooking, knitting and sweeping, and then launched into one of her monologues. This, among other things, informed me that my cousin Harjit was up on an assault charge ('That boy will never learn, but he says the police hit him first'), my cousin Sukhjit had bought a house next to his parents ('Such a good boy, *looking after his parents*'), my cousin Daljit had been arrested for brandishing a sword in a petrol station ('You'd think a taxi driver would know that petrol stations have cameras'), an uncle on Dad's side of the family was having a bypass ('Thank God my heart is one of the few bits of me that still works'), a girl at the end of the road had been spotted talking to a boy on the Dudley Road ('No shame, those girls, no shame'), the white woman down the road was being divorced by her husband ('No sense of family, those *goras*, no sense of family'), my cousin Hardip had secured a £70,000-a-year job after graduating with an accountancy degree ('Why couldn't you've studied something useful?'), the council had put up signs saying people couldn't feed pigeons in the park any more ('What harm do a few seeds do? They're God's creatures'), my cousin Jasbir in India had been injured under the hooves of a bullock ('He may have been drunk'), and a boy who had been in my class at primary school had got married to a nice simple village girl from India ('Will I live to see your children?') . . .

The monologue went on and on and on, through the remainder of the music programme, through the BBC News national bulletin, as I went upstairs to unpack, even as I went to the toilet.

'. . . I'll call you every day when we're away . . .'

'Mum, I'm on the toilet.'

'. . . make sure you keep your phone on . . .'

'Mum, I'm on the toilet.'

'. . . otherwise, your father and I, we'll worry . . .'

'MUM. I AM ON THE TOILET.'

Thankfully distraction arrived in the form of my three elder siblings, who, like me, were visiting, as custom and duty dictated, to wish my parents well on their trip to India. They came in age order, beginning with my eldest sister Narinder, known as Puli, followed by my elder sister Balbinder, known as Bindi, and my elder brother Jasmail, known as Rajah. My Punjabi isn't great, but I'm proficient enough to suspect my siblings haven't been lucky with their nicknames: 'Puli' means 'cutie' or 'slightly dim', depending on who you ask; 'Bindi' seems to be the word used to describe the mark that some Indian women wear between their eyebrows, and okra; and while 'Rajah' rather snazzily means 'King', it's old-fashioned and my brother is forever trying to rebrand himself.

I'm free of a nickname, but then I'm the family freak in most respects. My siblings got jobs straight after school and settled in Wolverhampton, whereas I left the town for university as soon as I could and never came back. My siblings were all married to spouses of the correct race, religion and caste by the age of twenty-one, whereas I, at twenty-four, was secretly dating someone of the wrong race and religion and of no caste whatsoever. And while they had two children apiece, I had . . . well, a rather large record collection, the highlight of which was every track ever recorded by George Michael.

On arriving, Puli, a housewife, left her two kids and market-trader husband downstairs in the living room and went upstairs for a lie down. Bindi, also a housewife, left her taxi-driving husband and two kids downstairs in the living room and went to fix some food in the kitchen. My brother's wife, Ruky, who was then working as a bank cashier but is now a driving instructor, joined Bindi, while Rajah, a middle manager, took a seat with his two kids downstairs and did what he always does best: looked way too good for his age. My brother has always been a hand-some boy, but with the man-hours he puts in at the gym, and with the rest of us disintegrating at a great pace, the gap seems to be growing. Seeing him at home is sometimes like watching Brad Pitt making a cameo in *EastEnders*.

The house had suddenly gone from being too quiet to being

too noisy, with kids screaming and bouncing on the sofas and adults bellowing across the room at and over each other,* reminding me that while I found the quietness eerie, I preferred it to the mayhem I grew up in. When the noise reached such a pitch that I thought my hangover headache was going to turn into an aneurism, various Indian neighbours I hadn't seen in ages, and in some cases had never seen before at all, started popping over with messages and parcels for their loved ones in the Punjab, the concepts of British Telecom and the Royal Mail evidently having eluded them during their decades of British residency. And then, when I thought the aneurism was going to morph into something even more catastrophic, various aunts and uncles started popping round too, to make last-minute deputations to my mother regarding an ongoing family dispute over inherited farmland in India – a dispute which seemed to have been raging longer than the Middle East crisis.

Not that my parents seemed bothered: Mum multitasked calmly at one end of the living room, simultaneously dealing with visitors' queries, complaining about her arthritis, and feeding two or three children; while Dad monotasked at the other end, blankly watching the Bollywood video channel that my brother had tuned into. Somewhere in the middle, I attempted to laugh off suggestions that my hairstyle and jumper were 'gay', tried to ignore the wild laughter that erupted whenever I uttered a word of Punjabi, resisted suggestions from various male visitors that we go and

* If we are to believe Lieutenant-Colonel Malcolm, writing in 1812 after spending several years in the Punjab with the British army, this is something of a racial trait. In his inadvertently entertaining 'Sketch of the Sikhs: A Singular Nation', Malcolm complains that Sikhs are 'bold and rather rough in their address; which appears more to a stranger from their invariably speaking in a loud tone . . .' In a note, he adds: 'Talking aloud is so habitual to a Sikh, that he bawls a secret in your ear. It has often occurred to me, that they have acquired it from living in a country where internal disputes have so completely destroyed confidence, that they can only carry on conversation with each other at a distance: but it is fairer, perhaps, to impute this boisterous and rude habit to their living almost constantly in a camp, in which the voice certainly loses that nice modulated tone which distinguishes the more polished inhabitants of cities.'

watch a blockbuster opening at the local multiplex or for a few drinks at the Glassy Inn down the road, and fielded a barrage of massively uninformed questions about my job ('So you write things and they appear on telly?') and my religious habits ('You still go to the *gurdwara* every Sunday?').

Throughout, I obeyed the three fundamental tenets of my Sikh household: never confess to religious doubt (you may as well confess to paedophilia); never get annoyed with repeatedly explaining what you do for a living (unless you're a doctor or an IT consultant, they won't understand); and never admit to a male relative that you don't want a drink.* In practice this meant omitting to mention that I'd never attended a *gurdwara* in London, that I'd already seen the film in question at a media preview, and ignoring the voice of the Londoner in my head saying: '*The only white wine they serve at the Glassy Inn is a Chardonnay.*'

There's only so much you can take, though, and when my mobile rang, and I saw that it was Laura, I instinctively walked out of the room, into the kitchen and out into the garden. Taking phone calls surreptitiously wasn't the only thing I did to ensure the relationship was kept secret. The concealing also involved: never doing anything with Laura within a 100-mile vicinity of the West Midlands; going on arranged marriage meetings to keep up the pretence that I was looking for a good Indian wife; only giving my family my mobile number, so I could pretend to be at home when I wasn't; keeping a flat of my own even though I was more or less living with Laura (just in case the family visited); and never introducing any of my family to any of my friends or vice versa.

It turned out she was calling to tell me: (i) she had thrown up three times; (ii) she was feeling better now; (iii) she was watching *A Room with a View* for the thirtieth time; and (iv) she wished I was there with her. I wished I was there with her too, even more so when I returned to the mayhem of the house. Indeed, unable to face the living room, I decided to have some quiet time in

---

* The opposite rule applies with female relatives.

the front room, occupying myself by making sure Mum and Dad's luggage met the stipulations of Uzbekistan Airways, the airline they had chosen to risk their lives with.

This was a simple task, complicated only by the fact that while Uzbekistan Airways stipulated that the packed suitcases shouldn't weigh more than 20kg each, for some reason – perhaps it can be traced back to Partition, when many Punjabis were forced to pack everything they owned and flee for their lives – Mum wanted to take the collective belongings of Wolverhampton's 18,000 Sikh residents with her. I plonked her battered suitcase – its age evident from the blue and white Pan Am stickers plastered down the sides – on to the scales, and the needle lurched to an obese 35kg.

Groaning, I re-entered the chaos of the living room to inform her. She was still sitting serenely amid the bedlam, engaged in conversation on the sofa with an auntie I didn't recognize. They appeared to be talking at cross-purposes: auntie-I-didn't-recognize conveying a complex and convoluted message she wanted delivered to the daughter of her great-uncle's second cousin, who lived in a village just outside Jalandhar; my mum describing at length a new pain in her left shoulder. I shouted over the din and waited for a reaction. Some time later – Mum's monologues are like ocean liners, they require time to change direction – she was peering at the scales over the rims of her large owl spectacles.

Standing next to me, she seemed smaller than ever before. Mum has always complained of being old and tired, was doing so when I was four and she was thirty, but she was beginning to look it. I felt a pang of protectiveness, warm feelings blotted out with the ink of irritation when she defended her overpacking with a shrug and the remark: 'But it's the first time we're going to India in two years!' After a pause, she added: 'Besides, there are two of us travelling, *hunna.*'

I bit my tongue. I lose my temper so easily with my family, and can't decide whether this is because my family are simply exasperating, or whether it is because I speak in Punjabi to them and my Punjabi skills are so poor that I get frustrated at my inability to express myself. * Trying to remember how to breathe, I placed my father's suitcase on the scales. Fifteen kilos. Underweight. Typical, I thought. It's astonishing how little my father owns – in the whole house, the only thing he uses for himself is one cupboard, which rarely contains more than a few jackets, trousers and jumpers. He owns no records, no books, no photos, no documents, no mementos. Anyone sifting through his things would think he didn't exist. And sometimes it is like he doesn't exist: while at five foot ten and fifteen and a half stone there's a lot of him to see, he pads around the house as soundlessly as a cat; he is as spare in his remarks as a monk, and more often than we'd probably admit, we forget he is there.

'Mum, even if you're allowed to combine what you take, which I doubt you are, together you're still ten kilos over.'

'Ten kilos?' I could make out the shape of the ceremonial dagger under her Indian suit. 'What's that? A few bags of sugar.'

I explained that ten kilos was quite a lot actually and that the Uzbeks weren't renowned for their happy-go-lucky attitude. Then I unzipped the case. The contents made me gasp, like I did when I flipped open the back of my first watch. It was hard to believe that so much could have been packed into such a small space. Among the expected clothes and toothbrushes and prayer books and documents, I could see two coconuts, a box of Typhoo teabags, a box of Rice Krispies, a pair of my old Prada trainers, three prayer books, six unsewn women's suits and six men's shirts still packed in cellophane.

* Or it could be that people have different personalities when speaking in different languages. The phenomenon was recently investigated by a psychology doctoral student at the University of Texas at Austin, who conducted a study monitoring the character traits of 225 Spanish/English bilingual subjects in both the US and Mexico as they responded to questions presented in the two languages. According to *Scientific American Mind* (June/July 2006), she found that when using English, the bilinguals were more extroverted, agreeable and conscientious than when using Spanish. Her conclusion was that people who speak two languages 'feel like a different person depending on which language they are speaking'.

My initial impulse was to ask how on earth my Prada trainers had ended up in the case, but as I could guess why – Mum had decided they'd make a good gift for my cousins in India – and as I know the importance of choosing which battles to pick with my mother, I instead raised the issue of the cellophaned shirts. I recognized them as the currency of Punjabi hospitality. Every time a Punjabi Sikh visits any relative on any special occasion, the host is obliged to give the visitor one of these shirts, plus a woman's suit, plus some cash. The woman's suit is generally unsewn – a section of material out of which a salwar kameez can be made. The amount of cash, for some superstitious reason, is usually £21. Meanwhile, the shirt generally has two characteristics: it is wrapped in plastic and is utterly unwearable. The only thing a recipient can do with such a garment, with its bizarre combination of browns and greys, stripes and pointy collars, is to pass it on as a gift to another relative. By the look of these shirts, they had been in circulation since 1973.

'Mum.' I tried to speak evenly and calmly. '*Why?*'

'I can't visit people empty-handed, can I?'

'But, look . . .' I pointed at a sticker on one of the shirts, and, struggling with my tone and my Punjabi vocabulary, continued. 'Made. In. India. This is like taking *retah* to the . . . what's the word? . . . in English they call it the desert. *Maruthal?* Yes. Like taking *retah* to the *maruthal*. They'd be cheaper to buy out there. Especially if you factor in what you'll have to pay for taking them, because you know you'll be charged for the extra weight . . .'

The mention of a possible fine did the trick. After all, this is the woman who will walk a mile to save 50 pence on a 10kg bag of onions, who will carry the 10kg bag of onions home on a bus and on foot rather than pay for a taxi, who considers carrier bags an extravagance. She allowed me to pluck the shirts and women's suits from the case, but clutched her chest as I did so, as if each abandoned item was a child she was having to give up for adoption. There followed lengthy negotiations over other items, but eventually the job was almost done and I was left to trim off the final few kilos, with the warning: 'But leave the coconuts – *okay*?'

With Mum gone, my editing became more brutal. Two of the three prayer books went. The teabags and Rice Krispies went. But then, underneath the cereal boxes, I came across something more surreal than even the coconuts: two 2kg boxes of East End Vegetable Margarine – 'made with 100% vegetable oil, no animal fat'. Incredible. Mum had allocated a fifth of her allotted luggage weight, on her flight from Birmingham to Amritsar with a five-hour stop in the horrific-sounding metropolis of Tashkent, to . . . margarine.

I laughed, made a mental note to tell Laura about it later, and tried to think of a possible explanation. Maybe she was planning to make chapattis along the journey to my father's village? Perhaps there was some superstition related to margarine? I flicked through my mental database of Punjabi folklore.

It was good luck to mutter '*Waheguru*' before you embarked on any task.

It was bad luck to wash your hair on a Saturday or a Tuesday.

It was bad luck to look at the moon.

It was bad luck to sneeze when setting off on a journey (a nightmare when you have allergies, like I do).

It was bad luck to step on money.

It was bad luck to leave one shoe resting on another.

It was bad luck to point your feet at a picture of a guru or a prayer book.

It was bad luck to spill milk.

It was good luck to scoop up the placenta of a cat that had just given birth.

It was bad luck for a nephew or niece to be in the same room as an uncle from their mother's side of the family in a thunder-storm.

No. I couldn't remember anything margarine-related . . .

But picking out the boxes with the intention of storming into the living room and remonstrating, I found they were lighter than

I'd expected. They rattled too. Phew. Mum was using the boxes as containers. She hadn't lost the plot completely. I opened one and found it contained medication: Mum's herbal pills for her migraines; non-herbal pills for her arthritis; antidepressants; vitamin supplements; paracetamol. The second one was heavier, and contained five boxes of tablets. The brands emblazoned across them meant nothing to me. But the name on them did. Jagjit Singh. Dad.

I thought this peculiar because my father is rarely ill. He has diabetes, but the condition is managed well. I had a fuzzy memory of him once being prescribed sleeping pills. But I thought that was a temporary thing. Indeed, I couldn't remember a single time that he'd complained of feeling sick. Couldn't recall him ever having a lie down during the day, for that matter. Ferreting around the box for a clue, I found an envelope addressed 'TO WHOM IT MAY CONCERN'. I was a 'to whom it concerned', so I opened it. It was a note from Dad's GP, Dr Dutta.

This patient has been registered on my panel since 1969 and was re-registered in 1993. In fact, he is known to me from 1969. He suffers from paranoid schizophrenia. (He is often confused and cannot communicate facts and his wife has to assist him.) He is on regular treatment of injection and tablets (which he often forgets), and his wife has to keep an eye on his medication. He also suffers from diabetes for which he is having regular check-ups and treatment. He is visiting his family in India and he is going for a short visit.

Blinking at the words, I thought: fuck. *Schizophrenia*.
And then: *Christ*. That's what my sister Puli must have too.

2. Vertigo

So I didn't realize my father and eldest sister suffered from schizophrenia until my mid-twenties; I didn't start confronting what this meant until my late twenties; and it is only now, at thirty, that I feel the need to talk about it. How did this happen? How can someone grow up with two members of their family suffering from a severe mental illness, the most severe mental illness around, without realizing it? How can someone discover this fact and then not try to find out more for another five years?

If the following attempt at an explanation reads like a set of flatpack assembly instructions it is because there's something about my family – maybe it's the sheer number of characters, or the melodramatic nature of Indian family life, or the havoc schizophrenia causes in families – that makes talking about it come out in the form of lists. I'm still not entirely sure why I was so ignorant and then chose to remain ignorant, but at the moment it seems that the reasons included:

1. Cluelessness. I'm not talking about everyday cluelessness here – the kind that leads people to believe that Marilyn Manson is a woman, or that George Eliot was a man. I'm talking about an epic, wide-screen, high-definition, Dolby 5.1 Surround Sound cluelessness. When I was six or so, I remember asking my eldest sister Puli, who would later fall ill herself, why it was that our dad didn't go to work like other dads. 'He's diabetic,' she replied. And for the next two decades 'diabetes' was the word I mumbled if anyone enquired about my father's unemployment or strange habits.
2. The language divide. Punjabi, the language my parents

speak, is the one I learnt first. However, I left home nearly twelve years ago and have since become less and less proficient in it, so much so that now, even asking for a glass of water sometimes has me burbling incoherently like a GCSE French candidate on a daytrip to Calais. I can make myself understood, but subtle conversations about delicate matters are difficult. Moreover, since my parents cannot read or write English – and since my father is entirely illiterate – they've never had the word 'schizophrenia' to give me, although this is less of an excuse with my sister, who is entirely proficient in English.

3. Relative youth. As the youngest member of the household, any questions I did pose were often batted away on the grounds that I was 'too young to understand'. On some occasions this was undoubtedly true – I was young and I was stupid – but I realize now that there were occasions when the expression was used as a way of shielding me from uncomfortable truths.

4. The sometimes subtle nature of the illness. The term 'schizophrenia' may bring to mind images of young men smearing themselves in faeces in lonely bedsits and pushing hard-working media professionals under the wheels of oncoming trains, but in actual fact, most of the time, when sufferers are receiving treatment, and when they are taking their medication, the symptoms can be subtle. Or, at least, subtle within the context of my family's perpetually raging soap opera.

5. Lack of inquisitiveness. This may seem an odd, perhaps even perverse, trait in a journalist who is paid to ask intrusive, often very rude questions of strangers, but if you do something for a living, you don't necessarily do it in your spare time. There are people, for instance, who race motorbikes who don't have a licence to ride them on the roads, and chefs who rarely cook for their own family. Similarly, I would dismiss information even

volunteered by my relatives with a grunt, a tendency accentuated by the enormous size of my extended family (there are so many relatives there's often no point in even *trying* to keep up with the news), by the lack of self-examination in Punjabi culture, and by the difficulty most children have in seeing their parents as personalities. Which isn't to say we don't see and love them as parents. But when it comes to thinking about them as human beings with ambitions, motivations and stories of their own . . . those closest to us are often the people we know least well.

6. Self-absorption. As will become evident.

7. An aversion to delving into the past. As will become evident.

8. Procrastination. There were occasions during the five years after I discovered Dad's illness when I thought I should find out more. Saying goodbye to my parents the morning after finding that note, I even asked Mum if she would mind me asking her about their past when they returned from India, and Mum, after a slight pause which suggested she considered the request a little peculiar, said she wouldn't. But on their return I was paralysed by inertia – surely the strongest determinant of male behaviour alongside lust – and did nothing.

9. Low pain threshold. I'm not quite at the stage of getting all the news I need from the weather report, but I am a coward. I avoid news reports about disease like the plague. Gritty episodes of Channel 4's *Dispatches* about rape and murder are likely to be dispatched in favour of MTV. And I'd rather have my face rubbed in dirty nappies than read a misery memoir. It's not that I don't care. I just find depressing things . . . depressing. The technical term for this is probably: denial.

10. Wariness. As far as my religious mother is concerned,

or at least as far as I *think* my religious mother is concerned, I've never had a girlfriend, I've never had sex, I pray every day and I keep away from meat and egg products on Sundays and Tuesdays to appease the ancestor spirit who apparently roams the Punjabi farmland I will one day inherit. In order to keep things this way, I was reluctant to get too close in case I ruptured the walls I'd built between my two lives. It was safer to restrict conversation to the banal.

11. Happiness. Despite the strain of having to keep my London life secret from my family, I was reasonably content. Loving my job, having interesting friends and being in a fulfilling relationship, the notion of going back to Wolverhampton, a town I was desperate to leave as a youth, to delve into my family's problems with schizophrenia wasn't appealing.

Looking back over these reasons, or excuses, it's evident now that some factors played a bigger role than others, and the one thing that sticks out in particular is point 7, the aversion to delving into the past. If I was going to confront the fact of my father's and sister's illness, I was also going to have to rake over my childhood, work out whether everything was as it seemed, and I had no desire to do that.

The reluctance was in part down to the nature of my childhood memories, which, like most people's, were chaotic, hallucinatory, varied in tone and detail, disconnected and littered with inconsistencies. Here I was, for instance, at the age of three or four, sitting in a bath with my two sisters. But how could this be? We didn't have a bath or a bathroom until much later, when the dilapidated terraced house we grew up in, located in the inner city Park Village district of Wolverhampton, was renovated courtesy of a council grant. Here I was at the same kind of age being read a Mr Men book by Puli. But how could this be? I didn't understand English until I started school, much later. Was she translating into Punjabi?

Then there was the fact that, while disconnected and incoherent, my memories were nevertheless generally warm. I know it's fashionable nowadays to lay claim to a miserable youth, to confess to having been fed cat litter by your parents and posted off to Pakistan at thirteen to be forced into a marriage with a moustachioed sixty-four-year-old uncle. But I had a happy childhood and was pleased with the fact. Which isn't to say there weren't bad bits. There were tears and times during my adolescence when jumping off the Mander Centre car park seemed tempting. But most teenagers feel like that, and a childhood is what you choose to remember of it, isn't it? A reappraisal through the prism of schizophrenia would have been an act of vandalism.

But the main reason for the reluctance to delve was that the past felt so disorientatingly different. The gap between my London and Wolverhampton lives was uncomfortable enough: travelling the 124 miles to Wolverhampton after a month or two often felt like flying in from a different continent. But travelling the 124 miles and twenty years from London to Park Village was like re-entering the earth's atmosphere after a year in space. I'm getting a sick-making sense of vertigo even thinking about how to explain.

I suppose the obvious place to begin would be to point out the economic differences. In London, due to my career, I enjoyed a lifestyle of expensive restaurants, foreign travel, brushes with celebrity and nice cars. In Park Village, on the other hand, because my father didn't work, because there were four children to feed, and as my parents were immigrants, we were poor. We never ate out, never owned a car – sitting in one was an event; 'holidays' were trips to relatives' houses; once a week the whole family walked for an hour back from the town centre with shopping bags to save 80 pence in bus fare; we had no telephone, no video player; our furniture was second-hand; school uniforms were often hand-me-downs; my sisters made their own dresses. Because of a lack of space I shared a bedroom with my parents; we grew our own vegetables; birthday presents were Matchbox cars and 20 pence water pistols; our house was infested with mice, a problem our grandmother, who lived four doors away with the family of my father's younger brother, my 'Chacha', tried to tackle with a cat (the unimaginatively named Pussy), which, being unneutered, quickly created the problem of an infestation of kittens; and one of my most humiliating memories is of taking my shoes off for a period of PE at primary school and two semi-crushed cockroaches crawling out of them. Even the teacher yelped.

But while this relative poverty would be an obvious place to begin, it would also be a misleading place to begin. For while we were poor, we were poor in the way that Punjabi immigrants are poor. In other words, not really. My mother worked hard, making what she could sewing dresses at home; she was incredibly good with money,* we spent little, and as no one in Park Village was well off, we never felt poor. Like most Indians on our street, we even owned our house – my parents bought it in the seventies for a few hundred pounds; we had no debt, and rather than go hungry, we were routinely overfed. On reflection, the more profound differences – I feel another list coming on – were:

1. Linguistic: I studied English at university and became a writer, yet most of my adult relatives didn't speak the language.
2. Religious: in London media circles, admitting you believed in God was taboo, whereas I was raised a devout Sikh and even kept my hair long as a symbol of my faith.
3. Educational: all my London friends were graduates, whereas no one in my extended family had attended university when I was growing up.
4. Professional: only one member of my massive family had an office job in the Park Village days, whereas I socialized

---

* I was not surprised to read a report from the Financial Services Authority in 2006 showing that among Britain's major faith groups, Hindus and Sikhs come out tops in terms of managing their own money and making ends meet. It transpires that some Sikh communities within Britain actually have low credit ratings, because so few of them have credit cards or credit records.

with no labourers, factory workers or tradesmen in London.

5. Culinary: in London curry was an occasional indulgence, but Indian food was the staple in Park Village, and fish and chips the occasional treat.

6. Literary: almost all my London friends talked about writing books, but I grew up in a world where no one read books, or owned them, let alone wrote them.

7. Geographical: everyone lived with their nuclear families in Park Village, and in most cases had their extended families living nearby too, but I could go for months without seeing relatives in London.

8. Sexual: no one 'dated' in Park Village, and marrying someone not of the same caste and religion was taboo.

9. Political: party politics always cropped up as a topic of dinner party debate in London, whereas everyone blindly voted Labour in Park Village, because they were 'for the Asians', while the Tories, it was accepted, were for deportation.

10. Superstititious: reason and rationality ruled in London, but in Park Village my life was governed by a million and one spooky rules and rites imported from India.

11. Journalistic: no one had newspapers delivered or watched the news in Park Village, and often we would only find out about major events such as the invasion of the Falklands days after they had happened, but in London I sometimes knew about things before they happened.

12. Racial.

The final point needs emphasis. You see, while almost everyone I dealt with in London was white, and while I sometimes forgot I was Asian – I had become, as the insult goes, a coconut – almost everyone in my former Wolverhampton life was Asian. The doctor, the dentist, the shopkeepers were Asian. Three-quarters of my class at primary school were Indian and even the few white kids exploded in laughter when the teacher used the word 'bond' in class, because it meant 'bum' in various Indian languages. The only white adults we had contact with were teachers, Mrs Burgess, who looked after the corner shop at the end of our street, and the bachelor who lived next door and rarely spoke to us. My grandfather, a giant oak tree of a man, would waddle down for tea from four doors away a couple of times a week, and regularly hold forth on the topic of 'the *goras*', talking about them as if they were a distant African tribe. They were a clever people who conquered our homeland, he would say. They had made many advances in technology, he would say. But they also had bad habits: they treated their dogs like children, and their elders like dogs; they charged their own children rent; and, unlike us, they didn't wash their bums with water after going to the toilet. Until my sister Puli, in her late teens, stunned us by developing a close friendship with an English girl, and was allowed, on a couple of occasions, to bring her home, I don't recall ever seeing a white person in the house. The mere sight of a non-Indian at the front door would send us into a panic: Dad opening the door and calling for Mum without even saying hello; Mum running to the door and saying, 'One minute . . . one minute . . .' to the bewildered stranger, before shouting up for Puli (who did all the translating in the house); three of us following Puli down the stairs to see what was up. The entire family would end up on the doorstep, gawping at the stunned white visitor as he tried to explain via Puli that he worked for British Gas and was visiting to read the meter.

To go from this to actually dating an English girl, to go from being singled out as the perfect Sikh child – my brother and father didn't have long hair, but Mum found God before she had me and decided to raise me as a religious experiment – to being the one member of the family who wasn't doing the expected thing, was difficult to confront. It wasn't something I could get my head around or wanted to get my head around.

I've tried to think of an appropriate analogy to describe this relationship with my past, and in the end decided it was a little like my relationship with my household insurance policy. I knew

I had childhood memories, like I knew I had a household insurance policy. I didn't entirely trust my childhood memories, in the way I didn't entirely trust my household insurance policy. And I had no more desire to sit down and rake over my memories than I wanted to sit down and read the small print of my household insurance policy. However, five years after the discovery I made in my parents' suitcase, events finally forced me to return to those old memories, and . . .

. . . I remembered sitting with my brother on the floor of the front room in our terraced house in Prosser Street, Park Village, in 1980 or 1981. I'm four or five, and Rajah is seven or eight, and we're bent over the brown radio cassette player – or was it black? – that Mum has told us never, under any circumstances whatsoever, to touch. Rajah has taken the end of the cord and plugged it into a wobbly wall socket, another thing that Mum has told us never, under any circumstances whatsoever, to touch, and the contraption instantly bursts into life, blaring out Mum's morning prayers. Somehow Rajah manages to find the volume knob before we're busted and for a few moments we just sit there, recovering from the panic, watching the two spools behind the clear plastic casing pass brown tape to each other, alternately slowing down and speeding up. Tentatively, Rajah starts tinkering with the buttons and dials again, turning the volume up slightly, and flicking the function switch from TAPE to TUNER, which suddenly bathes the radio dial in a soft orange glow and causes the speaker to emit a quiet burr. He turns another dial, which turns the burr into a hiss and then a chatter, and then, finally, there's the sound of something . . . musical. I can't tell whether the voice belongs to a man or a woman. Or whether the singer is black or white. Or what the singer is singing about. All I know for sure is that it sounds nothing like the *ragis* who sing Mum's prayers, and that I like it. I like it very much. My first pop song. But what track was it? I'd like to think it was something irrefutably cool like 'Rock With You' by Michael Jackson. But I have a horrible feeling it was 'This Ole House' by Shakin' Stevens.

. . . I remembered the view from the lip of a balcony. It's earlier, around 1979 maybe. The balcony must be on the top of something high – a building, a tower? – and someone is holding me up so I can get a good look, as Mum points and says: 'Look – can you see it? Over there – our home.' I follow her arm, with its bangles and gold bracelets, until I reach the tips of her polished nails. But while I can see houses and roads and bikes, I can't see our house. Puli juts forward and takes over the task of jabbing in the air. 'Look, THERE,' she squeaks. 'THERE.' Again, I follow her arm, the plastic bangles, the red thread around her wrist, until I reach the tips of her chewed nails. But still, nothing I recognize. Dogs, trees, fields. But no sign of our terraced house. My blank expression soon has everyone jabbing in the air: Bindi, Rajah, Puli, Mum, all pointing frantically. Somebody – it must be Dad – lifts me higher now, so I've got a clearer view. 'Look, there,' they chorus. 'There! Over THERE!' I'm desperate to see the house. Even at this age, there is an eagerness to please. But I can't see anything I recognize. No sign of the railway track that runs at the back of the garden, of the washing hanging from the lines, of Pussy. Why couldn't I see the house? Could it have been because we were not, as I thought, in Wolverhampton, but in India? Were we actually at the top of the tower in the middle of my father's village? I'm not sure.

. . . I remembered, clearly, Mum giving me some money and telling me to buy myself a packet of crisps – and while I'm at it, could I get her something? She gives me a piece of plastic wrapping, ripped off from the something she wants me to get, and tells me to show it to the woman behind the counter at the corner shop. The shopkeeper will work out what to give me, she says. I scamper off to Mrs Burgess's, push open the door, which sets off a bell, and stand before the crisp rack, which I refer to as the 'crips' rack, for five, maybe ten minutes, trying to work out what to go for. Cheese and Onion Walkers Crips are my favourite, but Monster Munch last longer. Salt and Vinegar Golden Wonder Crips are pretty tasty, but then it's tempting to go for two packets of 5 pence onion rings on grounds of sheer volume. In the end I plump for Hula Hoops – I will put one hoop on the end of each finger and polish them off one by one – and join the queue of three white women (this being the only place where you see *goras* shopping), passing the time trying to read the letters on the plastic wrapping Mum has given me. Maths is my best subject, but I'm not bad at reading, and can make out a few of the words, even though they are quite long. I mouth the letters and sounds syllable by syllable under my breath, and when my turn comes to pay, I hand over the Hula Hoops to Mrs Burgess, and instead of showing the wrapping as instructed, shout: 'Could I also have a packet of SANTY . . . SANITY . . . SANTRY TOWELS, please?' Interpreting subsequent hesitation as deafness, I shout the request out louder, above the coughing and shuffling in the queue behind me. 'COULD I HAVE A PACKET OF SANTRY TOWELS AS WELL, PLEASE?' Mrs Burgess pouts like a goldfish.

. . . I remembered the family settling down at bedtime. I'm not sure of the year. And we're not settling down for bed at home: we are gathered in the *gurdwara* on the Cannock Road, a few minutes away. And it's not just my immediate family settling down for bed. Everyone from my uncle's house four doors down is there too: Baba and Bibi (my father's parents), Chacha and Chachi and their two daughters. It's cosy and exciting: it's not often we're all in the same room. Chacha will pop over to fix things and do DIY, and Baba and Bibi will come over for a meal and a chat every few days, and I might get to play with my cousins occasionally in the back yard, but we are usually only ever all together on weddings or birthdays or Diwali. Thick duvets have been laid out across the floor, to act as mattresses. The adult men – my uncle and father and grandfather – are lying on one side of the room, out of sight behind a tiled pillar. And the women and children are lying on the other. I'm tucked between Puli and Mum, with my feet pointing away from the shrine at the end of the room, because it's disrespectful to point your feet at the Holy Book. There are coloured lights skirting around the room. Pictures of saints and gurus in various states of torture and martyrdom on the walls. And the central heating is on full blast, though the overhead fans are still whirring – some Indian habits die hard – making the Christmas decorations that remain in the rafters all year round dance. Lifting my head I see my grandmother, thin and sprightly, tiptoeing back to her space between the bodies, carrying a mixture of *misri* and almonds in one hand and a mug of something – boiled milk? – in the other. Why are we here?

Maybe for an *akhand path*: an uninterrupted reading of the Sikh holy book, the Guru Granth Sahib. Sometimes when someone in the family paid to have a reading, the whole family would spend the weekend in the temple. But there's an associated memory of chained gates and boarded-up windows. A priest standing guard at a door with a sword at his side. Mum saying, 'Don't worry.' There were race riots in Birmingham in 1981. Did the tension spread to Wolverhampton? Could we have gone to the temple for safety?

. . . My most detailed early memory is of the family at breakfast time. It's 1979, I'm three years old, and like all breakfast times during my youth it begins with Mum combing my hair, a ritual for which I have to sit down on the second-hand, floral-patterned settee, and lean forward, like I'm presenting myself for execution. She starts by unravelling the preceding day's topknot: removing the hanky, uncoiling the bun and unravelling the plait, before smothering the black curtain between us with jasmine oil. She then takes one of the large plastic combs scattered around the living room – its teeth permanently clogged with long black hairs – and runs it mercilessly through the knots and tangles. The first tug makes me yelp. The second makes me whimper. By the third, the pain is subsiding, but it would be a mistake to relax, for the agony of my hair being pulled out from its roots will soon be replaced by the twinge of a ponytail being tied too tightly on the top of my head, and then, just as I'm recovering, there'll be the torture of breakfast: a saucer of *dalia*, porridge cooked in the Punjabi style, thick with milk, saturated with sugar, an almost human skin formed over the top.

I'm not interested in *dalia*. I'm interested in watching cartoons on the black and white telly that sits on the shelf opposite the settee. I'm interested in bouncing up and down on the settee. And I'm interested in watching my three elder siblings get ready for school. And as Puli and Bindi and Rajah file down the stairs that run straight into the living room, I abandon my plate of

gloop to watch them, over the back of the settee, in awe, my mouth open. Never one to miss an opportunity to overfeed, Mum breaks off from wiping the table clean to scoop a teaspoon of *dalia* into my mouth. To help it down, she gives me some tea in a glass, which, being brewed in the Punjabi style (thick with milk, saturated with sugar, an almost human skin formed over the top), just tastes like a liquid version of the *dalia*. Coughing and spluttering, but managing to swallow the concoction somehow, I clamp my mouth shut, escape Mum's clutches, and return to watching my siblings.

They're all there now, milling. Rajah, already the best-looking boy in Park Village, who has my mother in a permanent frenzy of chilli-twirling, is carrying a leather schoolbag which I think is cool. Puli, in a skirt that has an extension sewn on to the hem for the two inches she has grown in the past year, is sporting a bright red badge on her hand-knitted cardigan, which I think is even cooler. Meanwhile, Bindi – thin and sniffly as she is in all my memories, wearing a uniform that she has, most likely, slept in, to give her an extra ten minutes in bed – is talking to Puli in English, which I think is the coolest thing in the world, the solar system, the galaxy, the universe.

This is why, I think, the memory is unusually vivid. It's the only time I remember not being able to understand English, wanting to speak it, if only to be part of my siblings' club. If I could speak English, I think (in Punjabi, presumably), I would speak it all the time. And as my siblings say goodbye to Mum – hugs all round – I pretend I can.

'Herdy gerdy werdy,' I burble at Rajah, adding the little English I know. 'What's up doc? Beep beep!'

Preoccupied with checking the contents of his schoolbag, Rajah doesn't respond.

'Herdy bwhoop werchy? What's up beep?'

My reward for these linguistic gymnastics is merely another spoonful of *dalia*. The longer it lies on the plate, the gloopier and more disgusting it gets. If you leave it as long as I have, it develops the texture of jelly. Creamy milky disgusting jelly. But my subsequent mewling is at least enough to coax Puli into coming over and giving me the attention I crave. She picks me up under my fat arms and holds me above her, where I stretch out and pretend to be a plane: a game that renders me as wobbly as the *dalia* in my stomach.

Things look different from up here. I can see the radio cassette player, kept deliberately out of my sight and reach, next to the TV on the shelf. I can see my brother's Matchbox lorry, kept deliberately out of my sight and reach, next to the TV on the shelf. And I can see the top of my mother's sewing-machine, with its adventure playground of tension dials, spool holders, bobbin winds, clutch wheels and reverse levers. I'm enjoying the change of perspective, but Mum barks at Puli, telling her to put me down. She'll be late for school, she says. She'll make me sick throwing me around in the middle of breakfast, she says. But if there's anything that's going to make me sick, it's the *dalia* that Puli plonks me back in front of. By the time I look up again, she is scrabbling out of the room with Bindi and Rajah.

'Bye bye, Puli,' I say, showing off my other bit of English.

'Oi,' Mum interjects. 'Puli *pehnji* – she's older than you. Have some respect.'

'Bye bye, Bindi.'

'Oi, Bindi *pehnji* . . .'

'Bye bye, Rajah.'

'Oi, *pahji*!'

Not being good at goodbyes – I will never be good at them – I burst into tears again, my gaping mouth again proving a perfect target for my mother's *dalia*-laden teaspoon. I cough and splutter and shriek to such a degree that Mum eventually gives up, takes the end of her *chuni*, wraps it around her index finger and uses it to clean the corners of my mouth, rubbing and rubbing until it stings. Ignoring the sobbing, she takes her bottle of Oil of Ulay, glugs a dollop on to the tips of her fingers and smothers my face in it until it is swimming in grease.

'What's the rush?' A chuck under the chin. 'There's plenty of time to learn Angrezi. You'll be going to school next year.'

The remark intensifies my weeping. I hate the way Mum force-feeds me, cleans my mouth, sticks a dishcloth in my ear to get rid of the wax, only gets me Sugar Puffs and Lucozade when I'm ill, or pretending to be ill, doesn't let me play with the sewing-machine she sits at all day. But I love having her to myself, sharing her only with the bundles of cloth delivered once a week by the man with the van and the gold watch. The idea of not being here all day is heartbreaking. On reflection, I think I'd rather not learn English. On reflection, I think I'll weep at the kind of pitch children normally reserve for the death of a kitten.

Dad comes into the room as I wail and, at Mum's bidding, picks me up. He is dressed in a suit and tie. He smells of shaving foam and Brylcreem. And, with me on his arm, he moves to the hexagonal brass-framed mirror above the mantelpiece, takes a small black comb out of his blazer pocket and begins perfecting the quiff that is already perfect, sculpting the parting that is already straighter than the rows of vegetables in the garden.

In one of those sudden mood changes that young children

specialize in, I spontaneously forget what I'm crying about and become suddenly engrossed in watching Dad's reflection. His eyes are bloodshot. And there is a dark stain in the middle of his forehead. When he leans, I catch my own reflection, and spot I'm wearing red plasticky shoes, red socks, a black hanky on my topknot, and . . .

Whoa!

My mother appears to have dressed me in a . . . SMOCK.

A tartan smock!*

I'm still trying to take this in as Dad puts me back on the settee and completes his home-leaving ritual. He glances at the electric wall clock, its wires feeding directly into the socket to save the cost of a plug, and then back at his watch, fastened upside down on his left wrist. He switches his gaze back and forth five or six times. Then he puts his hand into his trouser pocket and pulls out his keys and puts them back. He does this five or six times too. And then, as he moves towards the front room, and the front door, I ask him, through snot and *dalia*, sitting in my tartan smock, where he's going.

---

* The fashion crimes Punjabi immigrants inflicted upon their offspring were picked up on by one of the earliest appraisals of Sikhs in Britain. 'The taste in baby wear is unusual to European eyes,' wrote Canon Selwyn Gummer and John Selwyn Gummer in *When the Coloured People Come*, an analysis of Sikh settlement in Gravesend (1966). They continued: 'One baby appeared at the age of three weeks wearing a white knitted mob cap, a colourful flowered dress stamped "Pride of Bombay", a black and yellow coat knitted in key pattern and blue and red striped leggings.' Unfortunately, this is the only worthwhile observation in the book, which continues with remarks about the low intelligence of Sikh children ('The percentage of literate Asians in the older age-groups is infinitesimal. Naturally the children of such parents are backward . . . Many of them . . . are of *low intelligence* as distinct from illiterate'), the racket Sikh women make during childbirth ('When the women are in labour they make a lot of noise which appears to be traditional rather than activated by pain'), birth control habits ('Rubber condoms and caps irritate the skin of these people and for that reason they are not very popular'), and concludes that 'the Sikhs are strangers in a strange land and they are intellectually and educationally ill-equipped to deal with the complexities of a modern civilization'. John Gummer later found fame as a squeaky-voiced Tory agriculture minister, a tenure which was memorably marked by an attempt to demonstrate the safeness of British beef by feeding it in public to his daughter.

'You going to work, Dedi?'

'—'

'Do you work in a factory?' Something makes me think that dads work in factories.

As she does so often, Mum answers for him. 'Yes, son. Your Dedi's off to work.'

'Can I work there when I grow up?'

'Of course, son.'

'With Dedi?'

'You can do whatever you want.'

And then, as soundlessly as he came into the room, he's gone.

For more than two decades I would refer to this memory if anyone asked whether my father ever worked. Yes, I would say. He was working when I was three. He was working in a factory. If they pressed for further information, I would add: yeah, he worked at the Goodyear tyre factory in Wolverhampton. I'm not sure where I gleaned this detail from. It was, in part, true. My father did, for a period, work at Goodyear's. But by this stage he had been unemployed for six years. If anything, that morning he was off to New Cross Hospital. If anything, he was going to have his weekly injection of Modecate, otherwise known as fluphenazine decanoate, which belongs to a group of drugs known as pheno-thiazine antipsychotics and acts by blocking receptors in the brain.

3. Love Will Tear Us Apart

As soon as my mobile began vibrating on the arm of Laura's sofa, I knew it was going to be bad news. People don't, in my experience, ring at midnight unless there's been a death, unless they've been drinking alone and have decided it's time to share some home truths, or unless they're a newspaper editor calling to explain that you've referred to a musical called *Bombay Dreams* as *Bollywood Dreams* fifteen times in a piece being published tomorrow about . . . *Bombay Dreams.*

In the event it was worse than all these things combined.

'Aareet Sathnam?'

'Hi . . .' I couldn't place the voice '. . . who's that?'

'Jugi . . .'

'Jugi?'

'Jugi . . . your *bua.*'

'Oh.' One of my army of aunts, who had moved from Wolverhampton to Newcastle fifteen years earlier, who, disconcertingly, had learnt to speak English (with a Geordie accent) in the meantime, and who, even more disconcertingly, had never rung me before.

'I'm neet botherin' you, am I?'

'No, no, no . . . How are you?'

'Fine, thanks. Long time, no speak.'

Long time, never speak, more like, I thought, before realizing from the resulting static on the line that I'd said it too. 'I mean, it must be what . . . um, four years?' I always seem to say things were four years ago when I can't remember when they were.

'Longer mebbies.'

'I'm sorry I didn't make it to er . . . your . . .' God, I'd forgotten the name of someone I used to play with every day '. . .

daughter's wedding. Was away with work.' Liar, liar, pants on fire.

'Y'mean Manjeet's wedding?'

'Sorry, your son's wedding. Last year.'

'You shouldn't be sich a stranger. You know, if you ivvor wanted to cum up an' spend a weekend wi' us . . .'

'Yeah, thanks . . .'

'So where'bouts in London d'ya live?'

'Central London.'

'Where'bouts?'

'Oh . . .' I could never risk an unannounced visit '. . . in the middle . . . quite near Big Ben.'

'Nice. Hope you don't mind me calling.'

'Not at all.'

'I'm just worried about yer mum.'

'Mum?' I had been splayed across the sofa in post-work exhaustion but suddenly bolted upright. 'What's happened?'

'I've just come back from Wolves an' she was very upset.'

'Upset? Why?'

'Someone told her something about you.'

'Something about me?'

'Someone told her you're going out with a *gori*.'

'What?'

'Someone told her that you were seeing a *gori*.'

'Who said that?'

She gave the name of a distant relative, and my calves began to perspire: something I'd never experienced before. 'I've nivvar seen her so upset – she's neet even eating.'

'Really?'

'Yeah.'

'*Christ*.'

'So?'

'—'

'Hello?'

'—'

★

I really should've known what to say given that I'd been worrying about something like this happening every minute of my waking life since I'd come to London and started dating Laura. Actually, to be strictly accurate, I really should have known what to say given that I'd been worrying about something like this happening every minute of my waking life since I started university, which may seem odd given that my three years at Cambridge, as well as being marked by a precocious amount of journalism, a gut-destroying number of microwaveable macaroni cheeses, a retrospectively depressing number of early nights, a certain amount of lovely punting to Granchester, and a surreal period as music editor of the university newspaper, during which I confused the readership by commissioning articles on Michael Jackson and Suzanne Vega in the middle of the Britpop phenomenon, was characterized by a total failure to have sex with anyone or anything at all. I'm still not sure how it happened – the George Michael posters can't have helped – and because three years is a bewildering amount of time for a young man to not get his end away, I'm not keen to dwell on it. But somehow, during this spell on the plains of the Sexual Sahara, my mother still managed to torment me for having inappropriate relationships.

Two incidents are etched into my memory like torture scars, the first of which occurred during a rare evening when an attractive young woman – an actress, no less – penetrated the almost visible forcefield of my sexual desperation and spent a night drinking in my room. Needless to say, the attractive young actress in question wasn't there to see me: she was a girlfriend of a friend, who was also there. And, needless to say, the drinking done was of the timid variety: over the course of several hours, the three of us may have polished off half a bottle of gin between us. But one thing led to another and when the attractive young actress revealed that she did voiceover work to make money on the side, in my drunken stupor I suggested she record a sexy message for my answering-machine.

I forgot about it until the next day, when I returned from my morning lecture to receive a distressed call from Ruky, my brother's wife, informing me that Mum had rung me, heard the voice of a *gori* simpering on the line, and had taken to bed in tears, convinced I'd betrayed my upbringing and culture by hooking up with a white girlfriend. Explaining the reality of the situation was almost as agonizing as having to explain a girlfriend. I'm not sure if Ruky believed me, but she passed the story on to Mum, I erased the message, and after a week of passive aggression, Mum was almost prepared to talk to me again.

The second incident occurred on the day of my graduation, when a day already steeped in the melancholy of partings, and, yes, the harrowing realization that I really had managed not to sleep with anyone for three whole years, took a turn for the worse when a former female housemate, unaware that even Punjabi husbands and wives don't make physical contact in public, broke through the circle of my family to plant a congratulatory kiss on my cheek. In the chilling instant that followed – Mum's cold scowl, her brow scrunched up in wrath – I felt what it might be like to have her affection withdrawn. It was like standing naked on an Alaskan peninsula, in a blizzard, on a patch of disintegrating ice, while being encircled by polar bears.

Given this, I suppose it was no surprise that when my biblical period of involuntary celibacy finally ended I approached my new romantic life with a certain degree of paranoia. And I realize now that for everything I did consciously to ensure my family didn't know about Laura – continuing with the arranged marriage meetings to keep up the pretence, only giving my family my mobile number, keeping a flat of my own, etc. – there was something I did unconsciously to strengthen the walls between my two lives. Is it a coincidence, for instance, that I never visited Indian areas of London? That I developed no close friendships with Punjabis? That I was touchy-feely in private, but had an aversion to public displays of affection? It makes me cringe now to think how quickly I would let go of Laura's hand if offered it on walks, how I would kiss in public with my eyes wide open, always on the lookout for someone who might spot me, how I would sometimes tell myself the relationship didn't matter, that I could end it whenever I wanted, without difficulty.

But gradually, I realized I was deluding myself: I was in deep, and had to start thinking about whether I should tell my mother I wasn't going to have a marriage, arranged or otherwise, to a Jat Sikh girl.

And of course, when I was with Laura in London, there was no debate. Every time she made me laugh, thrilled me with her appetite for life, it was obvious I had to do it. Almost every day I would hear a song or see a film or read a book or watch an episode of *EastEnders* which reinforced the clarity of the situation: you have to live with the person you love; individual happiness is everything; you can't live your life for other people. But the moment I considered the consequences and practicalities of actually talking to Mum about it, I lost my nerve.

The closest I would get to raising the subject with her was to make an incredible fuss whenever there was a story on the TV news or in the papers about a forced marriage or honour killing. On the surprisingly frequent number of occasions this happened, I would turn up the telly, or cut out the piece in question, and translate loudly, emphasizing the most dramatic bits, in the hope she would concede that the values which led to such violence were absurd.

'They hacked her into pieces just because she wanted to marry a Muslim!'

'Her brother strangled her with a skipping rope!'

'They stabbed her eighteen times before cutting her throat and made her little sisters watch!'

Mum would always, because she is intelligent and curious, listen to the details of the stories carefully, and she would always, because she is kind and humane, express horror at the violence. But I could never get her to state explicitly that the morals behind such honour crimes were wrong. Her sorrow was that of an American president apologizing for civilian casualties in a necessary war against terror.

As time passed, it became evident that if I did anything, it would have to be dramatic. I would have to throw the equivalent of a petrol bomb, and if the petrol bomb didn't work, I would have to throw another. Among the options I toyed with were: taking a foreign posting with work and disappearing with Laura; presenting my marriage to Laura as a fait accompli; having a baby – if there's one thing Mum understands, it is the importance of looking after children; marrying a Sikh girl who was in a similar situation, and then living with our respective white partners in secret; putting it about that I was gay, but then presenting the much more palatable reality of my heterosexual relationship; and contracting a near-fatal illness, during which I declared that my family's acceptance of my relationship with Laura was my last dying wish . . . only to recover suddenly.

I guess you should be careful what you wish for, because, one day . . . I contracted a near-fatal illness. Namely, neurocysticercosis, a brain parasite. I probably caught the bug from an undercooked pork dish I ate on a visit to central America or India. Apparently, once inside my stomach, tapeworm eggs in the meat penetrated my intestine, entered my bloodstream and travelled to my brain, where they caused scarring, swelling and focal epilepsy. But even then, in hospital, half senseless with fever, pneumonia, daily lumbar punctures, and, as it turned out, a near-fatal reaction to the anti-epileptic drugs I'd been given, I still didn't confront my mother. Somehow, I managed to keep the illness from my family, and when it became too serious to hide, I managed to arrange it so that few of my friends bumped into my family during visits. In my sick state, I even managed to make sure my flatmate at the time printed out pictures of Guru Nanak from the internet and put them up around the flat we shared.

You see, when it comes down to it, death is a more appetizing prospect than crossing my mother. I recovered completely, only to anguish further.

Not that I was ever short of advice. Close friends who knew about my predicament seemed to raise the subject at every dinner party. Or maybe I raised it at every dinner party. Either way, maybe because the love versus family duty thing is a universal dilemma, or maybe because Indian and Punjabi family life has been so demystified by the media, people seemed eager to provide suggestions.

But two things hampered the quality of the advice, the first being that most media portrayals of Punjabi family life, either in the form of all those news stories about Sikh fathers murdering their estranged daughters in the name of honour, or lighter depictions in programmes like *The Kumars at No 42* or *Goodness Gracious Me*, didn't really relate to my situation. I was hardly being forced into marriage to an Indian villager. What usually happened with arranged marriage meetings was that I was given the mobile phone number of an approved girl and asked to make my own arrangements to see her. It was less a case of forced marriage than blind dating with parental approval, egged on with emotional blackmail.

And the semi-comical fictional portrayals of Punjabi family life didn't reflect my situation either. Take *Bend It Like Beckham*, for instance, a big Punjabi crossover hit. Lots of things in the film, which tells the story of Jess, a British Indian Sikh girl who struggles against her family's orthodox mindset to fulfil her dream of playing professional football, tallied with my experience: the hysterical mother objecting to her daughter wearing shorts and 'running around half naked'; the eavesdropping aunties; the despairing parent looking up to a picture of Guru Nanak and intoning, 'What did I do in my past life?'; Jess pretending to be in Croydon when she was in Hamburg (I've done the Transatlantic equivalent); the pressure even from siblings and contemporaries to marry someone from your own culture; the chintzy furniture; the inevitable fight at the end of every wedding.

But few of the scenarios in the film could have occurred in my family. If Jess had been one of my sisters, for instance, she wouldn't have dared to have pictures of David Beckham up on her wall, let alone been allowed to play football. The scene where the Irish football coach is caught hugging Jess would have ended in Jess being disowned: whereas, in the film, Jess's father just gets

a bit moody about it. And as for the Benetton advert denoue-
ment at Heathrow Airport, where Jess and the coach kiss within
eyeshot of the parents, and Jess says, 'I'm back at Christmas . . .
we'll tackle my parents then.' Well, hahahahahahaha. My mother
would have a heart attack if one of my siblings kissed their *spouse*
in front of her.

Which brings me to the other thing that affected the quality
of the advice: part of me wanted to give my mother what she
wanted. Though I never would have admitted it to my friends,
to Laura or even to myself, the biggest obstacle was not my family,
but me. I saw myself as the dutiful son and I wasn't ready to go
from being the family hero to being considered the apotheosis
of evil, aunties pointing me out to children as an example of
how not to turn out. I also worried that the unhappiness caused
by any confrontation with my mother, the grief that would over-
whelm me if I was disowned, might poison the thing I was trying
to preserve: my relationship with Laura. Would we become one
of those couples who had chosen each other so much against
expectations that we were always unsettled and edgy? Did I want
to have children who would never know the culture and the
family that had shaped me?

The more I thought about it, the more irresolvable the dilemma
seemed. It was like being on a riverside, watching all the people
you love drown and only having time to save one of them. I was
torn, split down the middle like Bhai Mati Das, one of the saints
depicted on the wall of the Cannock Road *gurdwara*, who declared
that Islam was false, that Sikhism was true and was consequently
sawn across from head to loins under the orders of the Mughal
Emperor.

The one thing that might have helped would have been if
someone in the family, or someone my parents knew, or someone
I could introduce to my mother, had 'married out'. And I did
know of some people – even some of my male cousins – who
were surreptitiously dating English people. But time after time
they chose duty over love, went from wanting emotional fulfilment
to wanting a girl who was good in the kitchen and would agree

to give up her career after childbirth. I took news of these betrothals badly. They would call expecting to be congratulated, and I had to give them the congratulations they expected, but what I actually wanted to do was shake them and ask: *why?*

At the time, the odds struck me as odd. Surely it was just bad luck that they all succumbed to family pressure. But I recently came across a study that confirmed my darkest suspicions. Entitled 'A Study of Changes in Marriage Practices among the Sikhs of Britain', the thesis, completed in 1998 by Jagbir Jhutti of Oxford University, concluded: 'In this study, no evidence of a complete assimilation into British society has been found. The study shows that rather than rejecting their cultural traditions, i.e. arranged marriages, the second and third generation Sikhs have played an active role in maintaining such traditions.' In other words, I may have been as alone as I felt.

In desperation, I resorted to looking around my family for someone who might at least support me in the event of a confrontation with my mother. My brother was a natural person to consult, but relationships weren't something we had ever discussed and I worried he would tell her. I thought I'd found an alternative when, during an interminable wedding, a respected elderly friend of the family remarked: 'You know, we have to move with the times when it comes to marriage. We can't behave like Punjabi villagers any more.' But just as images of a white wedding flashed through my mind, me in morning suit, Laura in white, my family in the pews, he added: 'For instance, if one of my sons wanted to marry a girl who wasn't the right caste, I would try to understand it.'

The right *caste*?

He would TRY to understand?

The man had enjoyed a successful career in Britain, had spent nearly thirty years in Britain, and this was how far he'd come. The message came through loud and clear: marrying someone who was not a Sikh was the very worst thing you could do. I was as sensationally fucked as I had been sensationally unfucked at college.

Despite this, sometimes, tired out worrying, I would allow myself to think positively. Sometimes – encouraged by friends – I'd decide things weren't that bad. The Sikh faith, founded by Guru Nanak, was liberal. It taught monotheism, the brotherhood of humanity, rejected idol worship, the oppressive Hindu concept of caste, and had tolerance at its heart. Its *gurdwaras* were open to anyone; it was unique in respecting other religions and other people; Guru Gobind Singh, the tenth guru, had preached equality and proclaimed that his disciples should 'recognize the human race as one'. Besides, Mum must have worked out what was going on. She was so sensitive that sometimes she could tell if something was up at work from the tone of my voice on the telephone. She had to know about Laura. Maybe when she said, 'I just want you to be happy,' she actually meant it, without the thousand caveats. Maybe I was just being neurotic.

But these moments of optimism were the worst. With metro-nomic predictability, a crash would follow. I would visit Mum and she would present me with gold jewellery she'd bought for my future bride, or would insist on a particularly depressing arranged marriage meeting. The worst crash came when she rang in tears, announcing that a great scandal had afflicted the family in India: a pretty and lively cousin of mine had run away to marry a boy. When I pressed for further information, it transpired, between her sobs, that the problem with this boy was not that he was from another religion, or from another caste, or the wrong age, or had bad prospects, or was even the wrong height or skin colour. The scandal, it turned out, was that he was – get this – FROM THE SAME VILLAGE AS THE GIRL. Which, apparently, is a no-no.

More than anything else, this story brought home the bleakness of my situation. The only option I had was to ride things out, hoping my secret life wouldn't be discovered and that Laura wouldn't force the situation. And the thing is, she never did. Throughout she was supportive and understanding, even when I started suffering from recurring nightmares. In the nightmare – which I still have – I hear that my father is ill, go home to see him, only to have my mother refuse to let me into the house because of what I have done. The look on her face when she opens the door is the one she flicked in my direction at my graduation ceremony. It was a special kind of hell to wake up from this nightmare and to be comforted by Laura, to switch immediately from the guilt I felt about my family to the guilt I felt at what I was doing to her. I could almost hear the foundations of our relationship buckling under the weight of my indecision.

However, as I floundered, I found a way of plastering over the worst of the anxiety: work. With a deadline approaching, there was less time and space to worry about being found out, or having to come to some kind of resolution. And as I let my relationship drift, my career took off. I met my heroes, was promoted, won some of the awards that journalists love giving one another. Holidays were difficult: things would always catch up with me then. But I found an effective solution for these too: I stopped taking them. Laura complained, but seemed to understand. She always *seemed* to understand.

But, eventually, I had been caught. There were so many heart-stopping moments during those years, when I thought I'd been spotted, and it could have been any one of them, but there is one moment that frightened me more than any other. I was sitting with Laura on the Tube one Saturday morning, and in a rare, possibly guilt-induced, display of public affection had my arm around her, when I noticed an Indian of my kind of age sitting opposite, staring. The staring was not in itself notable: Indians always glare at other Indians. But there was something about this man – I thought I recognized him from somewhere – and something about his smile, almost a smirk, that made me think he was making a mental note to pass on some gossip. Having said that, it might have been speculation or gossip that instigated the crisis. Who knows. All that mattered was that Mum had found out, and now my aunt was calling me, asking me about it.

'Hello. You there?'

'Yes, sorry, bad line . . .'

'What did you say?'

'—'

As I held the phone away from my ear, the initial shock gave way to something else: anger. Suddenly, I was furious about Mum's reaction (the hysterical mother is the ultimate Indian cliché), my extended family's involvement (who were these people calling me, judging me? I barely knew them), the distant relative who had supposedly passed on the information (gleefully, no doubt), the way in which the media always portrays men as the beneficiaries of arranged marriages (some of us were just as trapped as women), and the racism of the word '*gori*', a word spat out as if it were interchangeable with 'whore', a word being used to describe someone who had only been kind to me, who had done more for me than many members of my extended family had ever done.

As I put the receiver back to my ear, the anger gave way to a sense of the imminence of a turning point, one of those rare critical moments in life, where you can change things for the better, or carry on badly, as you have done. I stood up, thought of Laura lying in bed next door, of how warm she would feel when I slid into bed next to her, and then I thought of my mother sobbing at home. In the end, I did what came naturally. I lied. I lied three times, like Peter.

It's not true.

I'm not seeing anyone.

I don't know why they would say that.

Asking my aunt to convey the message to my mother, I hung up, sank to my knees and knocked my forehead against the floor. It was my sincere hope that the laminate boards would splinter, that the splinters would penetrate my skull, and that I would die an instant death.

4. The First Time Ever I Saw Your Face

There was a time when I would have accepted the accepted wisdom about the end of love affairs: that, as with bereavement, there are five stages – denial, depression, anger, resignation and acceptance – and that one must go through each stage in order to reach the happy ending. At least, my response to Laura's inevitable decision to end our relationship followed that emotional arc. But with subsequent failed relationships it has become evident that things are more complicated.

There are, I realize now, many more intermediary stages between denial and acceptance – relief and bitterness, for instance; in some cases you can go through the grieving stages before the relationship actually ends, you don't necessarily go through all the stages with every relationship, and one's journey through them varies according to an impenetrable chemistry of: (i) the quality of the relationship; (ii) how you met; (iii) your initial expectations; (iv) timing; (v) whether someone else is involved; and (vi) the vital fact of who dumped who first.

Indeed, after Laura, there was a five-month relationship with a lovely recruitment consultant, which ended quite pleasantly; there was no denial or anger when we decided to give up, just immediate and mutual resignation and acceptance. There followed a three-month relationship with a Sikh doctor, the entirety of which, both before and after the break-up, was characterized by irritation and anger. Then four months with a blonde solicitor, the culmination of which bought acceptance; but then, five months later, on hearing she was engaged to a good-looking and successful acquaintance, I was suddenly punching walls. After this came four months with a brunette teacher, the termination of which mainly made me sad because she was so adorable and so upset. And when my sixth relationship ended in as many years – let's say her name was Alison, that she was a lawyer and that she at least had the courtesy to dump me on a Friday evening, just before a holiday, which, experience has taught me, is the best time to end a relationship, as you at least give the dumpee time to lick their wounds – initially I felt nothing at all.

I simply took the bag I had packed for France from the flat that I now owned in Brixton, south London, got into the canary yellow Porsche 911 Turbo I was test-driving as a new element of my even more ridiculously perfect job, slumped into the firm contours of the sporty bucket seats, and made off in a racket of engine noise and wheelspin which must have looked deliberate but was in fact caused by the combination of my unfamiliarity with the car and poor driving skills. Before I knew it, I had shot past the excessive number of fried chicken outlets in south London, over the silver-gleaming Thames, past those always-empty so-called steakhouses in the West End, through leafy north London, up the M1 and the M6, and, after the hills and spires on the horizon began to be replaced with shabby factories and the shimmering tops of newly built *gurdwaras*, I once again found myself in Wolverhampton, the arse of the Black Country, in itself the bumcrack of the West Midlands, in itself the backside of Great Britain.

Within moments of pulling up outside my parents' semi-detached home, the spoiler crunching expensively against the steep tarmacked driveway, one of the ever-declining number of white residents on the street had come up to say hi – 'Alroight, cock?' – and an Indian neighbour I hadn't seen in ten years or more, on his way back from the Three Crowns, asked with a directness that was almost physically winding what kind of salary I was on. 'Must be on a fair whack to afford those wheels.' I shrugged vaguely in a way that intended to convey frustration with the Punjabi obsession with status symbols, but in actual fact implied, incorrectly, that my salary was so large that I didn't want to talk about it, and then tugged my LVMH bag through the double-glazed UPVC porch door of my parents' house.

Even though the visit was unannounced and it was at least

three hours past Mum's bedtime, she insisted on the usual ritual of hugs, running hands through birdseed, having chillies twirled around my head and curry, during which I told her I'd be spending a week in Wolverhampton.

'. . . your brother-in-law's cousin Harbjit was let off the kidnapping charge in the end . . .' she was saying, as I informed her.

'Mum, is it okay if I stay for a while?'

'. . . it was ridiculous it went to court. I mean, all he did was drive them a few miles out of town . . .'

'Mum – did you hear what I said?'

'. . . I just don't think the police like Indian taxi drivers . . .' A pause. 'Did you say you're staying for a while?'

'I've taken a week off work.'

'A week?' She looked delighted. The longest I'd managed to stay in Wolverhampton in the preceding years was forty-eight hours. '*Chunga, chunga.*' It was evident from the faraway look in her eyes that she'd already begun planning the menu. 'Though God knows why you can't live here. There are newspapers in the Midlands, you know.'

I went to bed straight after dinner and didn't get up until midday. Mum must have heard me stirring because when I got to the bath, it had already been run and Mum was standing next to it, pouring holy water into it. I was downstairs in the living room an hour later, where I waved a doll at one of my nieces, remarked on the weather to Dad, munched my way through lunch – more to appease Mum than out of any desire to sustain myself – and returned upstairs. I did a version of the same thing the next day. And the day after that too. God knows what my parents thought I was up to. Maybe they thought I was working. In reality, I was either sleeping or staring at the wall-mounted gas heater.

I suppose the symptoms could be interpreted as those of depression. But my mental state differed from melancholia in one crucial respect: while the spiralling, endlessly looping thought processes of depression are negative, I wasn't really experiencing any real thought processes at all. I thought of nothing as I lay in bed. I thought of nothing as I stared at the wall-mounted gas heater. I thought of nothing as I went downstairs and stared out of the patio doors at the cats in the garden, which spent their days staring at the birds in the garden, which spent their days staring at the mounds of food and seeds my mother put out at 7 a.m. every day. I've tried to find a word that might describe this not pleasurable, not unpleasurable state of intellectual and emotional suspension, and an online dictionary suggests 'hebetude', which apparently means 'dullness of mind; mental lethargy'. But the offline *Collins Dictionary* suggests the word doesn't actually exist, which seems apt somehow, for a state of blankness.

There was a breakthrough on day four, however, in the form of a thought. Not a particularly profound one, but a thought nevertheless. It was: '*God.*' As with buses, soon several other thoughts had arrived. They included: 'Maybe all my relationships have been a waste of time and energy'; and 'Maybe I would have been better off marrying one of those Indian girls I'd been introduced to'; and 'Why have I been putting my family life at risk for nothing?' I'd thrown myself wholeheartedly – well, a little neurotically, perhaps – into a series of relationships, put everything on the line, though admittedly I'd never come close to telling my parents about any of them, and where had it got me? It had got me back to my mum's.

And because, in my mind, I connect relationships to work and London, I had a concomitant downer about these other things. Where had journalism got me? I had the mobile numbers of several celebrities who would struggle to remember who I was if shown photographic evidence of our meeting, and a tiny flat in a violent neighbourhood. As for London, I'd fetishized it for years, had wanted to live there before I'd even been there, had written a dissertation on London in the modern novel at university. But if I was honest, was it fun to live there? The parking wardens were tossers. Brixton was scary. Everything was too expensive. No one ever popped over to see how you were. If you were in trouble, you had to ask for help. And what was the point of that?

The low point came the next day, when, for the first time since I had left home, I was struck by the idea that I could move back. I could work freelance from Wolverhampton, I told myself. Become one of those members of the 'boomerang generation' that newspapers were always writing about. A 'kidult' who moved back home after university. After all, my parents wanted me to stay. And wasn't living at home like living in a hotel? A hotel with an extremely intrusive and attentive proprietor, admittedly. A hotel with bizarre rules – no alcohol, no meat on Sundays and Tuesdays, etc. – but a hotel nevertheless. If I sold my flat and pooled it with my parents' money I could buy a mansion in Wolverhampton. A *mansion*. With a car and a cat. Maybe I could give up work entirely . . .

It took three separate but virtually simultaneous developments to drag me out of this vortex. First, I looked in the property section of a local paper and realized I wouldn't be able to afford a semi-detached in Wolverhampton, let alone a mansion. Second, I remembered an episode of *Seinfeld* in which George approaches an attractive woman and says, 'Hi. My name is George. I'm unemployed and I live with my parents.' And then, watching an episode of *Bargain Hunt*, my father slurping his tea loudly next to me, several nephews and nieces using me as a climbing frame, and my mother prattling on about the importance of listening to prayer tapes ('Even if you don't understand the words, it is good to listen') and the engagement of the girl down the street, who had apparently graduated with a 'digiree' in pharmacy – 'TWENTY-NINE YEARS OLD AND STILL NOT MARRIED' – I remembered that as well as being the most wonderful people in the world, my parents were also the most infuriating, and literally bolted out of the house.

I walked for hours that afternoon. Down the dual carriageway on which I failed my first driving test, past the pub where I witnessed my first glassing, past the record shop I queued outside – if you can have a queue of just one person – for my copy of *Listen Without Prejudice Vol. 1*, past the library where I once took out a copy of *Making Love While You're Pregnant*, past the branch

54

of Burger King where a sadistic supervisor once made me clean a single toilet five times in half an hour, past the entrance to the Mander Shopping Centre where two boys once set a Doberman on me for amusement, past the bench where I once kissed a date – she tasted of apples, I tasted of battered sausage – past the concert hall where I once paid real money to see Lenny Henry perform and *actually laughed out loud at some of the jokes*, and finally into Queen Square, where, of all things, in a space where I think there used to be a charity shop, I found a building claiming to be the 'Wolverhampton Tourist Office'.

It's hard to put into words just how much of a shock this was. I've always taken it as one of life's certainties, alongside the fact that water freezes at zero degrees, and the fact that Cliff Richard releases a single at Christmas, that Wolverhampton is the crappest town in Britain. And I'm hardly alone: Wolves, or Wolvo as it is known by many inhabitants, has been a byword for misery in books and stand-up routines for decades. But now it appeared it had, of all things, become a tourist destination. I couldn't think of anything more improbable, and went in, to be greeted by the sound of a DJ on 107.7FM, The Wolf, talking over the opening chords of 'Against All Odds' by Phil Collins.

Once my eyes had adjusted to the light I could make out the shape of a counter, two middle-aged women typing frantically behind it, and, opposite them, a large display of tourist brochures. I had no idea there were so many places of interest in Wolverhampton. And on closer inspection I discovered there aren't so many places of interest in Wolverhampton. Most of the brochures seemed to be related to attractions tens, and, in some cases, hundreds of miles away: Hampton Court; Snowdonia; Cornwall. There was a section dedicated to more local attractions, but it was more than a little padded out with bus timetables. I picked out the most promising-looking leaflet – 'Black Country Days Out' – and after reading about the delights of the Merry Hill shopping centre and 'Mad O'Rourke's Pie Factory', an apparently 'famous' pub which produces something called 'the Desperate Dan cow pie', I couldn't help but turn to the less severe-looking of the two attendants, and remark: 'I can't believe Wolverhampton has a tourist information office.'

'It ay a tourist informayshun office no more.' She was still typing frantically. An application letter? A suicide note? 'It's a *visitor informayshun centre*.'

'Right.' It must have been obvious from my tone that I was being a sneery Southerner, but I also had a point. 'And the difference is . . .?'

'"Visitor" sounds more welcoming, apparently. We started off as an informayshun centre, then it went to tourist informayshun and now it's visitor.'

'You sure they didn't change the name because Wolverhampton has never had . . . any real *tourists* as such?'

'No, no, we have lowuds of tourists. . . because of the university.'

'The university?' I resisted the urge to point out that, strictly speaking, the term for these visitors was 'students'.

'So how many . . . how many "visitors" do you get?'

She chose to answer a different question. 'We can only log the ones that speak to us.'

'Right.'

'So yow live local?'

'No, I'm from London.' It felt good to say it, so I said it again. So much for being a member of the boomerang generation.

'Y'am gunna be a national then?'

'Sorry?'

'Yow live in this country?'

'Yes.' It was like being in the back of a cab. 'London is . . . the . . . capital city of Great Britain.'

'So, y'am a national?'

'Yes.' It dawned on me that she was planning to register me as a tourist.

'I'm being recorded as an official visitor?'

''Cos yow spoke to us.'

'God.' I was still struggling to get my head around the concept of a 'Wolverhampton tourist' and now I was one. I replaced the

'Black Country Days Out' leaflet. 'What kind of things do people ask for when they come in?'

'Souvenirs.'

'*Souvenirs*?'

'Ar.'

'What do you sell?'

'Have a look behind yow.'

I had no idea what to expect. What could possibly symbolize my home town, a place that *The Idler Book of Crap Towns: The 50 Worst Places to Live in the UK*, had described as a city 'so divided along class and racial lines that it is hardly a city at all but a collection of tribal groupings'.* A pork sandwich? A curry? A knife recently used in a racially aggravated assault? Nothing would have surprised me.

As it happened, the glass cabinet behind me turned out to contain: sticks of Wolverhampton rock; Wolverhampton thimbles; Wolverhampton fridge magnets; Wolverhampton hairbrushes and Wolverhampton ponchos. The thing that made these objects specifically 'Wolverhampton' was that they all had 'City of Wolverhampton' emblazoned across them. The slogan alerted me to a fact I'd forgotten: in my absence Wolverhampton had become a city. When I lived there, it was a town – according to one of my primary school teachers 'the biggest town in Europe', a fact I'd never managed to corroborate – but it had been appointed city status in 2001. I bought some Wolverhampton rock – which turned out to have been manufactured in Harrogate, according to the label – and some postcards I thought I'd use as ironic thank-you cards. The attendant put the items into a carrier bag with the prayer 'Wolverhampton – our city – bright future' emblazoned across it and I walked out and sat down on a bench outside, to take it all in.

In the middle of the square, in front of me, stood Wolverhamp-

---

* The entry concludes: 'In the evenings, the smell of hops from Banks' Brewery permeates the town like the stench of a trapped animal slowly decaying in a drain pipe.'

ton's most famous landmark, a statue of Prince Albert, Queen Victoria's consort, referred to by locals as the 'Man on the Horse', the 'Mon on the 'Oss', and the 'MOTH'. Looking at it – someone had, as usual, put a road cone on Prince Albert's head – it struck me that apart from a few churches, it was probably the only thing that had remained unchanged in the city centre for the past century. It was there when Wolverhampton was a great industrial town, at the forefront of the Industrial Revolution. It survived the sanctioned vandalism of the post-war years, when many of the town's greatest buildings were destroyed in the name of progress. It was there during the brief period in the seventies when Wolverhampton was cool, with local band Slade riding high in the pop charts, and Wolves were doing well in the league. And it was still here now in Wolverhampton's oddest and most unexpected phase as a tourist attraction.

And then I was struck by a sudden need to talk to Alison. We had spent recent weeks half killing each other, and the Friday evening had been horrible, bloodier than the opening scene of *Saving Private Ryan*, but she was still the person I wanted to call if I saw something funny, and she used to listen to my stories of Wolverhampton with such suspended disbelief – the fascination of someone who had never travelled further north than Oxford. Actually, that's unfair – it was probably the fascination of someone who had never been allowed to see the home or meet the family of their partner. After extensive negotiations with myself, and realizing I had several postcards on my person, I compromised and decided to write instead. I picked one – a picture of the man on the horse – and began.

> Dearest Alison, I know you said you didn't want me to contact you, in person, by phone, email, or letter. But you didn't mention postcard! So I'm writing to you on the back of this picture of the man on the horse – remember? Anyway, you'll be glad to know I'm not writing to ask you to change your mind. I agree it probably wasn't going to work out between us, we wind each other up too much, but . . . (cont. on card 2)

. . . (and here we have another picture of the man on the horse!) . . . I just wanted to take you up on a few things you said on Friday. First, my family aren't 'racist' in not wanting me to go out with someone who isn't Sikh. My dilemma is more subtle than that. And it's depressing that after so much time you still don't understand that. Second, I am not, as you say, 'trapped in a dysfunctional pattern' with my relationships – you've been reading too many women's (cont. on next card)

. . . magazines (and here we have another picture of the man on the horse!) . . . I don't think my relationship history is untypical of a man of my age. Furthermore, I am not, as you say, 'running scared of confronting my mother'. I'm just waiting for the right person and the right time, and then I will do it, on my own terms. There's no point in sparking a family drama when I haven't got someone to commit to anyway. And I realize now that someone isn't you. I'm sorry we both wasted each other's time. Good luck. S

And here you have another thing about the end of relationships: yes, you go through phases of coping and not coping, but you don't necessarily go through them progressively or sequentially. Sometimes you can go from thinking you want to be friends with your former lover, to wanting to mutilate them slowly, in the time it takes to open a very necessary bottle of whisky. I had begun the postcard with warm intentions, but somehow, during the course of writing, had become furious and bitter. And by the time I got up with the intention of buying some stamps, for a set of postcards that would never get sent, I was in a stage of post-relationship torment I had not experienced before: horror. For it was while walking down Lichfield Street that it occurred to me that Alison was actually right.

Over the three or so years since my break-up with Laura, I had excused my hit-and-run approach to relationships with a variety of explanations. I was a romantic waiting for The One. I was, like lots of men, nervy about commitment. I was just doing what everyone else was doing: serial monogamy was the norm now. But looking back at the relationships, there was a dysfunctional pattern. They would all begin intensely: I would feel powerfully in love, suggest I was up for something long-term. But then, after a month or so, I would start finding faults, become more critical, and after a period of around three to four months, end things. And whoever said breaking up is hard to do didn't know what they were talking about. It was always easy. At least, always easier than confronting my mother. The relief I felt afterwards, at having got away without being discovered, always outweighed the stress of the break-up.

By the time I had trudged back home, things were clear: if I didn't confront my family about the arranged marriage thing, tell them I wanted to live my own life on my own terms, I was never going to be happy. My mother was the person I should be writing to, not Alison.

The realization wasn't a cheerful one. I felt as if I'd lost the use of several vital organs all at once. But unable to tell Mum why I felt awful, I claimed I was unwell, which, of course, sent her into a frenzy of nursing and cooking and brewing and praying – she has absolutely no sense of perspective when it comes to illness in her children – which made me feel even worse. I can't remember how long I spent in that crippled state, my thoughts muddled and disconnected, my mother offering handfuls of paracetamol. But, not being able to stand the strength of my own feelings, I do remember developing an acute aversion to any film or TV programme that featured any kind of competition or conflict, which in practice meant I couldn't even watch *Bargain Hunt* any more, and could for the first time share Dad's enthusiasm for *BBC Parliament*.

You may wonder why I didn't at this point get back into that canary yellow Porsche and deal with things by driving back to my secret and dysfunctional London life. After all, denial had got me through things before. But something had changed. After so many years of living a lie, and so many failed relationships, I had had enough. I'd got to the point when the idea of not doing something about my situation made me feel more ill than doing something about it. Desperation can lend you a kind of courage. And over the following days, the determination to write Mum a letter solidified: I would put down my frank and honest thoughts on paper, come clean, get it translated into Punjabi and hand it to her.

However, I realized there were precautions I had to take before putting pen to paper. I had to make sure I was sure, and to be sure, I had to make sense of how and why I had ended up in this position. I also had to find out about my parents' story. For if there was one thing I knew Mum would say, in the firestorm that followed a confrontation, it was: 'If you knew what your father and I had been through, you wouldn't do this.' They say it normally takes a death or a birth for someone to want to know about their family history. In my case it was six failed relationships and the prospect of an arranged marriage.

And so, some five years after discovering that note about my father's schizophrenia, I finally began to confront the fact of my father's illness. Though I make myself sound more dynamic and resolute than I was. I began timidly and awkwardly, almost by accident, by simply, for the first time in my life, looking at my father, closely, while I was lying across the sofa in the living room. And once I started looking, without moving my head, out of the corner of my eye, I couldn't stop. Rajah's mouth. Bindi's chin. Puli's eyes. My chubby cheeks. Skin browned by a summer's worth of walking to the *gurdwara* and back. A patch of red on his forehead. Ears that seemed to get larger, as the rest of him shrank. A growth of stubble even though he had shaved that morning. Handsome? Yes. Though he has one of those odd faces that varies in attractiveness. Sleep put a decade on him. A shave took a decade off. His clothes – green trousers tailored in India, a tight pullover hugging his pregnant belly – added a year or two. But if you stuck him in a suit and tie, got him to smile, he'd surely pass for a bank manager, a GP, or any other middle-aged Asian professional.

His pose was a familiar one. He was sitting in his armchair in the middle of the room, leaning over the table, poring over a copy of the *Daily Mail* my brother had left while popping over on the way back from the gym the day before. I realize the sight of my illiterate father reading a newspaper should have struck me as strange before this point. But as I've said, I took so many things about my parents for granted, and families can absorb infinite amounts of dysfunction. If I thought about it at all, I just accepted reading as one of Dad's odd habits, like adjusting his hair – he stands in front of the bathroom mirror, combing it for hours though there isn't much hair to speak of – wolfing down tea as soon as it has come to a boil, waking up at 6.30 a.m. even though he rarely has anything to do, refusing to go to bed during the day, even if ill or exhausted, watching *BBC Parliament*, even though he doesn't know the name of the Prime Minister and is instructed by Mum where to put his cross at election time.

Besides, like air and gravity, the reading thing had always been there. When we were kids, once a month, at Mum's insistence – she has always had a powerful belief in the importance of education – Dad would walk us two miles to the local library, and, as Bindi flicked through *Gobbolino the Witch's Cat* for the eighty-seventh time, as Rajah hunched over books about cowboys and horses, as I prepared for my future as a public schoolboy by immersing myself in Wodehouse and Jennings, and as Puli flicked precociously through the adult fiction section, and regressively through the Enid Blyton books she thought were actually written by 'Grid Blyton' until a teacher pointed out that she'd misread the signature on the front, Dad would sit in the corner, reading the newspapers. He wouldn't flick through them, or glance at the pictures and graphics, but would find some text, stare at it for a while, his eyes moving neither left to right nor right to left, and then turn the page.

When I was older he did the same with school textbooks I left lying around and, when I started having *The Times* delivered, for my A-Level politics course, I would often find him staring at it at breakfast. It annoyed me – sometimes I would hide the newspaper as soon as it arrived – but I never asked myself what might be going through his mind. It was just one of Dad's things.

But lying there watching him for the first time – because we never look at our parents closely, do we, just as we don't see them as people – I wondered whether the reading might be a symptom of his illness. And for the first time I asked him about it. Though again, I shouldn't make this sound too conscious or courageous an act. I was staring at him when he looked up, so suddenly that I couldn't pretend I was doing anything else. And to break the moment of awkwardness, and the habit of a lifetime, I asked: 'What you reading about, Dad?' There was an interval before the reply.

'I'm reading about America.' He pointed at the page. 'It's talking about the Prime Minister of America, isn't it?'

There were two stories on the page – neither of them about America.

He continued: 'There are two governments run by the white people and they both work closely, don't they?'

My turn to hesitate. 'You mean the American and British governments?'

'Yes.'

'You're right there, Dad.' A pause. 'Can you read, Dad? Do you understand the words and letters?'

'A little bit. We have lessons at the day centre.' Ah, the day centre. The Asian men's mental health group, every Monday and Wednesday morning. I had heard him talking about it, and once even received an email from Gurbax Kaur, the woman who set the group up – an overwhelming email that had me shutting my office blinds* – but I still hadn't tried to find out more about what he got up to there.

---

* I kept a copy. 'I currently work closely with your dad at the Croft Resource Centre. He arrived this morning carrying an article you had written in your newspaper. On previous occasions he has approached me with your articles and expressed joy at seeing your photo in the newspaper. Your article made me smile. Your father has a great sense of pride and smiles from ear to ear as he enters the room full of ten Asian males to say, "Look, my son has written this" . . . '

'That's great, Dad. I wish Mum would learn a bit of English.'

He folded the newspaper away neatly. Dad has always handled printed matter with care. And then, because the conversation had made me feel uncomfortable, I reached for the TV remote control. I was about to turn up the volume when he added: 'I want to tell you something.'

A missed heartbeat. 'Oh. Okay, Dad.'

'Your Mum tells me not to talk about this with you . . .'

'Okay.' He'd moved forward and was sitting on the lip of his armchair now. He raised a hand in the air, like a lecturer wanting to emphasize an important point.

'When the sun rises it's all okay.'

'*Ki?*'

'When the sun rises on the farmland there is so much *shakti* that everything is okay.'

I couldn't tell whether Dad was trying to convey a simple concept, that the sun had great power, whether I'd misheard what he said (Dad's speech is a little slurred sometimes), whether my Punjabi was once again proving deficient, or whether he was, terrifyingly, claiming he'd power over the sun.

'I'm not sure what you mean, Dad.'

'I mean, in the morning, when the sun rises it is because of *shakti*.'

'Is that something you learnt in the day centre?'

'No, I worked it out myself.' He lifted a finger and rubbed an area of inflamed skin on his forehead.

'Okay, Dad.' The implications raced through my mind and I fell back to the comfort platitudes. 'Are you going to the temple later?'

'Yes.'

'Nice day for a walk, isn't it?'

'Yes.'

The next day I was up and about, or at least had returned to staring at the wall-mounted gas heater in my bedroom, an improvement of sorts, thinking about possibly heading back to

London, when there was a soft knock on my bedroom door. It was Dad, who had just come back from his morning walk, one of the fixed elements of his daily routine. There's a question I always ask the people I interview for newspaper profiles: can you run me through a typical day of your life? I always ask it because it's an inoffensive opener and because it amuses me that the answer is always the same: 'Actually, there's no such thing as a typical day in my life,' they say. But Dad is different: he really does have a typical day. He wakes up at 6.30 a.m., drinks his hot tea straight from the stove, watches *BBC Parliament* for an hour or two, goes for a walk to the day centre or the temple, comes back, has a sausage sandwich, goes for a walk to the temple, walks from there to a shop to fetch some apples for himself or a few groceries for Mum, walks back home, watches a few more hours of *BBC Parliament*, has supper, watches a little more *BBC Parliament* and then goes to bed.

He sloped towards me with a folded piece of paper between his fingers. It was apparent from his body language – those hunched shoulders, that stealthy glance – what he was going to ask. He had a hospital appointment approaching and wanted me to read out the details from the appointment card. Often, when there's a meeting with a medical professional coming up – I assumed the three-monthly appointments were to do with his diabetes – he will show the card to several of his offspring in turn, trying, like an investigative journalist, to corroborate the time and date through multiple sources, or perhaps just trying to commit the time and place to memory through sheer repetition. If you're illiterate and have no way of keeping a diary, or keeping a note, repetition can be a way of remembering things.

I read it and conveyed the information: it was a card from the Wolverhampton City NHS Primary Care Trust, reminding him he had an Out-Patient Appointment to see Dr Patel, apparently a psychiatrist, on Monday at 1.20 p.m. in a month's time, in Bilston.

'The appointment is for Monday at 1.20,' I said. 'A month from now.'

5. Sign Your Name

If we're to believe the experts – and I've trudged through the books – the fact that my father didn't ever take me fishing or teach me to ride a bike or at any point take me aside and tell me father-to-son, or even man-to-man, about the birds and the bees, means he was a 'passive type' father, which, in turn, means I was 'under-fathered', which, in turn, means I had problems with bedwetting and soiling as a child and have grown up having difficulties with emotional expression, aggression and/or under-confidence.

While I can see how over-mothering could screw you up – my

current predicament may even be a testament to the fact – I can't say I've ever felt under-fathered and damaged as a consequence. I know there is a view nowadays that if a dad doesn't offer his children everything a mother offers, up to and including breast-feeding, he's not doing his job right. But if you asked children what they want and need, I think you'd find the answer was simple: time. The best offering a father can make his children is himself, and in this respect mine was fantastic. He was always around. He was there at breakfast and at teatime. He was there, because of our admittedly potentially psychologically damaging sleeping arrangements, all night. He was the person who took us to dentist's appointments, to the library, and during the school holidays he took my brother and I to the park every single day, standing watching at what we thought was a brook, but was in fact a sewage outlet, as we raced around and around and around on our bikes.

He also walked me to school every day. Several times a day, in fact: he would be with me on the ten-minute walk from home to school in the morning; on the ten-minute walk back from school to home at lunchtime; on the ten-minute walk from home to school at the end of lunchtime; and on the ten-minute walk back from school to home at the end of the day. Factoring in the fact that he had to walk for ten minutes, in order to walk me for ten minutes – like so many Indian children I had a predilection for mathematics – at least eighty minutes of his day were dedicated to walking me to and from school.

By the age of seven, when I started primary school, and the casual tartan smockwear my mother made me wear to Woden Infants was replaced with the Woden Juniors' uniform of grey shorts, grey shirt and red tie, I was old enough to make my own way. And, this being an age before kiddy-fiddlers were believed to be lurking behind every parked car, most children across Park Village did so. But when, on my first day, Dad appeared at the front door as usual – five minutes early, staring at his watch, repeatedly checking his pockets for his housekeys, as usual – I took his hand gratefully. So terrifying was the prospect of a new school and so feeble my hold on reality, I may well have ended up in a distant borough of Birmingham had he not assisted.

This is another thing that adults often get wrong about childhood: yes, it is the most carefree time of your life, but, at the same time, if you consult the small print of your memory closely enough, you'll probably recall it was also the time you could be at your most anxious. Your problems might have been smaller and fewer, but your ability to deal with them was correspondingly weaker, and something like moving schools – even to a school next door to the one you had been attending for four years – could feel like the end of the world. It certainly had me breathing bricks of fear.

Which was not to say there weren't things to be excited about. I liked the new uniform, especially the elasticated tie and the rather girly grey slip-shoes, which, with the protective metal studs that had been hammered into the heels, made me feel like a tap dancer as my father's hands guided me to the school gates. Also, having listened to my siblings talk about their time there – they were all at Heath Park High by this stage – I was excited by the prospect of pottery, the possibility of learning the recorder, and school trips to stately homes and museums. At Infants, we only ever seemed to be taken to Dudley Zoo, a prospect that was beginning to make us as listless as the primates shivering behind bars.

But there was a great deal more to worry about. Specifically, compulsory cross-country runs, which, according to my brother, involved running in your pants if you forgot your kit; compulsory swimming lessons, which, according to my brother, involved being thrown into a pool in the nude if you forgot your kit; and older kids throwing you into dustbins – in the nude too, doubtless – just for the hell of it. And then there were the teachers: Mr Burgess (no relation to Mrs Burgess, the corner shop owner), notorious for making children stand in corridors sporting a 'dunce' hat; Mr Ball, the headmaster, whose weapon of choice was apparently something terrifying called the 'jimmy slipper'; and Mrs Caring, whose lessons seemed to revolve around a perpetual series of shouts, slaps and wooden rulers smashed against the backs of hands and legs. In my mind she was a combination of the Wicked Witch of the East and the Child Catcher from *Chitty Chitty Bang Bang*, and the prospect of getting her as a form mistress made me want to go to the toilet repeatedly.

I clutched my schoolbag tightly as I walked along with Dad, as if my life and dignity depended on its contents (which, in a way, they did), mumbled the Japji Sahib, the beginning of the Guru Granth Sahib Mum had taught me, and watched Dad hum to himself – Hindi songs I didn't recognize from Bollywood films I'd never seen – click his fingers to some beat I couldn't hear, and smile, at people going past, at nothing in particular. Dad's hands were hairier and darker than mine – thick, yellowing fingernails curving down like the ends of banisters, his Seiko watch hanging loose on his wrist like a bangle – and at the school gates, I had to be prised away from them slowly. And then I would only let go when I caught sight of another member of the family: my cousin Pumi, the eldest of Chacha's children, who was a year behind me at infant school, but had been bumped up this term. Her extravagantly looped and ribboned plaits made her instantly recognizable among the sea of oiled and shampooed heads. We stood silently against each other in the playground – she'd heard the stories about Mrs Caring too – speechless with nerves as older kids ran around us.

It was a comfort having Pumi there. A member of the family was never more than an arm's length away in those days. But as a teacher rang a bell at the end of the playground, I felt a pang of longing for my siblings. What was the point of having older sisters and brothers if they were always going to be at a different school, always out of reach, when I needed them? The self-pity turned into panic when I was put in a different group from Pumi, and sent down a disorientating sequence of polished corridors.

But finally, behind the green door of the classroom next to the girl's cloakroom, relief arrived in the form of my new form mistress's kindly face rising like the moon against the blackboard, and the sound of her saying, warmly: 'Good morning, class. My name is Mrs Jones.'

'Good morning!!!' we chimed back, an army of American cheerleaders. Twenty-six brown, black and white – though mostly brown – faces smiled in relief and adoration.

'Now then, let's see who we have here this year . . .'

She glanced at her coffee mug. Or rather, she appeared to be glancing at her coffee mug, but given that she was cross-eyed, was actually consulting the register.

'Nicholas Cope?'

'Yes, miss.'

'Zareena Dhillon?'

'Yes, miss.'

'Debra Jones?'

'Yes, miss.'

'Kamaljit Kaur?'

'Yes, miss.'

'Kulvinder Kaur?'

'Yes, miss.'

'Sukhbir Kaur?'

'Yes, miss.'

'Arvinder Singh?'

'Yes, miss.'

'Baldev Singh?'

'Yes, miss.'

'Dalbinder Singh?'

'Yes, miss.'

'Tajinder Singh?'

'Yes, miss.'

'Oh dear, oh dear, oh dear . . .' She put her red pen down on the table. 'This won't do at all. Now then . . . Can those of you called Kaur or Singh provide me with a surname, please?' She picked up her biro. 'Kamaljit?'

'Sandhu, miss.'

'Kulvinder?'

'Dhaliwal, miss.'

'Sukhbir?'

'Bains, miss.'

When she got to me I squeezed my legs together, pushed my hands deeper into my pockets, and fingered the remnants of the boiled sweets that Mum had given me to hand out, to help make new friends.

'Sath-nam? Is that how you say it?'

'Yes, miss,' I lied.

'Your surname?'

'Singh, miss.'

'Come on now, don't be a silly sausage.' A ripple of giggles across the room. 'Everyone has a forename – mine, for example, is Hyacinth . . .' More giggles. 'Most people have a middle name . . . mine, for example, is Edna . . .' Open laughter now. 'Yours is Singh. And you should also have a surname or family name. Like Jones?'

My mouth opened and closed like the goldfish in the tank at the back of the room.

'Maybe you can ask your father or your mother and then let me know?'

I nodded.

'Maybe you could ask at lunchtime? Are you one of the children who goes home for lunch?'

Of course I was one of the children who went home for lunch. There had been a brief period at infant school, after Puli had filled out the appropriate forms, when I'd spent lunchtimes being served free school slop in the hut next to the playground, but, pathetically, I was poleaxed by homesickness – being away from my parents for a whole day seemed too long – and when I happened to mention to Mum that I thought I might have eaten a beefburger by accident, and that I'd been told off by a dinner lady for scooping up mash with a spoon (we didn't use knives and forks at home), Mum reacted with the rage I'd hoped for, pronouncing that free or not free, no child of hers would be force-fed the Holy Cow with a fork. By the end of the week I was coming back home for lunch and a shiny set of knives and forks was sitting in our cutlery drawer.

At the gates, I got the expected response from Dad: 'Ask your

Mum when you get home.' Which is what I did, as Mum stood in the kitchen preparing chapattis, her apron shaded with flour, the *paoncha* of her salwar dipped in dust, a *sabzi* of carrots and potatoes on a rear hob and an iron griddle, a *tuva*, on a front one. Certain British staples – chips, beans, sausages – were creeping on to our menu by this time, any meal with an English element being labelled 'dinner' by Mum, and in some cases being combined with Punjabi staples (Mum's Heinz Baked Bean curry was to die for, and tomato ketchup goes brilliantly with yellow lentil curry), but at lunchtime it was always Punjabi cuisine. Chapattis with curry. Flour and fat and gravy.

Mum didn't respond at all initially. She just pinched a globule off the mound of dough that had probably been kneaded that morning, patted and rolled it into a perfect circle, threw it on to the *tuva*, cooked it on both sides, flipped it on to a naked gas flame until the steam inside made the chapatti balloon, and then tossed it on to a waiting cloth. I interpreted the hesitation as a sign of tiredness: by lunchtime she would have done two hours' housework, an hour of cooking, three hours' sewing and got us ready for school. But it was probably exasperation. Mum hadn't had much success when it came to registering the names of her children in England. Rajah's full name, Jasmail, was mistakenly recorded as 'Gasmail' on his birth certificate, my illiterate father having been sent to register it. And while my first name is common among Sikhs, I've never met anyone else with an 'h' in the middle of it, a quirk once again attributable to my illiterate dad, or to the relative who wrote the name down on the piece of paper he took to the Civic Centre.

'Your surname is Singh,' she said eventually, running a slab of Lurpak over the most recently baked chapatti. 'It means lion. A name shared by every Sikh man and a name to be proud of.' She pinched another piece of dough off the globe. 'Don't you remember the story I told you?'

I remembered the story. It was one of the many religious tales Mum told me at night, when my siblings were still downstairs watching telly, and we lay in the room above, my father on the double bed, my mother on the three-quarters bed pushed next to it, and me trying not to slide into the gap between. It involved Guru Gobind Singh, the tenth and most militaristic of the Sikh gurus, a test of faith involving the slaughter of a goat, and ended with Guru Gobind Singh pronouncing that all male Sikhs would henceforth share the surname 'Singh', and all female Sikhs would henceforth share the surname 'Kaur'. I remembered the tale but it didn't really help with my predicament.

I waited for Mum to finish baking another chapatti before pressing further. She made cooking look so easy: whenever I tried making *rotis* – I would have to beg to be allowed, whereas my sisters were forced to learn – I could never get the dough to roll out evenly or transfer the chapatti from the sideboard to the *tuva* in one piece, and the bits that did make it would always end up burnt and tasting like the back of an oven. Mum would invariably attempt to rescue my effort by carving an animal shape out of the bit that looked least burnt and would try to reassure me with the remark: 'Don't worry, son, you'll have a wife to cook for you.'

As another steaming chapatti deflated, I decided to press my point by exploiting my mother's instinctive and total respect for authority. 'My teacher says I must have a family name,' I ventured. Just in case this didn't convey the urgency of the matter, I followed it up by pressing another of her buttons: implying that, somehow, we weren't as good as other families in the neighbourhood. 'All the other Sikh boys in class have one. You know Arvinder, who lives at the end of the street? His family name is Chahal.'

She sighed. And shrugged. And then, with one hand on her hip, said: 'Ask Puli when she gets home.'

There was a wait before I could ask Puli. It was more than a mile to Heath Park High, which meant, with the walk of more than a mile to school in the morning, the walk of more than a mile back from school to home at lunchtime, the walk of more than a mile from home to school at the end of lunchtime, and the walk of more than a mile back from school to home at the end of the day, that my siblings walked four or five miles every day. They rarely had more than fifteen minutes to eat at lunchtime, and sometimes my sisters had to make their own chapattis in that time too. Puli was scraping her bowl clean with the end of her roti, in her preferred dining position – at the foldaway table underneath the telly – when I asked her. She gave me a version of Mum's huffing and puffing before asking for a piece of paper – I tore a strip from one of the blue airmail letters that arrived in the post for Mum once a fortnight – and I watched as she transcribed my surname slowly on to it, the tips of her fingers iced with flour. I read it out to myself as I struggled through my lunch of two chapattis – 'You can't just have one roti now you're at big school' – and announced it to Bindi and Rajah.

'That's our name,' said Bindi, sniffling into a hanky between mouthfuls, sitting in her preferred dining position: the settee opposite the telly.

'I know, you plonker,' said Rajah, from his preferred dining location: the armchair, a plate placed on a tray resting on his lap. 'We all have the same family name. That's the point. Durrrrr.' He stuck his tongue under his bottom lip. '*By nabe's Sathnam dun d'im a SPACK.*'

When they'd gone, leaving separately as usual – *why did they never go to school together?* – I continued practising my name on Pussy as she danced around my father's feet in the kitchen, his preferred dining position, where he received his chapattis red-hot and sooty, and where he could belch and fart to his digestive system's content without having to endure disapproval. I continued practising as his hands took me through the streets of Park Village again, and would probably have practised all the way to school had we not had a happy interruption in our routine outside Mrs Burgess's corner shop.

Sweets were something my father and I had in common. Or rather, not having sweets was something we had in common – me because, as an eight-year-old boy, I could never have enough; and my dad because, as a diabetic, he was under instructions to avoid them. But sometimes, usually after lunch, he'd crack.

'Don't tell your mum, okay?'

We didn't enter until I'd promised.

A bell tinkled as we pushed open the blue door, and Mrs Burgess, as thin as the cigarette hanging from her mouth, older even than the lino that cracked across the floor, came hobbling out of her stock room.

'Alroight, cock,' she trilled, examining me from the tip of the brand new silk hanky on my topknot, to my already-grazed knees. 'Coo. Look at yow, trimmed up like a ham bone! Yow look just like ower Steve used to.'

I loved Mrs Burgess. For her crazy expressions, for the crazy way she said I reminded her of her son Steve, even though her son Steve, judging by the picture on the shelf behind her, was a middle-aged officer with the Metropolitan Police. But more than anything I loved Mrs Burgess for her shop, which unlike the Indian shop on Crowther Street, or the Indian newsagent on Cannock Road, was almost entirely dedicated to sweets and snacks. As well as its display of crisps, one whole wall was stacked with jars of chocolates and sweets measured out by the quarter pound – barley sugars, cola cubes; another was taken up with a deck of sweets coming in packets – Mojos, Black Jacks, Love Hearts; and at the far end of the shop stood a display of what my siblings and I called the 20 pence sweets – Twixes and Mars Bars – which we continued calling the 20 pence sweets even when they started costing much more.

The combination of lots of sweets, greediness and feeble purchasing power might have been frustrating, but I always found the activity pleasurable, as it allowed my fondness for confectionery to be combined with my enthusiasm for maths. I must have spent a quarter of my childhood running through the combinations and permutations of what I could get with my 10 pence a week pocket money. If you wanted to go for sheer quantity, you could go for twenty Mojos, at a half pence each. If you fancied something savoury *and* something sweet, you could go for a 5 pence bag of crisps plus five Black Jacks. Then there was the possibility of those 20 pence sweets – the emperors of chocolate bars, for which we occasionally pooled our pocket money. The resulting purchase would be cut in half with the kind of precision reserved for diamond cutters, the process usually monitored by an independent adjudicator – Mum. We still nearly always ended up in blows over the crumbs. Thrillingly, it was this display that my father padded towards.

'Shall we get the coconut one?'

He meant Bounty. I should have guessed. Coconuts, along with butter, mangoes, guavas and raw sugar cane, were among the foods that sent my parents, grandparents, uncles and aunts into fits of ecstasy and nostalgia for India. I didn't think much of the real-life hairy coconuts Mum brought home, but Bounty . . . it was like it said on the pack, the taste of paradise.

'Comes in two chunks,' I said. 'So you can have one and I can have one.'

At the counter, Dad reached into his trouser pocket and handed over some money with a slow smile and a 'hello', one of his few words of English – the others being 'thank you'. The 20 pence coin that passed between them, only recently in circulation, was almost as mesmerizing as the chocolate bar it entitled us to.

'Cheers, cock,' trilled Mrs Burgess, taking the coin from Dad, but addressing me, and putting it into the wooden tray that served as her cash register. She sang us a local farewell – 'Ta ra!' – before disappearing, whistling, back into her stock room.

Outside, I relished ripping open the wrapper and sliding the bars out from the cardboard slip inside, but Dad wolfed down his share in two gulps – like a pig chobbling coal, Mrs Burgess would have said. There was no chance of me doing that. I was going to make it last as long as I could, even if it meant being late for school. Crawling along, with Dad glancing repeatedly at his watch, I nibbled the milk chocolate off the top first, then off the sides, and then – trickiest bit here, the chocolate is at its thinnest – from the bottom. Finally, a cuboid of sugary coconut caught between the tips of my fingers, themselves stained with the yellow *haldi* of lunch. I polished it off in quarters.

'That was *sohni*, Dad.'

I kept the black cardboard slip from inside the wrapper with the intention of sniffing it and reliving the experience later, but it drifted on to the classroom floor during afternoon registration, as I ransacked the pockets of my shorts for the strip of blue airmail, with my name written on it. Mrs Jones waited.

'How do you spell that?'

'Ess, ay, en, gee, haitch . . .'

'You mean aitch . . .'

'Gee, haitch . . .'

'Not *haitch*. Aitch is pronounced without an haitch. . .'

Again, my mouth opened and closed wordlessly. Fortunately, she changed the subject.

'I see your name alliterates . . .'

She looked over the whole class now. Or rather, she looked at the wall and I assumed she was looking over the whole class.

'Does anyone know what alliteration means?'

A sea of blinking eyes. We knew nothing.

'Alliteration is a stylistic device, or literary technique, in which successive words begin with the same consonant sound or letter.' She may as well have been speaking Mandarin. 'For example, the phrase: the sweet smell of success. Actually, Wordsworth springs to mind.' She closed her eyes. '*And sings a solitary song, That whistles in the wind* . . . Can any of you think of an example of alliteration?'

The blinking intensified.

'Come on, I'm sure one of you can think of something. A

dime a dozen is another example. Bigger and better? Jump for joy?'

It was only when I noticed my classmates laughing that I realized I'd inadvertently replied. 'Silly sausage!'

'Yes! Excellent example. Well done. One house point to you.' Ten house points meant a visit to the headmaster's office to claim a bright red maxi badge, which you could wear on your pullover as a demonstration of your swottiness. 'Very well done.' Smiling, Mrs Jones returned to the register. 'Now then, that name sounds familiar. Are you Narinder's brother by any chance?'

'Yes, miss.'

'Gosh.' Her tiny cross-eyes almost disappeared into her large face when she smiled. 'One of the best students I ever had. We'll be lucky if you turn out half as good . . .'

I beamed idiotically. It's not every day you get a new name, learn that it aliter-thingy and find out that you're related to a genius. The good feeling stayed for the remainder of the day, with its new exercise books, the sound of someone murdering 'Au Clair de la Lune' on the recorder next door and the smell of hops wafting across from the brewery on the other side of the playing fields. When the bell rang, our steel-framed chairs screeched against the floor and Mrs Jones said, 'That bell is for me, not for you, sit back down,' just like the teachers did at infant school, before letting us go after the customary pretence that she didn't want to get home as soon as possible too. I pelted out at a hundred miles an hour for *Bananaman* and *Jackanory* and luncheon meat sandwiches, dunked in Indian tea.

Dad was standing at the gates – probably had been for ten minutes already – and next to him was the unexpected figure of Chacha, who, presumably back from a morning shift at his copper tubing factory, had come to pick up Pumi. Seeing them next to each other, you'd never have guessed they were brothers: my father stocky and sombre, his hair brushed back into a bouffant; Chacha younger and thinner and smily and sporting a turban. But then, my brother and I hardly looked related: Rajah was at this stage in the middle of his Ralph Macchio phase, bearing an uncanny, possibly deliberate likeness to the Karate Kid, while I, the family's religious experiment, was still in my prolonged Ranjeet-Singh-the-Punjabi-Tube-worker-from-*Mind-Your-Language* phase. Years later I would be surprised when people asked why I was singled out for having long hair when my father and brother didn't. I never wondered why, the difference between Dad and Chacha having normalized it. It was just the way of things: some people in families had turbans, some didn't.

On seeing me, Chacha smiled and did what he often did – plucked a single hair from his black beard and pretended to plant it in my cheek. 'There you go, sahib!' he laughed. His Punjabi was speckled with bits of English gleaned during his few years at a British comprehensive as a teenager. 'A full and bushy beard within a week!' He stepped back to size me up. 'You will look like a saint.' A stroke of his own beard. 'Like Guru Gobind Singh, perhaps. People will travel from the four corners of the world, from the three corners of India, from the two corners of Wolverhampton, just to worship under the enormous shadow of your beard!'

If I knew what 'ironic' meant, the remark would have struck me as so, because, with his thin, handsome face, sculpted beard and regal turban, Chacha often reminded me of Guru Gobind Singh, who in portraits was portrayed as a majestic figure on horseback holding a royal falcon. Indeed, when I was very young, I thought Chacha *was* Guru Gobind Singh – in the way that I thought that the *granthi* at the Cannock Road *gurdwara was* Guru Nanak, the founder of the Sikh religion – a confusion accentuated by a photograph in our front room, in which Chacha was shown posing with a budgerigar. But I laughed at the joke anyway, like I laughed at all of Chacha's jokes – after all, he was the one who taught me to ride a bike, who took us to the open day at the local bus garage sometimes – and was still laughing when Pumi's sad figure crawled into view.

I'd forgotten about her in the relief and excitement of my day, but now it was apparent from the way she couldn't even summon the energy to pull up her white socks that something terrible

had happened. The worst thing imaginable, in fact: she'd got Mrs Caring as a form teacher. I might have offered sympathy, but it would have been easier to offer consolation to someone who had just lost their entire family in a freak tornado. Besides, I'd yet to develop the necessary skills of human empathy, so I ignored her entirely and skipped home, my father within reach, Chacha and Pumi following close behind, my thoughts as cheerful as they had been anxious in the morning. I tried to walk all the way without standing on cracks in the pavement, looked for empty packets of Hula Hoops (collect twenty and send off for a free Wham! T-shirt), peered into the windows of the cool Ford Granada at the end of Nine Elms Lane, considered important questions such as 'What did Boy George mean when he sang: "Karma Chameleon"?' and 'If planets are in the sky, are we in the sky too?', and played a game of spot the difference with the houses along the route – the council was making renovation grants available and the smooth rows of Victorian terraced houses were beginning to be disrupted by the addition of Edwardian effects, mock Tudor doors, cottagey bow windows and porches. Instead of looking straight ahead at the street, some houses appeared to have developed a squint.

As we turned the corner from Crowther Street into Prosser Street – the local pub, the Lewisham Arms, and the family houses at numbers 60 and 68 within view – my thoughts returned to the events of the day, and I found myself babbling them out in a stream of consciousness to Pumi, who had caught up with Dad and me: telling her about the lovely Mrs Jones, who seemed to have the gentleness of Princess Di and the twinkliness of Mary Poppins, about my two house points (I'd got another for answering a maths question), and about my new name.

'S. A. N. G. H. E. R. A.,' I elaborated. 'You see, everyone has a forename, a middle name and a surname. You must have the same surname? It's a family name, you see.'

Chacha interjected. 'That ain't how you spell it, Dumbo.'

I looked up at his face to see if he might be joking. He'd recently tried to persuade me that eating bananas would literally turn me into a monkey. But he seemed dead serious.

'Honestly, ask your mother. There's no aitch in the middle.'

6. Everybody's Got to Learn Sometime

I filled in the month between my resolution to visit the psychiatrist with Dad and the actual appointment by conducting some rudimentary research into schizophrenia. Or rather, I filled in the month between my resolution to visit the psychiatrist with Dad and the actual appointment by . . . *returning to London, where I worked during the day and filled the evenings worrying about how I should word my bombshell letter to my mother, and her possible reaction, until I could stand it no more and came back hoping for some kind of insight in Wolverhampton, where I worked during the day and spent the evenings being nagged about getting married before it's too late, until I could stand it no more and stomped off to my bedroom, deciding I had to write the letter right there and then, get it translated immediately and deliver it straight away, regardless of Mum's possible reaction, only to change my mind when brought cups of tea and Penguin bars by way of apology, coming back downstairs to watch* BBC Parliament *and listen to Mum go on about the declining quality of tomatoes in shops on the Dudley Road, until I could stand it no more and left the house to visit my sister Bindi, an awkward conversation with whom kick-started me into* . . . conducting some rudimentary research into schizophrenia.

I decided, in an attempt to burn off the gallons of ghee that had been cascading into my stomach, to walk the mile or so to Bindi's house in Goldthorn Park, a leafy suburb in the south of Wolverhampton, slightly to the north of the leafy suburb in the south of Wolverhampton where my parents reside. Initially, little seemed to have changed. But gradually it became evident that the little changes – net curtains framing windows that had previously been bare, front and back gardens concreted over, parked cars mostly of German extraction – in fact pointed to a significant social shift. In my absence, this part of town had become heavily

Asian. Wolverhampton has long had one of the largest Sikh populations in the country – 8 per cent belong to the faith according to 2001 census figures – but when I lived there, the Asian areas were concentrated in pockets near the town centre. My family, specifically my eldest aunt, Pindor, who lived on the same street as my parents, was among the first to drift to the southern suburbs, but now the whole area had a distinctly Indian flavour.

And, on the scale of Indian flavours, Bindi's house was a vindaloo. Designed and fitted out by her husband – a turbaned taxi driver from India to whom she was arranged in marriage at twenty-one – her semi-detached home was an exposition of almost every Punjabi design cliché. Trees had been yanked out of the back garden to make way for slabs. The front lawn had been block-paved over, to make parking space for not one, but two Mercedes. Inside, wallpaper had been replaced with painted plaster, the newest bits of furniture retaining their cellophane packing for protection, and while thousands had been spent sprucing things up, the family actually spent most of their time in the least swish room: the converted garage. But as I was a visitor, Bindi – thirty-four now, not as thin as before, but just as sniffly – took me into the posh living room.

'How's things?' she asked as we squeaked against the cellophane.

'Fine,' I lied.

'Busy?'

'Yeah,' I lied.

'Would you like a cup of tea?'

'Yeah.'

One of the uncomfortable revelations of those early days of being back home was the realization that I'd lost the ability to talk fluently to my sisters. Bindi and I used to be close. When I was around twelve, and she around seventeen, we were probably the closest members of the family. Trapped in the house together (as a young Asian woman approaching marriageable age, she wasn't allowed to go anywhere, and, being new to the area, I often had no friends to hang out with), we spent our spare time making cakes and trifles in the kitchen – following the recipes from her old home economics books like chemistry experiments – and indulging in our pop music obsession together. But once Bindi got married, we stopped talking, and while I'd become increasingly estranged from Punjabi culture, she, with an Indian husband, and two boys being raised as religious Sikhs, with topknots like I used to have, had become entirely immersed in it. Now, the gap between her life (housework, children, TV) and mine (words, music, media tosspottery) felt insurmountable. The few conversations we had were always through her children, and with them away delivering newspapers on this occasion, I flailed through a list of possible conversation topics as she went to make the tea. *Housework?* God. No. I had a cleaner anyway. *Pop music?* Nope. The first thing that goes when you have children is music. *Telly?* I'd realized years earlier that my kind of shows (*Curb Your Enthusiasm, Six Feet Under*) were not her kind of shows (*X Factor, EastEnders*). Besides, my telly aversion was still simmering.

I ummed gormlessly as Bindi reappeared bearing tea and a plate of Jaffa Cakes, and because I couldn't think of anything else to say, I found myself asking: 'So when did you realize Dad had schizophrenia?'

I'd blurted out the same question to Rajah some nights beforehand. We'd been playing a round of Scrabble in our parents' living room at the time, a game which, owing to the fact that some of the players didn't speak good English, and the fact that some of the players were under the age of ten, and the fact that we don't have a dictionary in the house, we were playing with the usual family rule that any word is allowed, as long as the other players agree it is a word. As ever, proceedings had begun cheerfully, but the game had disintegrated amid recriminations. A nephew had stormed off when I'd objected to 'adress'. I'd successfully thrown a strop when it looked like 'SIFT' was about to be disallowed ('I DO WRITE FOR A LIVING, YOU KNOW'). But having begun with four players, it was now just down to the two of us.

'Actually,' he'd said, putting down a thirty-two-pointer and winning the game. 'I didn't realize until quite late. At first I just thought he was depressed. It was three or four years ago that I realized what schizophrenia was. I went to a few appointments with Dad and read some stuff.'

And that was it. No elaboration on how he found out, no suggestion of trauma, no five-year period of denial and, apparently, no desire to tell his younger brother what he had discovered. I've envied Rajah for many things over the years. For his looks, his easy way with people, his patience, his Punjabi skills, the way in which he has managed to balance his love life with family requirements, his successful career in business with hobbies: despite being busy at work, he manages to find time to work as an extra on film sets around the country and is a keen bodybuilder. But at this moment I envied him for something new: for his ability to quickly confront things and get on. I wish I could be like that.

Bindi, meanwhile, fell into a rather ominous silence after the question was posed. I'd scanned the whole of her living room, with its fake ivory ornaments, family portraits superimposed on to palace interiors, and portraits of Sikh freedom fighters, by the time her response arrived.

'Schizowhat?'

I suppose I should extend what I said earlier: I didn't realize my father and eldest sister suffered from schizophrenia until my mid-twenties; I didn't start confronting what this meant until my late twenties; I didn't share this knowledge with my other sister until I was in my late twenties and it is only now, at thirty, that I feel the need to talk about it. After drinking my tea and recovering from the surprise and relief of discovering someone as clueless as me, it struck me that Bindi's question was actually a good one. What did schizophrenia mean?

I wasn't, at that stage, entirely ignorant about mental illness. I knew, for instance, that people who have depression are often sad, not because of their circumstances, but because of a chemical imbalance in the brain. Mum took antidepressants. But that, I'm ashamed to admit, was the extent of my insights. Like many young

and healthy men I regarded the mentally ill as a distant, difficult and sometimes even amusing aspect of other people's lives. I would occasionally remark, in a way to highlight my urban streetfighter credentials, that Brixton, the area of London I lived in, hosted 1 per cent of the UK's mental health patients – a fact gleaned from a Sunday newspaper feature. I could regularly be heard referring to difficult colleagues and ex-girlfriends as demented, maniacal, hysterical, psycho, deranged, mentalist, whacko and bipolar (though in one case the person concerned did actually turn out to be bipolar). I didn't really understand the difference between 'psychotic' and 'neurotic', though again I used the words to describe ex-girlfriends and colleagues, and while I thought Puli had had one, the phrase 'nervous breakdown' confused me. As far as I could tell, it seemed to refer to everything from a bad hair day to a full-on catastrophic mental breakdown.

As for 'schizophrenia' . . . Well, I'd watched *A Beautiful Mind*, the biopic of John Forbes Nash Jr, the maths prodigy who overcame schizophrenia to win the Nobel Prize. I knew it was the title of a bad album by JC Chasez, a former member of 'N Sync. I occasionally used the word as an adjective – to describe ex-girlfriends and colleagues, and also, ironically, my split life between Wolverhampton and London. And, of course, media coverage had given the word certain connotations of terror, violence, and of sufferers sitting hooting and tooting in the secure wings of prisons and hospitals around the country.

In other words, I probably knew as much about the disease as Punjabis know about landscape gardening. So when I returned to London after that visit – Bindi and I actually spent a nice afternoon flicking through old family photographs and old copies of *Smash Hits* (she'd kept everything) – I did something I should have done years earlier. I logged on to a database of newspapers and looked up recent articles that mentioned the term. It's hard to imagine another phrase in the English language that could have elicited a more depressing set of headlines.

CITY MAN GETS LIFE FOR HACKING NEIGHBOUR TO DEATH
(*Allentown Morning Call*)

NUDE WOMAN ARRESTED NEAR MALL
(*Brownsville Herald, Texas*)

ARREST MY SON BEFORE HE KILLS SOMEONE
(*Daily Mirror*)

EYE-GOUGING MAY LEAVE MUM, 73, BLIND
(*Dominion Post*)

Once again I struggled to tally the apparent violent reality of schizophrenia with my sensitive sister and my always-gentle father, but, keen not to lose momentum, I continued the research by consulting a medical dictionary. Unfortunately, though I didn't realize it at the time, the one nearest to hand in the London library I sometimes worked in – *Encyclopaedia of Aberrations: a psychiatric handbook* (1953) – was also woefully out of date. Somewhere between entries on 'sadism and masochism' and 'sexual activity. Relation of olfaction to', I found several entries related to schizophrenia, and settled on one headed 'schizophrenia latent'. It mentioned something called the 'Rorschach test' (which I now know is a controversial and possibly unreliable method of psychological evaluation), and an outline of fifteen features 'generally indicative of latent schizophrenia'. That was exactly what I needed, I thought – a list of symptoms. I ran through the list, putting mental ticks against the symptoms I thought might be exhibited by Dad:

Minimal loss of reality contact (maybe, not sure what this means though)

Deviations from the common ways of thinking, expressed by bizarre associations or looking at the cards from unusual angles (yes)

Lack of mental energy, with reduction of intellectual initiative (yes)

Anxiety, often based on awareness of mental borderline state (maybe, he does sometimes look anxious)

Fantasy living (maybe, but not sure what this means)

Estrangement from reality (yes, probably)

Hypochondriasis (I had to consult another dictionary to find out this meant 'hypochondria'. No. Dad never complains of being ill)

The tendency to attribute reality to the cards (maybe, but not sure what this means)

Ideas of reference, often expressed jokingly (no – don't think so)

Projections of inner hostility (no – the most passive man I know)

Projections of asymmetry (maybe, no idea what this means)

Religious themes, or interest in related fields (no – he goes to the temple a lot but seems more interested in the social aspect)

Chaotic sexuality, with preoccupation with sex and loss of social sense (really hope not)

Homosexuality (no)

Withdrawal from people (no)

Putting the book down, it seemed to me that Dad was hardly conclusively schizophrenic – seven 'nos'; three 'yeses' and five 'maybes'. If anything, I seemed to exhibit more of the symptoms than he did: I lacked mental energy, had anxiety, was a hypochondriac, had inner (and outer) hostility, was interested in religious themes, was as preoccupied with sex as any other man, was often mistakenly thought to be gay, and had, since the break-up with Alison and the subsequent realization that I had to confront my mother, withdrawn from people. Meanwhile, the second point – 'Deviations from the common ways of thinking, expressed by bizarre associations or looking at the cards from unusual angles' – could have been my job description.

I'd only pursued this line of thought to amuse myself, but a scary possibility became lodged in my mind. If both my father and my sister had been struck with schizophrenia, did it mean I was at risk from mental illness too? Come to think of it, was I already halfway there? Didn't friends and family often accuse me of being *neurotic*? Wasn't I too quick to anger with my family, too quick to tears in confrontations? I felt guilty for letting such selfish concerns overshadow the more pressing matter of finding out about my father's and sister's respective sanity or insanity, but from that point, the quest to find out about schizophrenia became, at least in part, a personal hypochondriacal one. I ordered a set of books about schizophrenia on the internet.

Opening the parcels was a depressing business. Lord knows why publishers feel the need to decorate the covers of books like *Recovered, Not Cured: A Journey Through Schizophrenia* and *The Quiet Room: A Journey Out of the Torment of Madness* with pictures of faceless women sitting bleakly on bare floors, of distorted faces staring distractedly at each other. The subject matter is bleak enough. A few waving bears or lolloping kittens really wouldn't go amiss. But if the covers made me want to self-mutilate, what lay between them made me feel worse. Time after time I would launch into a new title with enthusiasm, only to hit a phrase so bleak – such as 'each of us lives a life of quiet desperation' or 'Jonathan died of a drug overdose when he was twenty-four' – that I would have to stop and immerse myself in *Fur Fighters* on my Sony PlayStation to get over it. The task was made additionally difficult by the invariable turgidity of the writing (it seems a psychiatrist will always use twelve words when three would do), the arbitrary and impenetrable classifications (talk of 'paranoid'/ 'hebephrenic'/'catatonic'/'simple'/'type 1'/'type 2' schizophrenia was of little help), and the lack of consensus. I'd think I'd finally got my finger on an aspect of schizophrenia, only for it to be contradicted by another psychiatrist in another book.

It was a comfort and delight, therefore, to come across E. Fuller Torrey's *Surviving Schizophrenia: A Manual for Families, Patients, and Providers.* The book didn't appear promising. There was the uninspiring title, for a start. And the author's name, too: how much can you trust a man who initializes his first name? Also, like so many writers on the subject, Torrey, a clinical and research psychiatrist specializing in schizophrenia and bipolar disorder, laid on the misery with a trowel: 'Schizophrenia is to psychiatry what cancer is to medicine: a sentence as well as a diagnosis . . .'; 'Schizophrenia is the modern day equivalent of leprosy . . .'; 'Schizophrenia is a cruel disease. The lives of those affected are often chronicles of constricted experiences, muted emotions, missed opportunities, unfulfilled expectations. It leads to a twilight existence, a twentieth-century underground man . . .' *Stop now. I've got the point.*

But after a little more reading, it became clear that Torrey was unlike other psychiatrist-writers. He was capable of writing sentences of less than fifty-seven words. He was authoritative and opinionated but still managed to frame debates fairly. The science bits were detailed and clear. And, maybe because his sister was afflicted with the disease, he didn't give the impression that he was only gracing the subject with his time and attention because he considered it a diverting intellectual exercise. The discussion was imbued with sensitivity and warmth, the acknowledgement that schizophrenia is not only an interesting disease, but is also one that devastates the lives of sufferers and their families.

It was particularly interesting to read his thoughts on the effect the illness can have on siblings or children of schizophrenics. '[They] often try to compensate for their ill family member by being as perfect as possible. In a study of the children of mentally ill parents, Kauffman et al. labelled the extremely competent offspring as superkids . . .' I'm not (quite) vain enough to call myself a superkid, and I didn't have the word 'schizophrenia' until the age of twenty-four, but I recognized the desperate urge to be as trouble-free as possible, to compensate for trauma elsewhere. It was also a comfort to read Torrey acknowledging that 'most siblings and children of individuals with schizophrenia are themselves haunted by a fear that they too will develop the disease . . .'

Most unexpectedly Torrey managed the almost impossible task, in a field where people seem almost to wallow in misery, of writing about schizophrenia with humour. A chapter on 'Fifty of the best and fifteen of the worst books on schizophrenia', which mercilessly skewered some of the books I'd wasted my time on, was a particular treat. All in all, reading *Surviving Schizophrenia* was like being told painful news by an insightful, sympathetic and humorous archbishop. It gave me a targeted reading list and with that a realization that most of my preconceptions about the illness had been wrong. It turns out, for instance, that:

1. *Schizophrenics do not have a 'split personality' in the Dr Jekyll and Mr Hyde sense.* The word actually derives

from the Greek for 'split' and 'mind', refers specifically to disordered thought, and was coined in 1911 by Swiss psychiatrist Eugen Bleuler, who observed that sufferers had difficulties in sorting, interpreting and responding appropriately to stimuli. For example, when told that a relative had just been promoted at work, a person with schizophrenia might cry. Or they might laugh when told a friend's house had burnt down. There *is* a condition which results in something resembling a split personality, but, as Torrey explains, this is called a 'dissociative disorder', is much less common than schizophrenia, occurs almost exclusively in women, and is thought in most cases to be a reaction to sexual or physical abuse in childhood. Dr John Cutting and Anne Charlish also dismantle the common misconception in *Schizophrenia: Understanding and Coping with the Illness,* explaining that in schizophrenia, 'moods, ideas and actions may change dramatically from moment to moment, but it is very rare that there are distinct personality types to be recognized. It is better to regard the result as a shattered rather than as a split personality.'

2. *Schizophrenia is a complicated disease, with no definitive diagnostic test and no single defining symptom.* Unfortunately, you can't just get someone to sit a test for it to be diagnosed. The experience of the illness differs greatly from person to person. Having said this, there are certain common symptoms, many of which were laid out by German psychiatrist Kurt Schneider after the Second World War. These so-called 'first rank symptoms' include: hearing voices arguing; hearing voices commenting on your actions; feeling that your thoughts are being broadcast to the outside world; believing that your thoughts are being removed from your mind; believing that someone else's thoughts are being inserted into your own mind; experiencing

somatic hallucinations (such as feeling that insects are crawling beneath the skin); thinking that your feelings are not your own; believing an alien force is directing your will and actions; and drawing illogical conclusions from perceptual experiences – concluding from the fact that Chris Rea is playing on the radio, for instance, that the Martians are landing in Dudley.

3. *Recovery rates vary.* Predictors of a good outcome apparently include: having a relatively normal childhood; being female; having no family history of schizophrenia; having an older age at the onset; having a sudden onset; having a good awareness of the illness; and having a good initial response to medication. Conversely, predictors of a poor outcome include: having major problems in childhood; being male; having a family history of schizophrenia; having a younger age at onset; having a slow onset; having poor awareness of the illness; having a poor initial response to medication. This seems to tally with my family's experience of schizophrenia: my father, who exhibits many of the bad signs, is visibly not as well as my sister, who exhibits many of the positive indicators. But such precursors do nothing to mask the fact that schizophrenia is a life-long condition with no cure. Only a small number of people have only one episode and can then live their lives without medication.

4. *Schizophrenics do not necessarily want to kill you.* The link between mental illness and violent crime is complex. As Torrey explained in a recent article for the *Wall Street Journal*, 'to be precise, mentally ill individuals who are taking medication to control the symptoms of their illness are not more dangerous. But on any given day, approximately half of severely mentally ill individuals are not taking medication. The evidence is clear that a portion of these individuals are significantly more dangerous.' However, in addition to this, it should be

stressed that people with schizophrenia are as much a risk to themselves as to others. Between 10 and 15 per cent of people with the illness take their own lives.*

5. *Statistically speaking, I might be out of the woods.* Over the course of my reading I stumbled across many terrifying statistics, including claims that siblings of schizophrenics are on average ten times more likely to develop the condition themselves than members of the general population, and that children of schizophrenics are nearly fifteen times more likely to develop the condition. However, it is some comfort, I suppose, that schizophrenia is one of those chronic brain diseases, like multiple sclerosis and Alzheimer's, that has a particular age range of onset, and having an initial onset before the age of fourteen or after the age of thirty is not common.

I felt odd sifting through these revelations while killing time waiting to interview celebrities in London, and even odder sifting through them in Wolverhampton, while my father watched *BBC Parliament* across the room and my mother, resisting Western notions of comfort and furniture, snoozed under a shawl on the carpet nearby.

As someone who reads constantly, who starts scanning the washing instructions on the inside of his blazer if there isn't anything else at hand, I've long despaired at the consequences of my father's illiteracy and my Mum's lack of English ... it means not being able to work out the best-before date on groceries, not being able to complain when you receive bad customer service, not being able to call the emergency services, not understanding the bus driver when he explains that the bus is terminating short of its destination, not daring to travel anywhere you haven't travelled before, in case you get lost, not being able to help your grandchildren with homework, staring into the distance in waiting rooms because there is nothing else to do,

* Max Birchwood and Chris Jackson, *Schizophrenia*.

sending your son a 'for my husband' birthday card because the newsagent misunderstands your request, having to walk all the way to the doctor's surgery to make an appointment because you can't make yourself understood to the secretary, and then struggling to make yourself understood with basic words and hand signals, learning about 9/11 on 12/11, not being able to read what your son writes in a newspaper, being suspicious of strangers because you can never be sure what they mean or intend or want from you . . . But it struck me that not being able to read about a condition that has defined and restricted your entire adult life was the worst consequence of them all. I'd learnt more about the science and incidence of schizophrenia in a few hours of reading than my parents had picked up in more than thirty years of living with the disease. It was bewildering to think that even the word 'schizophrenia' remained foreign to them.

But something in another of Torrey's recommended titles – *Mad House: Growing Up in the Shadow of Mentally Ill Siblings* – subsequently moderated this unease. In one section, the author, Clea Simon, discusses something called the 'clasp-knife reaction', a term which describes how, in certain situations, mechanical joints will not move at all but then suddenly give way. The term is apparently used by some neurologists to describe a common family reaction to the diagnosis of schizophrenia. '[The clasp-knife reaction] is characterized by a slow build-up of rationalization that – when it starts to go – completely collapses . . . We go from thinking, "This is a person, this is my brother. He's just being a little strange . . ." Then all of a sudden, "He's schizophrenic." You've lost the person/brother part . . .'

I was guilty of this. If my father watched *BBC Parliament* obsessively, it must be because he thought his thoughts were being broadcast, I'd concluded. If my sister had a tendency to take things literally it was because Torrey said that people with schizophrenia sometimes struggled with taking a metaphorical approach to language. Among the other things that I ascribed to the disease were: Dad's slow and considered movements (apparently, the minds of sufferers sometimes get flooded with a rush of thoughts); Puli's indecisiveness (ambivalence is apparently a common symptom of thinking in schizophrenia); Dad's comments about the rising sun (grandiose delusions, such as the power to control the weather, are quite common); Dad's quietness (he was evidently exhibiting a range of 'negative symptoms' such as a flattening of emotions, apathy, slowness of movement and under-activity); Dad's unprompted smiles (the 'schizophrenic smile', which appears without obvious external cause, is apparently a response to an internal hallucinatory stimulus), and Dad's unwillingness to visit the doctor (paranoia).

In other words, my father and sister had gone from being my father and sister, two people who behaved a little strangely at times, but two people I loved, to being a collection of symptoms. I'd let the disease claim them entirely. On reading *Mad House*, it struck me that, maybe, in some ways, my mother was actually better off without the word 'schizophrenia'. At least her ignorance meant she didn't lose so much of her husband and daughter to the illness.

I subsequently made a conscious effort to stop jumping to conclusions. It was possible my father didn't like going to the GP because all middle-aged men are reluctant to do so, that my sister was indecisive because it was a trait of her personality, like it was a trait of mine. Instead, I let the remainder of my reading lead me to a series of questions, rather than answers, which I wrote down in a notebook. They included:

Why does Dad stare at books and newspapers when he
can't read?
Does Dad hear voices?
Does Dad think he is receiving personal messages via
BBC Parliament?
How well is his condition controlled by his medication?
Might he get better?
Has he ever been violent?

I would, I decided, put these questions to the psychiatrist when we met.

7. Mad World

As I was saying, schizophrenia is difficult to diagnose. The disease has not a single, but many different ways of beginning; some of the early signs – withdrawal, moodiness, etc. – are also the early signs of adolescence, when the illness tends to strike; there's no scientific way of verifying a diagnosis; the sufferer, because of the nature of the illness, cannot always help in describing the symptoms; and the early symptoms tend to be subtle. And it is this subtlety that bedevils attempts to talk about the beginning of my sister's illness in its context. You see, while Puli's early symptoms were barely perceptible, almost nothing else about our family life was so. Looking back, her madness wasn't half as mad as our apparent sanity.

One aspect of this collective lunacy came in the form of our innocence, which may seem, I realize, a strange thing to pick out. Children are, by definition, innocent, you may say. All kids have funny ideas about the world. But the thing that gave our childish innocence a demented edge was that our parents and grandparents and uncles and aunts, the adults whose role it was to ground us into reality, were, isolated by language and illiteracy and focused on survival, even more clueless than we were. How clueless? Well, I have a vivid memory of trying to explain to my grandfather that the flying monkeys depicted carrying Dorothy and Toto away in *The Wizard of Oz* weren't actually real flying monkeys, but created through special effects. The way he looked back at me, you would have thought I was telling him the sky was made of sponge. I also remember my brother struggling to explain the concept of fashion brands to my mother ('But why pay £5 for a T-shirt I could make for 50 pence?'), Bindi trying to convey the concept of veterinary surgery to my grandmother ('So you're saying there are people *pagal* enough to spend *real money* on treating dogs and cats?'), and Puli attempting to make Mum appreciate the significance of Santa Claus. 'You see, there's this old man, who lives in the North Pole . . . What's the North Pole? It's a very cold place, like the top of a mountain. Anyway, he lives there with these things called . . . elves. What are elves? Well . . .'

But it was a case of the blind leading the blind, as we didn't have a clue either. By the time I was eight, Rajah eleven, Bindi thirteen and Puli fourteen, I'd still never been to a cinema, used a telephone, been inside a church, used a shower, sat in a bath – we still used a bucket and jug – seen the countryside or the sea, read a newspaper, had a white friend, owned a book, met a Muslim or a Tory or a Jew. Among the things I'd never tried on the culinary front were: bacon, coffee, beef, lamb, Chinese food, pizza and McDonald's. When my primary school headmaster gave a lecture on the dangers of glue-sniffing, I thought he was refer-ring to the white paste we used in art lessons and for months afterwards I held the jars at arm's length, terrified that a whiff would have me dribbling like an addict. I thought the area we lived in was called the 'Black Country' because of all the black people living there (but at least I didn't blurt this thought out loud as one of my classmates did during a lesson on local history). And when I saw an NF sign scrawled on the wall of a nearby Indian butcher's, I liked the graphic design of the logo so much – the fancy way in which the F hung off the N – that I inscribed the symbol on to a balloon I'd been given to play with. Puli burst it on sight, but without explaining why.

'Don't EVER write that again.' Her fingers dug into my arm. 'EVER!'

Allied to this was the craziness of the culture clash that engulfed us. Again, this is hardly unusual, you may say. East meets West, East struggles to understand Western notions of liberalism and black pudding, West struggles to understand Eastern notions of enforced marriage and mango pickle, is an old chestnut now, as much of a cliché in multicultural Britain as class used to be in monocultural Britain. You could pave a path from Wolverhampton to New Delhi with books and films and poems on the subject.

But what made our culture clash unusual, I think, was that while we were subject to Eastern and Western influences, there was, at the time, absolutely no sense of a gap yawning open inside us. It was less a culture clash than a . . . culture concurrence.

And it's not as if we were fed bland versions of East and West, either. At home we were essentially raised as Punjabi village children. We didn't just get nagged about the importance of arranged marriages from an early age. Mum would snap at us if we even made eye contact with a member of the opposite sex while walking along the street. She didn't just warn us about the immorality of alcohol and cigarettes. Alcohol was very rarely allowed in the house and we weren't even permitted to buy chocolate cigarettes. There was compulsory Punjabi school on Saturday mornings, compulsory four hours of sitting cross-legged at the *gurdwara* on Sunday mornings, and it was made clear that our parents' word – or rather, Mum's word, as Dad didn't have many to offer – was the word of God.

However, at the same time, we embraced – and were allowed to embrace – many aspects of the West with wild abandon. There were Easter eggs at Easter, cakes and Bird's Eye trifles on birthdays, and every year at Christmas we'd have the full shebang: fairy lights on a plastic tree from Woolworth's in the front room, Christmas cards from our classmates throughout the house, and, on the big day, a giant turkey for lunch and in the early evening, the traditional family bust-up – Puli and Rajah nearly hacking one another to death over whether we should watch *Only Fools and Horses* on BBC1 or the James Bond movie on ITV. As soon as we were done we would do it all over again, waddling over to the Sang(h)eras four doors away for another Christmas dinner later in the evening. Though these Christmases, as now, always had an Indian flavour: we didn't eat meat on Sundays and Tues-days, so would sometimes have our Christmas dinner on Christmas Eve or Boxing Day; Mum would often try to jazz up the turkey with various spicing and tandoori techniques; among the trad-itional Christmas cards there would always be a few wishing us a happy new year and depicting Guru Gobind Singh astride a stallion; and when it came to presents Mum didn't really get into the seasonal spirit. She would give each of us some cash, and we would trot off to buy ourselves something (usually a Matchbox car in my case), wrap it up ourselves and place it under the plastic tree. As there was nobody stopping us, we invariably ended up opening the parcels before Christmas Day morning.

Meanwhile, among the telly programmes we never missed were: *Dallas*, *Rentaghost*, *The Dukes of Hazzard*, *Starsky and Hutch*, *Miami Vice*, *That's Life*, *Don't Wait Up*, *EastEnders*, *Hi-de-Hi*, *Blue Peter* and *Top of the Pops* . . . which brings me to perhaps the most extreme manifestation of our Westernization: pop music. We consumed it in whatever form we could get it, pooling pocket money for copies of *Look-In* and *Smash Hits*, listening to the Top 40 singles countdown on Sunday nights, and the album chart with Bruno Brookes on Wednesday nights. *Top of the Pops* was, of course, the absolute highlight of the week: we awaited its transmission in the way football fans might await the World Cup Final. Conversely, the choreographed bluster of professional sport passed us by like our competitors on the school playing fields. Often we'd only notice there was a major sporting fixture afoot when our favourite music TV shows were moved from their scheduled slots.

It didn't seem possible for us to become any more obsessed, but then, one Saturday morning, Michael Jackson's video for 'Billie Jean' was broadcast on BBC1. I was with my brother at the time, and thought we were equally mesmerized. But the sight of Jacko in those short trousers, that fedora pitched forward, those ringlets framing his face, triggered something more profound in Rajah. At the time he had been flirting with a variety of acts and movie heroes – there were Wham!, Ralph Macchio and Sylvester Stallone posters displayed in his bedroom – but within weeks the walls were plastered, from skirting board to ceiling, with Jacko. He saved up for a copy of *Thriller*. When we got our first video player, about five years after Chacha had got one, he taped every passing mention of his idol: from news bulletins as well as pop music shows. Eventually, watching the video for 'The

Way You Make Me Feel' became as much a part of our breakfast routine as tea and Weetabix. And finally, he began dressing like his idol too: abandoning his neat Ralph Macchio cut for an extravagant loose perm taken straight off the cover of *Bad*.

At the same time, Bindi directed her affection towards Bruce Springsteen and George Michael. With the former her devotion mainly took the form of recording his songs from the radio, collecting posters and making rather sinister-looking traced drawings of the posters. With the latter it went further: there were posters and sinister traced drawings, but other manifestations too. When we discovered Pussy had given birth to three shiny kittens, my brother called his Rocky, I called mine Lucky – because we had successfully saved it from Mum, who always tried to get rid of kittens as soon as they arrived – but Bindi called hers 'Georgina'. At some level, like my brother with Michael Jackson, I think she wanted to be him too. After the former Wham! star was depicted wearing Aviator shades in the video for *Father Figure*, for instance, she splashed out on a £2.50 pair for herself. And when the stubbly one appeared on the Nelson Mandela tribute, dressed in a black suit, Bindi started dressing in black suits too, though in her case they were of the Indian salwar kameez variety.

And then – it's embarrassing to continue, but only fair – there was me. Like Bindi and Rajah I went for the music thing with gusto, catching my sister's George Michael bug in the way you might catch chicken pox. My idea of the best time possible was to make mix tapes of his music, a common enough pastime among children in the eighties, I suppose, but an activity complicated for me by a lack of blank tapes, a lack of original music to copy and a lack of hifi equipment. I would begin by swiping a cassette from my mother's collection of religious music, then get Bindi to lend me her tape player and place it next to an old radio, and then lie in wait for his tracks to be broadcast like a detective on a stakeout. As I often wouldn't know a George track was being played until it had been part-played, and as I would often be on the other side of the room or the house when it came on, and as I would sometimes press PAUSE accidentally, or forget to press PLAY at the same time as RECORD, and as radio DJs would often talk over songs, my mix tapes took several months to make, and usually consisted of little more than fragments and snippets of songs, often interrupted with human voices calling me down for chapattis.

My idea of the second best time possible was to attempt to transcribe the lyrics of the songs I had managed to tape, a task that Bindi would often assist me with.

'He's saying "But don't worry, you come sometime,"' I'd say, having played 'Club Tropicana' for the 415th time.

'No, listen.' Stop. Rewind. Play. '"Fun and sunshine — there's enough for everyone . . . All that's missing is the sea . . . But don't worry . . . you can . . . SUNSHINE. . ."'

'"But don't worry, you can *sunshine*?" What does that mean? People don't sunshine. The sun sunshines.'

'Makes more sense than "you come sometime".'

When we'd finally agreed on a version, Bindi would let me use the typewriter she and my sister had been bought for the

typing course Mum had enrolled them on (to make them more employable and more marriageable), and I would spend an hour or two typing out a perfect copy on to a clean sheet of paper before filing the results away, imagining that some day they would come in useful.

Like my siblings, I matched this appetite for pop with a concomitant dedication to many of my mother's Eastern values, and the two things I went for in particular were religiosity and an intense eagerness to please. I think – actually, I know – all four of us felt the latter from the earliest age. We saw how hard Mum worked, saw that Dad didn't work, and wanted to help. But I think my sister Puli and I felt it particularly acutely. In Puli's case the sense of responsibility was nagged into her ('You're the eldest, so you have to set the tone,' Mum would tell her several times a day) and sometimes beaten into her. I was never hit, not once, a fact that had me singled out as spoilt by my siblings, but nevertheless tried to obey Mum in every possible way because I believed we had a special relationship. It's interesting that in conversations with my brother and sisters now, they all say they felt this way at some stage, which is a sign of a good parenting, if ever there was. But I felt it almost constantly, every time Mum combed my hair and told me my *kes* made me special in the eyes of God, every time she told me a story at bedtime in the bedroom I still shared with her, and every time she recounted the story of my birth. The tale went that just after my brother was born she'd gone to see the tea-leaf reader on Stratton Street, who'd greeted her with the remark: 'So, how are your four children?'

'I've three children,' Mum would say she replied. 'The burden of two girls and the blessing of a son.'

'You'll have another son,' said the tea-leaf reader on Stratton Street. 'And he'll lift the family out of poverty and misery.'

In other words, I thought I was the Messiah. And this saviour complex intensified suddenly when I came home from school one afternoon and found Mum splayed across the living room floor. Her hair was dishevelled, and Chachi was bent over her, seemingly trying to stop her digging her nails into her scalp. I'll never forget the sound . . . it was animalistic, the kind you might make if someone tried to cut your heart out with a knife. Puli, her eyes wide with fear, whispered an explanation in the kitchen, where the rest of the family were walking in frightened circles: Mum's eldest and closest brother, our *mama*, had murdered his younger brother, our youngest *mama*, over a dispute over farmland in India. Our cousin Manjit, our eldest *mama*'s only surviving son, had been implicated in the murder and arrested along with his father.

We were used to violent news from India. Several of my uncles had died from alcohol or opium abuse; several other uncles and aunts had died from (unidentified) illnesses; one of my aunts had lost three sons in violent circumstances – one falling under the wheel of a tractor while drunk; another killed in a motorcycle accident while high on opium; another losing his life in a house fire while high on opium. But most of that drama was on Dad's side of the family, whom we could barely remember meeting on our one trip to India in 1979, whereas Manjit had recently spent a month living with us. We felt the loss, were shaken by Mum's reaction, and the world was suddenly blanched of colour: white sheets spread out across the living room floor; Mum's reds and blues shed for the white suits and scarves of mourning; mourners, dressed in white, arriving to wail and express sympathy. I'd accompanied Mum on similar mourning visits to other people's houses and watched as she forced herself to cry – it is considered polite to weep – and then return to normal as soon as she left. I kept on expecting to turn around and find she was okay, but days and then weeks passed with no change. It was the only time, and remains the only time, I've ever seen Mum incapacitated: even when her mother and father died in the late seventies and early eighties, she carried on looking after us. But there were mornings during this time when she couldn't even comb my hair: I had to go to Chachi's house to have my topknot tied before school.

Looking back, that murder, and the subsequent imprisonment of my uncle and cousin, affected us all deeply. Dark rings appeared around Mum's eyes and she never wore nail polish or perfume again. My brother, in the pimply turmoil of early adolescence, disappeared into his bedroom. Bindi disappeared into her sinister drawings. Puli disappeared, I thought, into her studies. And I experienced an intensification in my sense of responsibility. Any resentment that may have been festering about having a topknot when my brother and father didn't have long hair dissipated. I became even more religious: muttering the Japji Sahib not just once at night before bed, but eight or ten times in the morning and night and accompanying Mum to the temple not just on Sundays, but at dawn before Punjabi classes on Saturday mornings too, to clean tables, wash dishes, clean floors, and serve tea to the tramps who had worked out that there was a constant supply of free food and drink at the *gurdwara*. If anyone had asked me why I did this, I would have said it was because '*sewa*', selfless service, was a central tenet of Sikhism, and I wanted to be a good Sikh. But it's obvious now I did it as much for Mum. In many ways, God and Mum were interchangeable in my mind.

At school, the swottiness I'd long displayed also intensified. It wasn't good enough to come top in the end-of-year exams any more. I had to come top in every single test and exercise. And my relentless sucking-up meant that over four years I was made milk monitor, litter monitor, stock room monitor – a prized job, for it meant being let off hymn practice – and tuck shop monitor. When the school got delivery of a keyboard synthesizer, even though I had no idea how to play it, I was the only child allowed to use it without supervision. One of my more surreal childhood memories is of sitting in my grey shorts and grey shirt and maroon tie and black topknot, on stage in front of a hundred kids during morning assembly, demonstrating the school's expensive new asset by playing it, a task which involved pressing the 'samba' button and sitting motionless for five minutes. In some ways the perform-ance echoed that of Chris Lowe from the Pet Shop Boys on *Top of the Pops*, albeit without the singer, the standing up, the fashion sense, the lyrics, the chord changes or the wild applause after-wards.

But perhaps the most extreme manifestation of my new intense Indian self, the bit that feels like false memory syndrome and makes me suspect we were actually brought up in a district of northern India and not the British West Midlands, was the sewing factory. For it was around the time of my uncle's murder, when I was about ten, that the bald, gold-watched man who delivered bundles of unsewn panels to our house opened a factory on the industrial estate behind the railway track that ran at the end of our garden – seconds away as the crow flies. Mum was persuaded to take up a job there, and it wasn't long after she started that she suggested, during a school holiday, that we accompany her.

'Give it a try tomorrow and see if you like it,' she said. 'You'll get paid.'

As with so many things, I don't remember the invitation to participate in the great Indian tradition of illegal child labour being extended to Puli. I assumed it was because she had lots of homework, or that working in a factory was another one of those things – like acting in school plays or playing in the garden – that wasn't the right thing for a girl to do. It was just the three of us – Bindi, Rajah and me – who sidled past the inquisitive glances of Mum's colleagues, through the cutting room, into a room containing four industrial ironing boards.

Opposite the boards was a rack on wheels carrying several white blouses, next to which the boss's bleach-haired teenage son explained what we needed to do. Our job, he said, was to make the sewn and ironed blouses shop-ready: to clip off rogue threads, button them up, attach a price tag using a plastic gun (£9.99), and wrap the whole garment in a cellophane bag. It was eye-straining, brain-numbing work, and Rajah didn't come back the next day. Bindi lasted a little longer: a couple of days. Then, with her forthcoming CSEs weighing on her mind, she quit too. But I came in day after day. By the end of the week I'd done fifty hours.

It was one of the most thrilling moments of my short life to receive my first pay packet – I could almost feel myself fulfilling my destiny, lifting the family out of poverty and misery – and one of the biggest disappointments to find it contained no more than a £10 and a £5 note. I hadn't expected a specific wage, but had let myself expect more than 30 pence an hour. My tears had Mum in the boss's office on Monday morning, after which my rate was raised to 50 pence an hour, an amount which was – it seems bizarre now – enough to keep me working for up to fourteen hours a day at that factory on weekends, evenings and school holidays. I can't say I felt exploited at the time: 50 pence was still five times the pocket money I got in a week. I loved hanging out with the boss's son and daughter. I had little else to do. But given the opportunity to meet my former boss recently – I should say he has helped my mother on many occasions and she regards him highly – I found myself grinding my teeth, going over those thousands of hours of work, unable to remember a single time when he rounded up my wages or gave me a bonus, even though I was doing the work of an adult, eventually operating button and button-holing machines. In the end I declined the opportunity of a reunion.

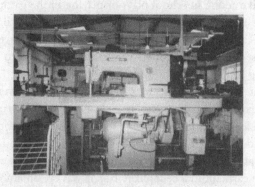

Nevertheless, I can still recall the excitement of being able to buy things for myself. I remember buying a tape recorder with two decks and a radio, which made making George Michael mix tapes easier. A white study desk with red handles – £29.99 from Argos. A picture of a Lotus Esprit – £5 from a shop on Queen Street. A white 35mm camera – £30 from Dixons. And a map of the world from W. H. Smith – £8 – which I fastened with Blu-tack above my desk.

'Think you're a right intellectual, don't you?' hissed Puli when she saw it, making me think, *where did that come from?*

I also remember buying Mum a green suit for Mothers' Day and my favourite picture from that time – taken with that camera from Dixons – shows her wearing it, while standing between me and my brother. Rajah hates the snap and will kill me for reproducing it, but for me, no other photograph captures the innocence, warmth, weirdness, bad taste, music obsession, dodgy decor, sticky-out ears, and filial devotion of that time.

There's another picture taken straight afterwards, showing me standing between Mum, Puli and Dad, but I'm reluctant to produce it, because my sister looks at odds with the world, as Dad so often does in pictures, and it is obvious she is ill; and looking at it now, I'm alerted to the fact that I've digressed from my point, which is simply that, in this context, Puli's behaviour, even when she was falling ill, wasn't striking. She enjoyed pop music but she didn't spend entire evenings transcribing the lyrics to 'Everything She Wants'. She was the teacher's pet at school, but unlike me, her sucking up didn't look as if she wanted the staff to take custody of her. Indeed, she was much more sober than us, an extension of Mum in many ways. It was Puli who washed and cooked for us when Mum was busy, who I ran to for comfort when Mum was busy, who wrote letters to school when I was feigning illness to skive off swimming classes made hellish by my reluctance to submerge my topknot under the water and Mum's attempt to help with the purchase of a rose-painted swimming hat. Yes, she had a bit of a temper, and, yes, the arguments she was involved in went on longer than they should have done, but we often needed telling off and often she was right, and when she began to get ill, the symptoms were so subtle that I didn't notice them. Even now, with the 20:20 vision of hindsight, and the floodlights of Puli's own account illuminating my memory, it's still difficult to pinpoint a time when things began to go wrong. Difficult, but not impossible.

To get to that point, though, I need to go back on myself, to a time before Mum got her job at the factory, before Rajah had that moment of epiphany with *Billie Jean*, to that brief period when, owing to a council improvement programme, we, like our Chacha before us, and many others on Prosser Street, briefly moved out of the disintegrating terraced home we owned into a council house on Springfield Road, a few minutes away, as professional renovators installed modern facilities such as bath-rooms, indoor loos and wall sockets that didn't explode when you touched them . . .

. . . It's a damp weekday evening in our temporary council dwelling, rain is slapping a wet, grey curtain against one side of the window-pane, an old bed sheet is wafting against the other; the smell of boiling *saag* is drifting in from the kitchen; a battered black and white TV is struggling to receive a signal from an indoor aerial; a bare 60-watt bulb is struggling to light the room; Mum's sewing-machine is blaring out a persistent mechanical whirr in the corner; and the whole family – except for Puli – is sitting in the front room.

Everyone hates the house. The loo keeps on overflowing. The meter needs to be fed a steady diet of 50 pence coins, which we keep on running out of. It stinks of the previous residents: cigarettes and dogs. No one can find their stuff and Mum keeps moaning, believing there is something morally reprehensible about living in a council house, even for a short while. But I like it: school is just twenty seconds away; my best friend is just thirty seconds away; the lack of heat means everyone huddling around the one functional heater in the front room, making it feel cosy; and a few months here seem a small price to pay for a transformed house.

Dad sits frozen in his armchair, the one bit of furniture that survived the move on the back of a milk float intact (we'd paid our Indian milkman in cartons of fruit juice). Rajah, deep in his Ralph Macchio phase, reads a martial arts magazine on the broken settee, a blanket over his lap. Bindi, panicking about a school test, consults a biology textbook, memorizing which bits of the reproductive organs go where. 'Ovaries,' she mouths under her breath, before sniffing. 'Vulva.' Sniff. 'Fallopian tubes.' Sniff.

I'd be embarrassed if I knew what any of the words meant or if I wasn't so preoccupied with the task of drying my hair in front of the electric fire. With my head bowed, I move around the heater with the efficiency of an automated kebab skewer, making sure each bit gets an equal amount of heat. At Prosser Street, in front of the gas heater, drying my hair would take an hour, but here it can take a whole evening, and involves blocking the one decent heater in the house.

'Can't you dry your hair in the girls' bedroom?' Rajah pulls his blanket over his nose.

'Moooooom.'

'But it's *freezing*. And he's stinking the room out.'

He's right about the smell. I've a chronic dandruff problem, which requires the use of a near-radioactive medicated shampoo, and which makes the house smell like a road works on bath nights. But Mum always takes my side when it comes to my hair.

'Oi.' She doesn't even turn round from her sewing-machine. 'Leave your brother alone.'

I continue, revolving my hair around the fire as Rajah hisses,

'You're a girl. You look like a girl, you sound like a girl, and you're a grass like a girl . . .'

The remark makes me whimper like a girl. Meanwhile, Dad does what he does more than anything else when he is in the house: he gets up from his armchair, walks towards the TV and switches from Channel 1 to Channel 4.

Bindi, Rajah and I groan in unison. 'De-diiiiiiiii!'

'None of you were watching.'

'But Dad, it's time for *Dallas*.'

'Oh.'

He does the journey in reverse, without protest, as he does everything.

I can't say I'm a big *Dallas* fan. Even though my favourite programme is *Knight Rider*, an American television series featuring a sports car with artificial intelligence of sufficient level to reason, talk and deliver sarcastic one-liners, I find *Dallas* far-fetched. But I watch it religiously, nevertheless, because it is the one thing Mum always watches, the one time of the week she isn't sewing or washing or cooking or praying or taking one or other of us to the dentist's or the doctor's. And I can see why she likes it: she clearly identifies with the long-suffering Miss Ellie Ewing, a strong woman at the head of an unwieldy household; being Indian, she has no problem accepting that a family with billions of dollars might still live together in one house; and like other programmes she takes a passing interest in – *Some Mothers Do 'Ave 'Em* and anything featuring Norman Wisdom – *Dallas*, with the angelic Bobby, and the evil JR, has a certain easy-to-follow pantomime appeal. The dialogue requires only minimal and occasional translation, a job, like so many jobs in our household, that falls to Puli.

There's a rush to get ready, as the time of the broadcast approaches. Wrapping my still-soggy hair into a fluffy towel, I take a seat at the end of the broken settee. Mum turns off the sewing-machine to join me – you don't notice how loud it is until it is turned off. Rajah pops off to the kitchen to fetch a bucket of hot water and jasmine oil, into which Mum will place her feet to soak. But as the *Dallas* theme tune blares out, and as Bindi and I sing along loudly and in tone-deaf fashion – de der, de der, de der de de der – there's no sign of Puli.

I shout up for her. 'Puleeeeeeee! *Dallaaaaaas!!* It's starting!!!"

'Oi.' Mum puts on her spectacles again. 'Stop blarting like a bullock and go up and get her.'

'Puleeeeeeeeeeeeeeeeeeeeeeeeeeeeeeeeeeeeeeeeeeeeeeee!!'

'Oi! You'll disturb the English *goras* next door. Go get her.'

'But Mum . . .' The reluctant Messiah. 'Why me?'

'Just go . . .'

I go, after receiving promises from Bindi and Rajah that they won't steal my prime seating position, tempering my speed only to make sure my towel turban doesn't collapse – calling as I scramble up the wonky stairs.

'Puleeee!'

'Puleeeeeeee!'

'Puleeeeeeeeeeeeeeee!'

The exclamation turns into a question as I push open the door of the bedroom she shares with Bindi.

'Puleeee?'

Bloody hell. She's in bed already. Totally submerged under her duvet, in the way I totally submerge myself when playing with the glow-in-the-dark stickers you get in packets of Sugar Puffs. I walk up to the bed and prod her.

'Oi.' Prod. '*Dallas* is starting in a minute.' Prod. 'Mum says come down.' Prod.

The prodding merely sends the human chrysalis rolling away from me, to the other end of the bed, so I jump up on to the mattress and pluck the duvet away, an act which reveals Puli curled up with her knees to her face and her hands against her ears.

'*Dallas* has started. Aren't you coming down?'

When she opens her eyes, there's something I've not seen in them before.

'Tell Mum I've gone to sleep.' She pulls the duvet back over her.

'So you're not coming down?'

She rolls away from me again. 'No,' comes the muffled reply.

And that was it: the beginning of the storm that would wash her away. No histrionics, no pushing of hard-working media professionals under the wheels of oncoming Tube trains. Her schizophrenia began with a need to withdraw, a need to sleep. 'I spent most of my waking hours looking forward to going to sleep,' she told me recently, speaking carefully and in full sentences, which is how she talks. Sometimes it sounds like she's reading. Often, she is reading: her illness can make her lose her train of thought, and she tackles the problem by making preparatory notes before conversations. 'I used to wake up and think sleep was the best thing in my life. When I was asleep my dreams were normal, the people were normal, my relationships with people were normal. I could recognize who I was in my dreams. But when I woke up, the nightmare began. Does that make sense?'

8. Doctor! Doctor!

Four of us ended up traipsing to Bilston on that frigid Monday: Dad, Mum, me and my youngest niece, who was off school sick but evidently not too ill to accompany her grandparents and uncle on a visit to the local mental health unit. We must have been an odd sight to passers-by: Dad, shuffling along in a cream anorak and brown trousers, carrying a T. J. Hughes carrier bag full of medication ('If you are taking any medicines or tablets please bring them with you'); Mum wrapped up like Sir Ranulph Fiennes on the cusp of an expedition to Everest; a four-year-old girl in a pink tracksuit and glitter-spattered hat, singing 'The Wheels on the Bus Go Round and Round'; and a twenty-nine-year-old man in a black French Connection coat and Prada spectacles, looking like, and sincerely wishing he was, on the way to a film screening in Soho.

Perversely, my parents took different routes to the bus stop: Dad, slightly hunched, walking with a limp which he refused to discuss with his GP, via the main road; Mum choosing to go via the park, walking a foot behind me, no matter how much I sped up or slowed down. We arrived at the same time, though, and Mum decided to pass the time waiting for the first West Midlands bus I'd caught in eleven years – I'd wanted to take a taxi but she'd refused to let me 'waste' £5 – by raising the infernal arranged marriage issue, this time by making an unfavourable and irritating comparison to a family friend who had recently had an arranged marriage to a fat girl from India, and had already produced a fat child to scamper around a £1m Barratt home purchased with the proceeds of a career in some mind-numbingly tedious sector of commercial law.

'Mum, he is a lawyer, he married a girl from India and he lives in Kent. I don't want to do any of those things.'

'I don't understand – you say you went to the best university and yet you only have a tiny flat in London.' A pause. 'He has a whole house!' Another pause. 'Plus a lucrative sideline in investment properties!'

'Mum, I did a degree in a subject I enjoyed. I enjoy my job. Some people would probably do it for half the salary. Every lawyer I've ever met is unhappy. Kent isn't London. And I like my flat.'

'You've one small flat. Noise in every direction . . .'

'Mum, you've only been the once. It's quiet.'

'. . . noise upstairs, noise downstairs . . .'

'Mum, it's quiet.'

'. . . noise next door one side, noise next door on other side . . .'

'IT'S QUIET . . . for Brixton.'

'. . . He has a Mercedes. You own no car.' Sensing she was about to win the argument, she combined her two complaints. 'GIRLS NOWADAYS LIKE TO MARRY MEN WITH HOUSES AND CARS.'

As much as I would like to own a Ferrari 612 Scaglietti and a house on the Thames, the way in which the wealthy are respected over the educated or the happy is one of the most irritating things about Punjabi culture. I can just about tolerate such values when they emanate from my extended family, and somehow managed not to lose it at a recent family funeral, when a cousin I hadn't seen in years greeted me with the remark: 'I've just bought a BMW M5 for fifty grand.' But I can't stand it when Mum implies I'm somehow wasting my life doing what I do. Not for the first time, I wished I had a wider Punjabi vocabulary with which to convey my exasperation, but having been taught the language by Mum, I didn't even have the Punjabi for 'dammit' to resort to – it's ironic that the first words one usually learns in any new language are the ones you shouldn't repeat too often, but with my first language, I don't have a single one – and had to resort to kicking the bus shelter in frustration. Dad, the peacemaker, attempted to intervene.

'Why do you always have to wind him up?'

Good question, Dad. Bloody good question.

But there was only the shortest of pauses before Mum and I started arguing about something else of vital importance: whether the fare to the town centre was £1.20 or £1.30. Mum based her view that it was the former on having watched people pay in the past (she herself has a free bus pass). I based my view that it was the latter on a notice in English at the bus shelter.

'Even if it is £1.20 and I give them £1.30, it's hardly the end of the world, is it?'

'But why throw away ten pence? That's ten pence that could be donated to the temple.'

'And what will they do with it? Build another hall for religious ceremonies that nobody understands?'

'Oi.' It was a cheap shot and I'm not sure I meant it. 'You shouldn't talk like that.'

'Trust me, it's £1.30.'

'It's £1.20.'

'It's £1.30. IT SAYS HERE.' I jabbed at the sign. 'If you'd agree to taking some English lessons, you'd be able to read the sign and find out for yourself.'

'You know I'm too old to learn English . . .' Sometimes my mother's defeatism defeats me. 'My head hurts too much to concentrate. Even making your father's meals is a struggle. Anyway, believe me: it's £1.20.'

Mortifyingly, when the bus pulled up there was a sign next to the hydraulic doors stating: maximum off-peak fare £1.20. As I foraged for the correct change, a receipt for dinner with a friend in London the night before – £150.48 – fell out of my wallet. I grabbed it before Mum spotted it – she can't read English, but has a superhuman ability to spot evidence of overspending – and, while she managed to resist crowing, I took a seat next to Dad, in the area usually reserved for the elderly and disabled, and spent the journey reading the adverts ('Earn up to £30 a week with EMA if you carry on learning after 16'; 'Targeting Benefit Fraud'; 'Army: Be the Best'), and noticing that the old unspoken seating plan was still in place (Indian women and pensioners downstairs, anyone under the age of eighteen upstairs at the back, the unemployed – presumably the only able-bodied adults of pre-pensionable age who use buses at this time of day – taking the remaining space).

We stayed on the bus to the station, where I noticed the colour scheme had changed from a migraine-inducing green and yellow to a vomit-inducing orange and blue, but where everything else was as I remembered from my teenage years of bus travel. Even some of the people milling around the alphabeticalized stands were recognizable from 1995: the *Express & Star* salesman, exclaiming, 'Townfinal! Townfinal!' (even though it should surely have been 'cityfinal') with a fag hanging from his scabby bottom lip; the lad with Down's syndrome who walked around asking to shake the hands of strangers. Another bus took us to the front door of the Croft Resource Centre in Bilston, where the receptionist, protected from the potentially violent clientele by a thick plastic screen, told us to take a seat in the waiting room.

A friend once remarked to me, in a rambling late-night drinking conversation, during my pre-schizophrenia-awareness days, that a sure-fire way of assessing whether someone was mentally ill was to yawn repeatedly in front of them. If, at some point, they didn't yawn in response – apparently the instinctive reaction of most human beings – it meant they were incapable of empathy, and therefore clinically insane. But judging from the people waiting to see a psychiatrist in that room, there was a more efficient way to diagnose loopiness. If someone walks into a hot room and doesn't remove their anorak, the chances are that they are nuts. In the middle of the room a middle-aged Indian man in an anorak stood still, utterly immobile, staring at his feet. He was wearing Denis Norden-style spectacles and humming to himself as if in pain. On the sofa opposite us there was an elderly, turbaned Indian man in an anorak. He was holding his hands up as if doing an impression of a cat. Next to him was an Indian boy of my age, in an anorak, with a fixed look of surprise on his face. The only person not in an anorak was a white teenager who shot in soon after we'd arrived and did several manic laps of the waiting room before heading to the hifi (how odd to have a stereo in a waiting room) and tuning it to a pirate station, adjusting the graphic equalizer until the bass line to 'Get Your Freak On' by Missy Elliot made the arms of my spectacles vibrate. The music had Mum massaging her temples (migraine brewing), and, until I grabbed her and forced her to sit down, had my niece demonstrating something she called the Barbie dance. Throughout, Dad, sitting next to me, looked into the mid-distance.

I tried not to appear phased, but it must have been obvious from my fixed smile that I was thinking: what the hell am I doing here? *Simon Cowell once called me on my mobile, for God's sake.* Moreover: what was my father doing bracketed with these loons variously twitching, standing catatonic, walking in circles, shaking, sucking, grunting, and dribbling?

Having since gone back to the Croft on several occasions, and spent time with Dad at his Asian Men's Group meetings, I'm ashamed at my attitude then. What was Dad doing with these people? He was one of them. It was just that I could see the man underneath the symptoms and side-effects. And when I made some effort to get past their symptoms and side-effects, these other men became as vivid as Dad. The man with catatonia – who stood in that position for the half-hour we waited – was a highly intelligent graduate with a degree in economics. 'I'm not physically sick, just mentally sick,' he told me during our first chat. 'The doctor diagnosed me with psychosis. I didn't know what it meant. I had to look it up in a dictionary.' A wry smile. Meanwhile, the Indian boy with the surprised expression on his face was dazzlingly articulate about his condition: schizophrenia. 'The worst thing is not being able to feel pleasure,' he said. 'Can you imagine what that's like? Not being able to feel happy on birthdays, at Christmas, when you see your friends?' It was, I think, the saddest thing I have ever heard.

Meanwhile, the staff, whom I had down as public sector parasites, making a living from the suffering of others, turned out to be angels. The thirty-eight-year-old man who helps run my father's day centre group at the Croft, Vuijay Malhan, is a volunteer, and has been working for free ever since his wife was diagnosed with bipolar disorder. Meanwhile, Gurbax Kaur, the glamorous young woman who set up the 'Positive Participation' group for Asians with mental health problems, fights a constant battle for funding, and reluctantly admitted to me recently that she sometimes uses her own money to fill gaps. You could mug these people, kick them in the face, vomit on their shoes and they would still have time for you. But all I could do as we waited to see the doctor – with my private health cover I'd forgotten how much hanging around is part of the NHS customer service experience – was sneer, and look away at the walls. Not that there was solace to be found there, as they were decorated with paintings by the patients of a distinct Hieronymus Bosch quality and poetry that went along the lines of:

Endurance

What is Life?
Life is Repetition.

What is Hell?
Hell is Repetition.

What is Life?
Life is HELL.

It was truly a relief when my father's psychiatrist called out for us.

'Jugjeet*sion*?'

What struck me the first time I met the Indian-born, Indian-educated, Indian-trained Dr Patel is the same thing that strikes me whenever I see him now: just how superlatively Indian he is. He hates to say no. He gets over-emotional as he talks about the home country and the glory of Indian culture. He does that yes/no headroll that sometimes means yes, sometimes means no and sometimes means nothing at all. You almost expect him to present you with garlands of white jasmine and orange marigold flowers as you enter his office. And it is an office, rather than a surgery: the ailments he treats not requiring the use of stethoscopes, blood pressure monitors, and other medical paraphernalia.

The three of us took chairs while Dad remained standing, as if in the presence of royalty. With varying degrees of patience, Mum and I suggested he sit down, as Dr Patel shuffled through the pile of folders on his desk.

'I haven't seen you before,' he said eventually, looking at me over the lenses of his rimless glasses. 'I think I met your brother once.'

'Yes.' An all too common pang of guilt. 'He has come the last few times. But I wanted to come today. I want to learn more about Dad's condition.'

'No problem, no problem. Yes, yes, yes. Now let's look at your father's notes . . .' The pile of papers in front of him was thicker than an edition of the Yellow Pages. 'Now, the last time I saw your father was . . .' He flicked through a few sheets on the top of the pile '. . . six months ago. Though, of course, he comes here to the day centre every week. He greets me sometimes and we say "*namaste*", "*sat sri akal*", etcetera, and he is under constant kind of review.' More flicking. 'I try and spend time with a person to get a rapport going. It's important you know your patient by name. My Punjabi isn't very good, but I can make myself understood to your father in Hindi.'

His attention reverted to the notes as Dad opened his carrier bag and started piling up his medication on the doctor's desk: the pills I'd found in that margarine box all those years earlier. Without looking up, Dr Patel said: 'You see, essentially, he's been on just one medication.'

'But aren't there five different pills there . . .'

'Ah, you see, this one [picks up one box] is for his blood pressure [slaps it down again], this one [picks up another box] is for his heart [slaps it down again], this one [picks up another box] is for his blood sugar [slaps it down again]. The only one for his mental health problem is this, the Quetiapine. And then there is the monthly injection of Modecate.'

'What's the injection for?'

'It has almost the same function as the Quetiapine.' The yes/no headroll. 'It ensures that if he misses out on the tablets – because people with your father's condition are very likely to forget about, y'know, the regularity of taking medication – there is a back-up to ensure he doesn't deteriorate beyond a certain point. Other than the calming effect, it is a mood stabilizer. The idea is to keep him on an even keel . . .'

The words 'even keel' ran through my mind with assorted images: no tears at his mother's funeral; being told to smile for pictures at my brother's wedding. But how many of these things were symptoms of the disease and how many side-effects of the medication? I was about to ask when my niece suddenly leapt up and exclaimed, 'Lollipop!' to no one in particular.

'No, no, that's the other doctor,' said Mum to her in Punjabi. 'No lollipops here.' My brother's children and my mother talk different languages but they still manage to communicate somehow, a little like Dr Patel and Dad with their respective Hindi and Punjabi. Dr Patel eventually peered up and shouted some Hindi in Dad's direction.

'And how are you, Jugjeet*sion*? *Teek, taak?*'

'*Teek, taak,*' Dad replied. He was smiling. 'I'm very well, nothing wrong with me.' He leant forward. 'I tell you, in our group . . . the day centre group . . . there's only two of us who are well. The rest are mad.' Dr Patel and Mum laughed. 'I've the sugar illness, that's all.' Diabetes. 'Nothing else.' Sitting back, he continued. 'I know what's what. The body, you see . . . is made of numbers, isn't it? And my numbers are absolutely fine. Dr Patel, sir . . . You know, what I told you yesterday? I was right, wasn't I? Remember what I told you about the sun, and about how our family comes fiftieth in the list of doctors . . . about the two governments run by the whites? I was right, wasn't I?'

Dr Patel smiled professionally, Mum rolled her eyes, and I

struggled to take it all in. Mum had warned me to be prepared to see Dad behave differently – he is always animated with doctors, because he worries they might hospitalize him, she'd said. But I was still stunned. I'd never seen him so animated. And I'd never heard him talk so incoherently.

'Does my father always talk like this to you?' I asked Dr Patel in English, knowing my father wouldn't know what I was saying. Sometimes a language divide can be handy. 'To be honest, I've never seen him like this before.'

'You know, he has been stable with no gross concerns for some time, but . . .' My niece jumped on to my lap '. . . I'm just going from what I see of him when he comes into the day centre, from the way he functions within the group – and I discussed this with your brother last time – I think we may need to have a look at his medication.'

'What does the medication actually do?'

'Controls the symptoms. His mental health condition, unfortunately, has no cure. In controlling the symptoms of his schizophrenia we try to see what is the best lifestyle can come out of it. But even with the most effective drugs, people with your father's illness continue to have problems and require a range of support from the family and the community.'

My niece began singing and I talked over her. 'I don't know if you've seen my father reading papers and watching TV – he's quite obsessive about watching *BBC Parliament*, for instance. Are these symptoms of the illness?'

'Yes.' Dr Patel removed his spectacles and looked at me. 'What can happen is . . . again, it's part of what we call the paranoid spectrum of behaviour. People with schizophrenia may think that things in the environment have a significance to them . . . they might see someone talking on TV and think, hey, this guy is talking about me. Maybe when they read the paper, they think they are being written about. Though it's hard to tell completely with your father at the moment . . .' He replaced the spectacles. 'His behaviour isn't out of control, but if he is becoming more delusional, it is better to nip the thing in the bud than wait for it to get worse. You see, he has only been on a kind of maintenance dose at the moment. But I've been monitoring the situation, and I think it would be good for him to increase it a little.'

I gave a synopsis of what the doctor had said to Mum, in my bad Punjabi, she agreed Dad needed extra help, I asked if she had any questions, and she said no, and then I asked the doctor if he could explain the medication change to my father, who was beaming as we talked.

'Oh, yes,' Dr Patel responded to me in English. 'We will explain to him gently in a language he understands . . . I will put it to him . . . I don't know Punjabi very well, but he tends to understand me. We have a positive relationship, which needs to be maintained for therapeutic reasons. He could become very paranoid about a new doctor. Continuity of care is a concept in schizophrenia, especially with the paranoid variety of schizophrenia. Change can lead to problems. Changes will always throw him off balance.'

Dr Patel raised his voice and changed his tone to explain the medication change to Dad in Hindi. 'Jagjit Ji – we need to talk about something. Your tablets. You take two tablets at the moment?'

'Yes, one at twelve, one at five.' Still smiling.

'You see, to keep you well, we need to change your medication . . . the same number of tablets but we are going to go from 200 milligrams to 300 milligrams.'

'The tablets are staying the same, but the number is changing?'

'That's it,' said Dr Patel. 'Is that okay?'

'Twice a day still?'

'Yes.'

'That's fine.'

Dr Patel gazed back at me, frankly, and reverted to English. 'You know, because of the chronic nature of the illness, your father is only doing as well as he is because he is in a family setting. Anything other than that would be very detrimental for him. Honestly.' Dad began putting his medication back into his carrier bag. 'Nobody's bothered about what you're doing in this society. Too much individualism has got its own flipside. You need your relatives, your family, your friends around you. Your mother will have been under a lot of stress during her life, to be honest.' I nodded as if I understood, but I didn't have a clue. 'Indian families manage to cope somehow, because the whole family rallies around to give the necessary support. In the Western population – families break up like mad and the outcomes are bad. A similar individual of white origin would be in a nursing home by now.'

At the time I thought this was just Dr Patel being patriotic. But it turns out he is right. Several studies have demonstrated that people who have schizophrenia in developing countries such as India, and people from such cultural backgrounds, have a better chance of improvement than those who live in, or are from, the industrialized world. Various hypotheses have been put forward. One is that there are more opportunities for employment in the third world, and a meaningful social role aids recovery. Another possible explanation is that families with so-called 'high expressed emotion', high rates of damaging emotional involvement with an unwell relative, are rarer in Indian than European communities. It may be that abnormal behaviour is tolerated to a greater degree by Indians, which is good for a sufferer. This has certainly been the case with Dad: his odd behaviour has been so tolerated by the family that I have been unaware of his condition for most of my life. Which raises the strange possibility that perhaps our lack of awareness has actually been good for him.

'But you should try not to worry,' Dr Patel continued, his eyes moving back to his sheaf of paper. 'His behaviour is very controlled for a big man. Had he turned violent, he would have been difficult to restrain.'

'Has he ever been violent?' I asked.

The yes/no headroll.

'Do you know about what happened to him when he was first diagnosed?'

The yes/no headroll gathered momentum. 'I don't really know that – no one has given me that information. And these . . .' He lifted up his thick file '. . . are sketchy things. What happened thirty years back I don't know, except that he was affected at a relatively young age and the younger you are when affected, the worse the prognosis.'

'I've read that.'

'And your father now, he is showing regressive behaviour. He is becoming childlike, you know. Not really senility, approaching senility.'

'*Senility?*'

'Having said that, his behaviour has always been very easy to manage in the community. He is very pliant. He is stable, at the moment. I don't see things changing for a while. As he gets older, little by little there will be more brewing concerns, of course.'

'Brewing concerns, of course?'

'Well, the disease . . .' He looked at his watch, and Dad stood up. 'It affects the intellectual functions. He will be more prone to developing dementia-like problems. Given his kind of illness, people do age faster that way. Intellectually, mentally. Anyway, I'll see him in six months.'

Before I knew it, I was shaking Dr Patel's hand and the consultation was ending in the way important meetings with doctors tend to: with more questions raised than answered. Not that I had time to fully formulate the questions in my mind, as I had to head back to London straight after the appointment, to interview a major recording artist about a new album I hadn't listened to yet, in a five-star hotel suite that had been hired especially for the occasion, a mountain of untouched food and drink sitting on a table between us. Indeed, it was only towards the end of that interview, some time after the record company PR executive had claimed, ludicrously, that the major recording artist in question was 'very excited' to meet me, just before the major recording artist had got my name and publication wrong for the third time, that I realized what I should have asked Dr Patel. Was there a way I could find out how Dad was first diagnosed? How much of Dad's behaviour was his personality, how much was schizo-phrenia, how much was incipient senility and how much was due to the side-effects of his medication? Before I knew it, I was being shuffled out of the hotel room, having forgotten to ask the major recording artist in question the vital intrusive questions newspaper interviewers always save for the end of interviews.

9. Opportunities (Let's Make Lots of Money)

Back to the mid-eighties now, when we have moved back into 60 Prosser Street after the council-sponsored renovation, when Rajah is picking his options at school, Bindi is working up to her CSEs, Puli is studying for her O-levels, and when, on a Sunday evening, while my siblings have been driven to their respective corners of the house by the crap telly, I am in the living room with my parents, bent over a two-tiered coffee table, the tip of my tongue protruding from my lips with the effort of concentration.

The living room, like the rest of the house, has been transformed by the Indian builders. The old orange and brown floral wallpaper has been replaced with smooth magnolia-painted plaster. Artex meringue effects dance around a fluorescent strip light, where once a bare bulb hung forlornly from a peeling ceiling. And I'm kneeling on a brand new wall-to-wall brown and white carpet, the brown bits of which disguise the extent of the incipient cockroach problem, which has taken the place of the rodent problem, and the white bits of which look as if someone has had an accident with a bag of chapatti *atta*.

The coffee table is as new as everything else. The family had yomped off to buy it at the opening of a new MFI store on the Bilston Road, where Johnny Briggs, the actor famous for playing Mike Baldwin in *Coronation Street*, had been hired for the official opening. We queued up with the rest of Wolverhampton for an autograph afterwards, and dissected our first ever brush with celebrity on the bus home, Bindi saying he looked smaller than he did on telly, Puli saying he looked older than he did on telly, and me clutching the flatpack at the front of the bus, trying to forget I'd heard him say 'Thanks, darlin'' as I trundled off with a signed photo. Typical. Even Mike Baldwin thought I looked like a girl.

Rajah helped Chacha assemble the table at home – it's ironic that we have a coffee table and yet Mum doesn't allow Nescafé in the house because she regards it as a narcotic – and this evening I have my most beloved item of stationery spread out over it, a folder given out by Barclays Bank to new customers. Some might regard it as a cheap piece of PVC-coated tat, barely up to its prescribed task of holding bank statements, but to my mind, with its flaps, compartments, and cool wipeaway memo pad, it is an object of considerable sophistication. I use it as a kind of Filofax, a personal filing system for my collection of misheard pop lyrics (which has expanded now into songs by Prince, Simply Red, and U2), my copy of the Wolverhampton Grammar School prospectus (given to me by my headmaster, who called in Mum and Puli – for translation – to suggest I was entered for the 11-plus entrance examination), my secret diary, and, in the main bit of the folder, my bank-related stationery.

However, this stationery isn't from Barclays Bank, telling me that my balance stands at £29, as it did the year before, and the year before that. All this financial literature – there's no way of saying this without it sounding odd – *relates to the bank I've set up in my spare time.*

Why have I set up a bank in my spare time, when other boys my age dream of becoming fighter pilots and marrying Daisy Duke, when my own brother's stated ambition – voiced out loud during a school careers lesson – is of becoming a member of *Miami Vice*? Well, I suppose I could blame the entrepreneurial streak that runs through Indian culture: we seem to fantasize about setting up businesses in the way other races fantasize about becoming pop stars and footballers. But this would be dishonest. I'm playing at bank manager because of my ongoing saviour complex. You see, Mum had recently returned from her annual pilgrimage to the tea-leaf reader on Stratton Street with news that one of her children was going to 'work with money', and as maths was my best subject, and as the only person we knew who worked with money was a cousin who worked in a bank, and as I can no more imagine a life away from my family than imagine a life foraging for porcupines in the Amazon, it was collectively concluded that this meant I was going to work as a bank clerk in town. And in preparation for fulfilling this destiny, between homework and the factory and playing with friends, I've . . . set up a bank.

Everything is in place. There is a logo: the radiation warning sign, with green triangles instead of yellow ones. There is a name: because young boys and Asian entrepreneurs love nothing more than plastering their monicker over things, I've called it: Sanghera Building Society. And knowing the way to attract funds is to offer the public interest-bearing accounts, I've compiled a leaflet outlining the rates offered by SBS – explaining over a page of foolscap how, if you deposit two pence, you will get one pence interest after three months, how if you deposit three pence, you will get two pence interest after three months, and so on. To add authenticity to the documentation, I've spent the evening copying out some small print from a bank advert in the *Radio Times* on to the back of each sheet of paper. *Rates may vary: correct at time of going to press. Interest is calculated on the total amount held for as long as this balance is maintained and is to be added on 31 December. Written mortgage details available on request.* Not that I know what a mortgage is.

All I need now is some cash on deposit.

My first cold call is Mum, who is sitting at her sewing-machine assembling heavy maroon velvet curtains for the new Tudor-effect windows. She is wearing a foam neck brace, to lessen the pains in her neck and shoulders that started when she began at the factory, and the lenses in her tortoiseshell glasses are thicker than they used to be. She presses the bright red 'OFF' button on her sewing-machine to hear me out and at the end of the sales patter asks whether SBS is just a way of getting extra pocket money. Satisfied it isn't, and reassured it's a stepping-stone in the direction of me fulfilling my destiny and saving the family from poverty and misery, she pinches my cheek, and pulls a 10 pence piece out from the pocket of the white slip she wears underneath her suits.

Ker-ching!

Flushed with success, I repeat the pitch to Dad, who, as ever, is watching Channel 4 on the still-new colour TV, and who, at the end of my spiel, looks back at me with such incredulity that for a moment it seems he doesn't even recognize me. Eventually, I get the predictable: 'Ask your mum.' Sometimes I think this would be his response if I asked him his name.

'Mum, can you tell Dad why I want some money.'

'Just give your son some money, will you,' she instructs Dad wearily, biting a section of thread with her teeth. 'He's set up a *bank.*'

Dad does as instructed: puts his hand into his trouser pocket and pulls out what he calls '*ek shelleng*' – one shilling, or five pence.

Wicked.

On to my siblings.

Rajah is going to be a challenge. Not easily parted with his cash and reluctant to indulge me in my whimsies, I am, further-more, almost never allowed into his bedroom. The only time he lets me in willingly is when he wants help with something, such as painting Adidas symbols on to the tracksuits given to us by Shindo *bua*, or programming his ZX Spectrum 48k+, a task for which he will allow me to sit at the end of his bed, from where I will recite lines of code from the *Sinclair User's Manual*. Just getting near his door is going to take the stealth of Pussy or Lucky.* One mis-step and he'll be storming out, chucking me, topknot first, down the stairs.

I pad as softly as I can down the corridor to his room, which, like the bathroom and the inside loo, is a new addition to the house, allowing him access to his bedroom without having to walk through the room I still share with my parents. At night the thing to look out for is the bucket, which Mum brings up so there is something upstairs to wee into, but in the day, the main thing to watch out for is the creaking floorboard.

Pad.

Pad.

Pause.

Pad.

Pad.

Pause.

I manage to get to the mahogany-effect door without being detected, close enough to be able to hear 'Part-Time Lover' by Stevie Wonder playing on his radio. I push the silver-effect handle down gently so as not to produce a squeak and manage to open the door a couple of inches without being noticed: a first. It's only a small gap, but the view is still tantalizing. The only things

---

* Rocky had died, and Georgina had, like so many kittens before and after, disappeared on an afternoon when Mum went for an unannounced walk. But somehow we persuaded Mum to let us keep Lucky.

of interest in my room are my desk, my picture of a Lotus Esprit, a map of the world and a solitary poster of Prince, which Mum is forever threatening to pull down because she says he looks like a witch and it gives her nightmares. But every inch of Rajah's room is fascinating. Apart from the Michael Jackson wallpaper, I can see the ZX Spectrum on the old kitchen cupboard that functions as his desk; his martial arts equipment on the floor – pads and gloves and robes – his cool Puma Dallas trainers next to it (*where does he get the money from?*); and a set of weights which, another nudge of the door reveals, he is using. Rajah's interest in bodybuilding and martial arts is the closest any of us have got to sportiness. Puli once attained third place in the sack race, with the aid of a freak back wind on the annual school sports day at Woden Juniors, and Bindi was, according to family legend, once seen catching a netball and passing it without dropping it, but that's it. Due to the fact that I have no co-ordination, and still can't tie my own topknot and therefore am still not willing to submerge my head under water, I'm now one of only three kids in my class who can't swim.

Watching Rajah pump iron, with his back to me, I decide there's no point trying to be subtle. I've got to take my chance while I can. Flinging the door open, and waving a leaflet in his direction, I blurt my pitch as quickly as I can.

'I've just started a b–'

'Gerrout!'

'Do you want to open an acc–'

'Gerrout!'

'Just two p–'

'Gerrout! Mooooooooom! Sathnam's in my rooooooom!'

He lunges at me. A dead arm. My turn to yelp for parental intervention.

'Aaaaaaaaaaaaaaaah. Moooooooom!'

A weary and muffled cry from downstairs. 'Oi! You two! *Hat-jao!*'

I leg it out of the room, down the corridor, past the top of the stairs, and into my sisters' bedroom, knowing he won't follow me there. He never goes there. And neither should I, really: with Puli revising for her O-levels, and my sisters constantly at each other's throats over cupboard space, or bedroom space, or household chores, or something or other, it's best to keep out of the way. But this time they barely notice me coming in, so I stand next to the radiator – the central heating system has transformed my life, for I can now dry my hair by inserting it between the filaments like ham in a sandwich, and watch telly in the armchair as it dries – and appraise the situation.

Bindi is kneeling at her single bed, reading *Jackie*, a magazine with a puzzling lack of pop music coverage. Puli is sitting at her desk – a dressing-table with the mirror removed, in the tidier part of the room, poring over an impossibly hefty textbook. There are no posters in this room: only pictures of the Gurus, though I know the inside of Bindi's wardrobe door is smothered with stickers from *Smash Hits*. In the corner, in front of the window, is our maroon telephone, another new addition to the house, and on Puli's side of the room, a set of recent birthday cards, Blu-tacked to the wall, a calendar featuring Guru Nanak and advertising Gainda Drapers, and her Halina camera, in its box.

Catching my breath, I approach Bindi, and, in a voice kept low so as not to disturb Puli, make my pitch, taking care to mention that Mum and Dad have already invested a grand total of 15 pence, reassuring her I will pay the interest, and reciting the small print that I don't understand, but which I've learnt off by heart. Because she is loaded (she got £10 for her birthday from our parents and grandparents) she gives me 20 pence – just to make me go away, she says – and flushed with cash, pound signs rolling in front of my eyes, I cross the invisible but heavily policed boundary that demarks Puli's bit of the room from Bindi's.

I know I shouldn't cross the line. Mum has told me to leave Puli alone as she revises; you can almost feel the atmosphere get heavier as you approach, and I can see from the careful way in which she has arranged her books and pens around her that she is tense. But I risk it anyway.

'Um.' A stage whisper. 'Will you give me some money for my
. . . *bank*?'

'I'm trying to work.'

'Just ten pence.'

'Look, I'm trying to work.'

'How about five pence?'

'I haven't got time for your pathetic games . . .'

'Five pence . . . I can see it there.' I point at her desk. 'That's
a quarter, or just 25 per cent, of what Bindi gave me.'

'Look. LEAVE. ME. ALONE.'

'Four pence?' I do the Indian yes/no headroll together with
the comedy Indian accent that used to make her laugh. 'Very
generous rate of interest, Auntiji!'

It doesn't make her laugh. There's that flash of something in
her eyes and with one arm still curled around her textbook, she
grabs the sheaf of paper from my hand, screws it up and throws
it towards Bindi.

'Think you're so clever, don't you.' I scrabble across the floor
for my notes. 'Always sucking up to Mum.'

'No I'm not!'

My eyes prickling with tears, I run out of the room, slide down
the stairs – it's quicker than running – to my mother's side, where
I receive absolutely no sympathy whatsoever.

'She's trying to study for her exams.'

Sniffling back at the coffee table, I straighten out my papers,
pull my secret diary out of the most secret pouch of my Barclays
folder, and underneath observations such as 'I think I love Debra
Jones' and 'I think Debra Jones is going out with Errol actually',
I scrawl: 'I hate Puli.' But the self-pity and anger dissipate the
instant I realize I'm 35 pence richer. And evaluating my fledgling
bank's new financial position I make a decision more in tune
with the ways of high finance than I realize: I do a runner and
blow the bank's funds on a finger doughnut from Mrs Burgess's
shop.

★

Another evening, some time later. At least, I think it's later. It must be summer, as I'm wearing a tight yellow T-shirt, and it must be late evening, as the street lights are flickering into life as I ride home on the racer I've inherited from Rajah. I don't know where I've been. Maybe I've popped into the factory after school, or I've been kept in by Mr Burgess, who has turned out not to be scary at all and is giving me extra tuition for the 11-plus, or I've been standing against the wall next to Sunita, the girl from number 70 who I love almost as much as Debra Jones, but who, unfortunately, has a crush on my brother.

The gold necklace Mum has made for me from her own wedding jewellery, and which she says will, in turn, be used to make jewellery for my bride when I get married a zillion years in the future, is flicking against my chin as I ride, and I'm out of breath as I wheel into the back yard. When I skid to a stop outside the kitchen, just in front of the living room window where Mum's sewing-machine stands, I can tell something's up. The kitchen windows, normally open while supper is being prepared, are closed, and there's no hint of the clashing and clanking that usually accompanies mealtimes. My suspicions intensify in the kitchen, where the connecting door to the living room is shut, Pussy and Lucky have licked their bowl clean, even of the breadcrumbs Mum mixes into their Whiskas to save money – they haven't been fed – and I can make out a voice that is somehow familiar and unfamiliar at the same time.

Removing my Hi-Tec trainers, I push the door to find Bindi and Rajah leaning against it. They move over, revealing an odd scene. Mum is standing, a *chuni* over her head, arms folded, underneath the mirror. Dad is sitting in his armchair, his eyes more bloodshot than normal, looking at his feet. In the corner opposite, next to the door leading up to the stairs, cowering, is Puli. And in the middle of the room, the voice: the father from the family next door, clean-shaven, but sporting a turban. He is towering over the two boys from next door, his sons, who are sitting on our settee – one is moustachioed, the other not, and both are around eighteen years old and tall – taller than me, even sitting down.

Something about the choreography of the scene suggests the meeting has something to do with Puli, and the first possibility that springs to mind is that the boys have been bullying her. There was an incident some months earlier when a classmate of Puli's had pelted her with pebbles as she walked home. Puli had told Mum, Mum had told our grandmother, and the Punjabi honour machine had kicked into gear: a visit paid to the boy's house, the boy confessing to the crime, saying he did it because he thought Puli was weird, and his father beating him in front of everyone, there and then.

The second possibility is that it is something to do with noise. The clamour we generate ourselves is bad enough: Mum at the sewing-machine or clanking saucepans in the kitchen; my brother listening to 'Beat It' on his radio-cassette player; me making mix tapes on my radio-cassette player; Bindi listening to 'Glory Days'; Dad watching Channel 4. But then there is the noise from 62 too: the Bollywood songs; the hollering that seems a necessary part of all Indian households. Puli, trying to study, is always complaining, telling us to shut up so often that we have christened her Sergeant-Major, after Sergeant-Major Williams, who blusters 'SHUT UP! SHUT UP!' throughout *It Ain't Half Hot Mum*.

But I'm wrong on both counts.

'What have you been saying about this girl?' shouts the father at his boys in Punjabi, his hands on his hips.

The two boys look on, astonished.

'Come on now . . . what have you been saying?'

Eventually, the moustachioed one mumbles: 'We ain't said nothing, Dad.'

'So you're saying she's lying?'

'—'

'Why would she make up these stories for no reason?'

'—'

'Why would she do that?'

The clean-shaven one speaks. 'We ain't said nuffink, Dad. *Kushnee.* We didn't even know her room was next to ours.'

'So what's your explanation for this good girl, who goes to the temple every week, who studies hard, who never causes her parents any trouble whatsoever, saying you've been talking about her, eh? Do you expect me to believe you over her?' He puts his face right up close to one of his sons'. 'DO YOU?'

I watch, agog. This is so weird in so many weird ways. It's weird seeing our neighbours in our house – a bit like seeing your teachers out shopping, or your parents in the school corridors. Just wrong. It's weird seeing Mum so quiet, seemingly not in control of a situation. It's weird that our neighbour is wearing his pyjamas, and a turban, when he has no beard. It's weird Puli has been saying she can hear what the boys talk about next door when you can't even make conversations out when you put a glass against the wall, as I have often done, out of sheer boredom. And it's weird seeing a man playing the role of the disciplinarian: like the shopping and the cleaning and the working, the shouting and whacking is something our mother takes responsibility for in our household. Dished out by a man it seems more unforgiving, scarier. I flinch when, after a few more nuffinks and *kushnees*, he raises his hand, as if preparing to hit the boys. But Mum stops him.

'*Nai, nai.* No need.' She sounds tired.

'Their mother spoils them . . .'

'Listen, no need.' I can barely hear her. 'I'm sure it won't happen again.'

'Kids nowadays . . .'

'It's okay.'

'Is there anything you want us to do?'

'No, no, let's leave it.'

'Maybe we could get the boys to move bedrooms?'

'*Suchi*, no need.'

'Make the boys sleep in the middle room. That way there'd be no problem.'

'No, no.'

'You sure?'

'Yes.'

'Well, if you have any problems, if you ever need anything . . . please just let us know. You only need to ask. If neighbours can't be there when you need them . . .'

'Okay.'

The neighbours snake out of the house; the father, unshaven, still dressed in his pyjama bottoms, cord dragging behind him; the two sons, bemused, in tracksuits, following like ducklings, through the kitchen, out into the back yard and away. As soon as they're gone, Puli runs upstairs, Rajah, Dad and I sit down in front of the colour TV, and Bindi and Mum start preparing supper.

In the week that follows, those dark circles reappear around Mum's eyes.

And no one hears a peep from next door.

Except for Puli.

★

More than twenty years later, I ask Puli for her version of what happened. She begins telling me – that the voices started when she was revising for her O-levels, that they were very loud from the beginning, that they tormented her more and more until she began coming downstairs to tell Mum about them, in tears – but then she stops, and says she would prefer to explain what happened in writing. Like me, she find things easier to lay out on paper.

A week later a brown envelope arrives at my flat in London, with the postcode underlined, and Puli's address inscribed on the back, in the way Mum used to get her to inscribe our Park Village address on to the back of airmail letters to India. Inside, three sides of lined A4, stapled, all covered in Puli's large, neat handwriting.

'Mum didn't take me to the doctor initially. She must have been terrified about what it meant . . . after Dad. But eventually . . . after that thing with the neighbours . . . she took me to see the doctor. It was Dr Dutta. I remember telling him I could hear people talking about me (in the background), judging me, laughing at me, criticizing me, while I revised. I wanted him to tell Mum that the voices were real, that I was talking sense. But his response shocked me.

'He asked: "Are you sure you're revising? You don't just sit there?" Of course I don't just sit there, I thought. I work very hard and have been working hard for years. But his question frightened me: what if I failed my exams after all the work I'd done?

'He didn't say anything else. There was this strange atmosphere in the surgery. And eventually he silently handed me a prescription for tablets, with no explanation. I couldn't make sense of any of it. But as we got up to leave I did pluck up the courage to ask a question.

'I asked: "Doctor, can you tell me if the voices are real or in my imagination?"

'"They are in your imagination," he replied, and returned his gaze to the papers on his desk.

'He said I'd be getting a letter from the hospital and it was important to attend the appointment.

'We left the room and walked home in the dark evening (at least it feels dark to me now, how I remember it). I was defeated. When I got home with my tablets – Largactil – I asked Mum if they were the same as Dad's. I had been going with Dad to the psychiatrist's for years – to translate – from as young as nine or ten. I didn't know he had schizophrenia, I wouldn't have known what the word meant then, but I knew he was mentally ill, and that his medication was for mental illness. But Mum said my pills were different. I still checked Dad's bottles of medicine though. And the labels said "chlorpromazine". I thought she was right, that both the medication and my condition were different. But I know now that chlorpromazine and Largactil are the same thing.

'So I started taking them, not knowing they were for schizophrenia. I didn't know my name had been added to the 'severely mentally ill register'. I found this out when I read through my medical records recently. It was a low dose compared to what I take now. By the summer holidays, I'd calmed down and the voices weren't such a problem. Things began falling into place. I passed nine of my O-levels. I passed them all.

'Then I entered sixth form to study for A-levels. Things began well – once I even surprised my chemistry teacher by solving an equation even the smartest girl in the class couldn't solve and she asked me to explain it to the rest of the class. But that was to be my last achievement at school. I started going downhill when Bibi died. I'm not blaming her passing away for my problems but I do know that it was at that time that I gave in. Life suddenly felt meaningless. Nothing made any sense any more. I didn't know why I was doing A-levels. I didn't know what I wanted to do as a career.

'What I didn't realize was that these were symptoms of my illness . . . the symptoms were changing. I was suffering from what they call severe mental anxiety. Life became a nightmare again. The mental anxiety was even worse than the voices. I visited a child psychiatrist at New Cross Hospital and she changed the pills I was taking. She gave me a prescription for haloperidol and said it should calm me down.

'It worked. But though I was given a small dose, I found it very strong and would find myself dozing off, in classes. In the mornings I'd wake up exhausted and run half the way to school because I was always late leaving the house, because I was always late getting out of bed. What surprises me now is that nobody, not my friends, not my teachers,

10. Something Got Me Started

I tell myself now that there were numerous logical reasons why I decided to write a family memoir soon after that appointment with Dad's psychiatrist. It would be an organized, disciplined way of finding answers to the difficult questions that had been raised. I had started talking to Puli about her story and wanted to rescue her experience from oblivion. Apart from being part of the strategy to explain myself to my family, I realized that my family story was important in itself. It felt increasingly ludicrous spending time writing about strangers when there were more important subjects at home. It was a way of bringing the various aspects of my life together. It would be a way of forcing me to write that letter – sometimes it's easier to be courageous when you have an audience. Making the letter a public act was a way of dragging my mother away from the Punjabi community into my world.

But I also wonder whether I am reinventing what happened to suit me. Was it less a reasoned decision than a kind of panic attack? I can't actually remember sitting down and going through the reasons for and against. Though I do recall asking Mum for her permission – calling her from a train, on my way to yet another interview.

'What, like of one those story books that you're always reading?' she asked.

'A bit like that.'

'Why would anyone want to read about us?'

'They might find it interesting.'

'It's not a very cheerful story. I wouldn't want you to get stressed out.'

'I won't get stressed out,' I said, having absolutely no idea what I was getting myself into.

'Would it mean you'll be around more?'

'I'll be around more. I'm thinking about going part-time at work.' The idea was to quit writing the interviews taking a sideways glance at the world of celebrity, and the car reviews, which involved driving sideways down motorways, owing to my poor driving skills, and concentrate on the column I was writing which took a sideways glance at the world of business.

'No problem.' She sounded keen. 'Maybe we can get you married off while you're back . . .'

'*Muuummm.*' I had to say something. 'Look, we need to come to an agreement.' The man sitting opposite me, irritated by my Punjabi bellowing, switched seats. I continued in a whisper. 'It's going to drive me mad if you keep nagging me. How about this: you don't mention the marriage thing and then, when I'm done, I'll give the matter serious consideration.'

'Okay, fine.'

'Promise?'

'Yes.'

'No nagging. No arrangements. Nothing.'

'You know, I just want you to be happy . . .'

I waited for the inevitable caveats, but the train passed through a tunnel and I lost reception before they arrived.

And I realize now how I should have begun my research: I should have sat down with Mum and got her version of events, as she remembered them. But what I actually did was sit down with Dad – Mum was lying on the floor, listening to the news on Panjab Radio via the Sky digibox – and began by asking him about his childhood. The conversation went like this:

Me: 'Dad, I wanted to talk about your childhood – for this book thing . . .'

Dad: 'When I was small?'

Me: 'Yeah. You know – what you got up to when you were little.'

Dad: 'I used to work on the family farm.'

Me: 'How old were you when you started?'

Dad: 'Two.'

Me: 'You were working on the farm as a baby?'

Mum (from the floor): 'He means five or six. That's when boys were put to work in those days. Your eldest *bua* told me your Dad would often be sent out with a calf to graze for a day. He didn't go to school, you see.'

Dad: 'No, I was working before five.' He moved to the lip of his armchair. 'Look, your mother tells me not to talk to you about this . . . but you know God, he has a mother and a father . . . there are two people . . .'

Mum: 'Oi . . . sssshhh. Don't talk rubbish . . . your son wants to know about your childhood, what you used to do.'

Dad: 'I used to ride to the farm on a bike.'

Mum: 'You can't ride a bike.'

Dad: 'I can. I used to ride a bike to the farm. Buli got one when he got married.'

Me: 'Who's Buli?'

Dad: 'My brother . . .'

Mum: 'Your *thiya* . . .'

Me: 'Oh.'

Dad: 'And then over here I used to ride with Shindi to Dudley.'

Mum: 'I don't remember that. You didn't have a bike.'

Dad: 'With Shindi, my friend who lived near the pub, remember?'

Mum: 'You didn't.'

Dad: 'I did.'

Me: 'When was this?'

Dad: 'When I first came here.'

Me: 'When was that?'

Dad: '1980. . .?'

Mum: (laughing) '1980? It was 1969! Or 1968.'

Dad: 'And I used to lift weights. I was one of the strongest men in the country.'

Again, I realize now what I should have done next: I should have sat down with Mum and got her version of events, as she remembered them. But instead, I resorted to stationery. Specifically: an 1800 x 1200mm professional dry-wipe magnetic whiteboard; a pack of 100 whiteboard cleaning wipes; five whiteboard dry-safe dry-wipe marker pens; and five 24mm round plastic-covered magnets. All in all, the order cost in excess of £100, and once I'd put the board up in my study in London – and shelled out another £100 for a man to re-plaster the bits of wall I'd demolished when putting it up – I felt ready to begin.

There was logic to the idea, beyond it just being a nifty method of procrastination, and a reversion to a penchant for stationery which probably goes back to that Barclays Bank folder, or to my time as a stock room monitor at Woden Juniors. What I figured was that with there being so much confusion about the basic facts of my parents' story, what I had to do, before sitting down with Mum and getting her version of events, as she remembered them, was to assemble an outline of the basic facts on to an 1800 x 1200mm professional dry-wipe magnetic whiteboard. And the thing to begin with, I reasoned, was a family tree.

I expected this to be a simple task: what could be easier than laying out the relationships that have framed my entire life? Besides, the precision of Punjabi family titles makes them easier to navigate than most. We don't just have 'uncles' and 'aunts', for instance, but types of uncle and aunt: your dad's sister is a 'bua' (her husband a 'phupre'), your mum's brother is a 'mama' (his wife a 'mami'), your dad's younger brother is a 'chacha' (his wife a '*chachi*'), your dad's older brother is a '*thiya*' (his wife a '*thiyi*'), your mum's sister is a '*masee*' (her husband a '*masur*') and so on. However, it gradually emerged that the titles we used as a family didn't necessarily correspond to the relationships – Shindo, for instance, my favourite '*bua*', who always bought us packs of Chewits when she visited and always pressed a pound note into my hand on birthdays, turned out not to be a relation at all. Meanwhile, my mother's references to '*nani*', the word for maternal grandmother, were in fact to her mother, and my deceased grandfather, the man responsible for the whole mess on my father's side of the family, was in fact called '*chacha*', by my mother, father and those of his thirteen children who survived.*

Such quirks wouldn't have been so problematic if my relatives' proper names allowed them to be identified, but not only do all my relatives, like all Sikhs, share common surnames – 'Singh' for men and 'Kaur' for women – but many of the men and women share first names too: my mother's first name, Surjit, is, for instance, shared by several of my uncles. At times, sifting through the list of names provided by Mum was like trying to sort through the family mailbox of George Foreman, the two-time world boxing champion who named each of his five sons 'George', and one of his five daughters 'Georgetta'. Also many nicknames did not correspond in any clear way to the official names: Mum's nickname, 'Jito', makes some sense, but Dad's – 'Cugi' – doesn't. A process I expected to take a morning – a process during which I learnt I'd a staggering fifty-four first cousins and half a dozen uncles/aunts I'd never heard of – took over a week and covered

* What happened, it seems, was a version of the phenomenon you sometimes witness in English families where a husband starts calling the mother of his children 'Mum'. My grandfather's contemporaries called him '*chacha*' as he was the youngest of four brothers – actually, he was an only child and they were cousins, but I'm trying to keep things as simple as I can – and his children copied them. In turn, some of their children – his grandchildren – called him '*chacha*' too, though Mum always insisted we called him '*baba*', the word for paternal grandfather, with a respectful '*ji*' added on.

three-quarters of the space on my 1800 x 1200mm professional dry-wipe magnetic whiteboard.

Not that I needed much space for my second task: a chronology of key events. Now I didn't actually expect this bit to be easy, as, still not having sat down with Mum and got her version of events, as she remembered them, I didn't actually know what some of these key events were, and I'd had enough difficulty constructing a chronology of events for my own lifetime. Recalling the date of my brother's wedding, for instance, took three telephone calls. 'I think it was around the time that Michael Jackson brought out *Dangerous*,' was how he remembered it eventually, to his wife's audible outrage. But assembling dates for key events in my parents' lives went beyond being 'not easy'. It turned out to be impossible. Not only do my parents have no date of birth – Mum's is simply down as 1950 on her passport, while my father has three different dates of birth, all from 1950, in various official documents – they have no marriage date either. My mother, consulting an old notebook, initially gave me the date of 17 December 1967. But using the advanced journalism skills which have enabled me to exclusively reveal that Gillian Anderson is pretty, that the Aston Martin DB9 is nice to drive and that Bernard Matthews is beginning to resemble one of his own turkeys (in other words, I looked at Mum's passport), I worked out that this couldn't be right, as Mum didn't land in Britain until fifteen months after this date – on 16 March 1969 – and one of the few certainties about my parents' wedding is that it took place in England. When I put this to Mum, she sighed and said it was possible the date she'd given me was wrong. She'd taken it down from some official documents at some point, but couldn't remember what these documents were. She may have mis-transcribed the date, she said. Or it may even have been that the person who filled out the document had purposely given an incorrect date to the author- ities – claiming, for some reason or another, that my parents were married on this date when in fact they were only engaged.

I subsequently became a little obsessed with the matter of this wedding date. Maybe because a journalist will always prefer

inaccuracy to ambiguity, or maybe because I was at some level scared of sitting down with Mum and getting her version of events, as she remembered them, I wanted to find out when it was, or at least take an educated stab at it, but with Mum only able to estimate that the wedding occurred 'about a fortnight or maybe three weeks' after her arrival in Britain on 16 March 1969, and Dad unable to recall even in which decade it happened, all I could do was narrow down the probable dates to: Saturday 29 March 1969, Sunday 30 March 1969, Saturday 5 April 1969 and Sunday 6 April 1969.

For reasons I can't justify, I spent an entire morning at a library in London looking up each of these dates in *The Times* – did I expect to find a wedding announcement? – and eventually settled on Sunday 6 April 1969 as a guestimate. I picked the date because it was an Easter Sunday – new beginnings and all that; and because it was a beautiful spring day – warm and sunny in Birmingham at midday – and felt a brief glow of satisfaction writing it down on the chronology section of my whiteboard. And then promptly lost the little focus I had left.

Having discovered several stories about Wolverhampton while flicking through *The Times* – and having always found books easier to get on with than people – and still unable to summon the courage to sit down with Mum and get her version of events, as she remembered them, it occurred to me that I could probably find things out about my parents' background from books and newspapers. And so I spent two weeks finding out what Wolverhampton was like when my parents arrived.

There turned out to be a great deal to read about because Wolverhampton was, at the time, enjoying its fifteen minutes of fame as the first town in Britain to be affected by mass immigration. Enoch Powell's 'Rivers of Blood' speech in Birmingham on 20 April 1968 had made immigration a subject of national debate and, since the speech mentioned racial problems in Wolverhampton, and because Powell was MP for Wolverhampton, the town became a focal point for discussion. In the year before my parents were married, the town witnessed marches both for and against Powell, was the subject of several TV documentaries, countless news reports and a devastating feature about racial tension in the *Observer* that ran under the headline of 'TOWN THAT HAS LOST ITS REASON'. On 5 March 1969, less than a fortnight before Mum arrived, the Parliamentary Select Committee of Race Relations and Immigration met in the town hall.

After reading the entirety of the minutes, I switched to books about the rural Punjab in the fifties, spending three weeks sifting through titles such as *The Punjab Peasant* and *Caste and Communication in an Indian Village*. This didn't turn out to be a total waste of time. At the end of each day at the British Library, I would fasten my notes on to my 1800 x 1200mm professional dry-wipe magnetic whiteboard and then at the end of each week I would take them up to Wolverhampton and ask Mum and Dad whether life was really like that for them as children. Through a complex system of ticks and crosses, confirmation and repudiation, I found out things about their lives I probably wouldn't have otherwise discovered.

For instance, I learnt that Dad was brought up in a world where young boys got given one item of clothing a year – a white *kurta* – made from cotton harvested from the family's own farm, and a pair of shoes every two years, which he would sometimes carry to prevent them from wearing; and though his father had a relatively large amount of land, there were times when he went hungry. During the summer months in particular, his family switched to a diet of Lenten simplicity. At first, cow's milk replaced buffalo milk. Then mustard oil replaced ghee. Then chapattis were eaten dry. At the worst point – this detail my father remembers most bitterly – they took their tea with powdered milk.

He was, as he had said, working on a farm from a young age, about five, and by the sound of things he was a difficult child. Sometimes he refused to bathe: when the stench became intolerable, his siblings would hold him down on a *munja* and wash him, though Dad would dart off to the nearest field to roll around in the dirt afterwards. When Baba, my grandfather, 'Chacha' to everyone else, who had taught himself to read by scratching letters in the soil, suggested school, Dad refused again, and couldn't be persuaded to stay in the classroom even with offers of sugar cane. Eventually my father announced that he would go to school if he could go and live with Pindor – his elder married sister, who was twelve years older than him, and who now lives up the road from my parents – and was sent to stay with her new family. But once there, he refused to go to school again, and was sent back to the home village of Bilga to a lonely life at the *khuh* – his father busy, his brothers often at school or otherwise occupied.

By the time he was eight, his days consisted of chopping *bhusa* for the bullocks, scattering manure for the crops, milking cows for the family and engaging in the perpetual battle to irrigate the land. He spent a good portion of his teenage years living not in the village home but on the *khuh*, the outbuildings on the farm, sometimes with his father and sometimes his brother Pyara, but mostly alone, his sisters, and, occasionally, his mother ferrying meals from a mile or two away. It wasn't all work: sometimes, young men at *khuhs* in the area, free from family scrutiny, would gather to chat, smoke hookah (and opium, if so inclined), drink strong tea (and moonshine, if so inclined), and, if a day of chopping, scattering, milking and engaging in the perpetual battle to irrigate the land hadn't exhausted them entirely, to wrestle (and play *kabaddi*, if so inclined). But many of Dad's recollections are dark: he says he often spent the pitch-black nights terrorized by fear of cobras and vipers and sightings of the spirits known to roam the land. Could these have been delusions?

It was fascinating to find this out. As a child my eyes would glaze over whenever India was mentioned – I found the stories almost physically painful to withstand. But now I couldn't get enough. But while absorbed, I still hadn't really got to the point – finding out what happened to Mum and Dad when they got married – and I think I still wouldn't have got to the point, had Mum not, on one of those visits home, in contravention of our agreement, presented me with a photograph of a prospective bride. The girl was arranged in the classic arranged marriage pose: standing in the corner of a room next to a rubber plant; her hands clasped in front of her; a *chuni* draped backwards over her shoulders. The side-on pose suggested the possibility of some kind of facial disfigurement out of view. The large, muscular hands suggested a history of lifting heavy objects. In spite of myself, I did what all men do with prospective mates: I mentally undressed her, tugging at the drawstring of her salwar, unhooking her kameez, probing her (pot) belly, until – agggggggggh! – I remembered where I was and yelped.

'Okay, okay. No need to shout.'

'Mum – we had a deal, remember.'

'Yes, yes . . .'

'No marriage stuff until I finish the book.'

'Very well, yes. It's just that I want you . . .'

'. . . to be happy, I know . . .'

'. . . and for you to marry . . .'

'. . . a nice girl who is the right religion, I know . . .'

'. . . and the right caste, the right age . . .'

She took back the picture and looked at it longingly, in the way an exhausted executive might admire a picture of a luxury spa in Tuscany. 'Of course, I didn't know what your father looked like until after we were engaged.'

I ran a hand through my hair. 'Really?'

'You know you can ask me about what happened. You said you wanted to talk about it. But you haven't asked.'

'Let's do it tomorrow.' I was reaching for the door handle.

'Tomorrow will be hectic. The kids are coming. What's wrong with now?' There seemed to be lots of things wrong with now: not least the stationery. My dictaphone, lying in the bedroom upstairs, needed new batteries; I'd left my best pen at home in London; the paper in the A4 pad I'd brought down wasn't of a good enough grade . . . 'I've thought about telling you for ages but sometimes I'm not sure you want to know any more. Am I wrong?'

The honest answer was no. The dishonest answer was yes. I went for something in between. 'Hmmfgh.'

'I'll tell you what happened, *hunna*.'

There was a cup of tea and a Penguin bar waiting for me when I came back down to the living room from fetching my notepad in my bedroom. Mum sat on the floor, and I moved to a sofa on the other side of the living room, sitting parallel to her, having found that conversations of any kind of intimacy are more comfortable without eye contact, put the TV on (mute) so there was something to look at if things got awkward – there was a programme about polar bears on BBC2 – and then feigned a sudden interest in the wrapper of my Penguin bar, a sudden interest which revealed that it wasn't actually a Penguin bar at all, but a 'Sealbar'. So many groceries in my parents' house, purchased from various discount stores, are like this. What I thought was a box of Kellogg's Rice Krispies turned out to be a box of 'Pip's Crispy Rice', and the bottles of Domestos in the bathroom had turned out to be 'Steritos'.

'So, tell me: what do you want to know?'

'Tell me . . .' I put my tape recorder next to the chocolate bar. 'Tell me . . . what happened when your marriage was arranged. What did you know about Dad?'

'Not much.'

'How old were you?'

'Fifteen. Sixteen maybe. My mother told me he came from a

good family, that he was going to inherit a good amount of land and that he lived in a village nearby – Bilga. Only four miles away from my village of Rurka. She said she would be able to take food to my father at the *khuh* in the mornings, walk the four miles to see me, and, God willing, my sons, and still be back in time to take food to the *khuh* in the evening.'

'Did she ask you for your opinion on the . . . match?'

'Ha!' I'd said something stupid. 'In those days children were no more consulted about marriage than a bullock asked where it would like to graze. Anyway, I trusted my parents. All that mattered was that they were pleased.'

'Did you really not even see his photograph?'

'Eventually, but when the marriage was fixed, they asked if I wanted to see a picture of the boy. And I said no.'

And there you have Mum's moral standards: she was brought up to believe that a person who could not respect their parents could not respect God, to such a degree that she even accepted her permanent separation from them with stoicism.

'Did the arrangement come as a surprise?'

'Not at all. Marriage was the point of everything for girls then. We didn't have the opportunities that girls have nowadays – careers and jobs. Marriage was the meaning of life.'

Mum elaborated and I listened. Among the many surprises of that conversation was that I'd managed – more or less – to shut up. My interviews at work are invariably punctuated with sycophancy, smarminess, desperate attempts to ingratiate and inappropriate laughter, and the longest I can usually get through any conversation with Mum without screaming in frustration is three minutes. But I was restraint itself that evening. It was almost as if I had reverted to being a child – those nights when, Dad snoring away in the corner of the middle bedroom at 60 Prosser Street, Mum would put me to sleep with tales of saints and gurus and talking birds and jungle adventures.

She explained that almost every task she'd been given, from making cow dung cakes for cooking fuel at seven, to embroidering at eleven, had been suggested with a view to preparing her for

the prospect of getting married to a strange man and moving to a strange home. Even her parents' decision to send her to school, when they themselves had no education, when her father worried that education would make children ashamed of being farmers, when her elder brothers were denied an education on the additional grounds of expense, was framed in terms of marriage. Her mother, whom I only have a vague memory of meeting in India when I was three or four, put it to her father, whom I cannot remember ever meeting, that if the first of their two daughters could read and count, she would be a more economical housewife and would be able to write back from her in-laws. Four years later, the decision to cease her schooling was also framed in terms of marriage. It was at that stage – she was just embarking on English lessons – that her girls' school was due to be merged with the boys' school, and the family decided to discontinue her schooling, worried that being seen with boys would damage her marriage prospects.

'It was never part of the plan to go to Britain,' she added, as back in Wolverhampton a fat ginger cat brushed past the patio doors. 'At the time we were fixed up, your *baba*, your dad's dad, was in Bilayat. And two of your dad's sisters were settled here with their husbands – your Bero *bua* and Pindor *bua* both came in the mid-sixties. Your *baba* was staying with Pindor in

Wolverhampton. At first, there was a vague suggestion that your *bibi* – your Dad's mother – was going to join them, but no one else. He hated it in Britain. The cold, the long hours in factories.'

'Why did he stay? He had lots of land in India, didn't he?'

'Ha!' Mum laughed. 'Lots of land in India just means lots of headache.'

A brief lesson on the economic realities of farming in the Punjab followed. Yes, Baba, as an only child, had inherited a large tract of land – three times the land that his cousins had inherited. But three times more land meant three times more taxes, three times more work, and a thrice more intense battle with the difficulties of droughts, floods, crop failures, locusts, sickness, rust in the wheat, moneylenders charging exorbitant interest, dying bullocks, carts needing new wheels, new plants drying up, unsprouted seedlings shrivelling in the earth, poor monsoons, excessive monsoons, animals drowning in the monsoon, black-smiths charging exorbitant rates for mending ploughs and cotton carders who kept more than their share of the cotton. Besides, Mum explained, it was good for the farm if members of the family emigrated: the more of them earning a prosperous living in England, the more money they could send back to buy new land and employ workers.

'But after the engagement we heard your *baba* had applied to have the whole family join him . . . all those allowed to join him anyway . . . his children. They included your *chacha* and your Rani *bua*. They weren't sure if your dad would qualify – his age was vague and borderline . . . but you know how it goes . . .'

'Sometimes it can be handy having a vague date of birth . . .'

'No one in the village, not even the family relations next door, your grandfather's cousins, knew that they were going to Britain. They didn't want to draw attention to themselves. They were worried that someone might report them, or they might attract *nazar*. You know what Indians are like . . .'

'Paranoid . . .'

'. . . Paranoid. But then they had a point too. You couldn't trust anyone in those days – brother betrayed brother for an inch of land in the Punjab.'

Mum's family – her mother, her eldest brother, an uncle and the matchmaker – went to Bilga to visit my father the night before he was due to try his chance at getting through immigration. I imagined the tableau as Mum described it. Four of them sitting on *munjas* placed against a wall: a tall, elderly woman with delicate features and a shawl over her shoulders – her mother; a man in his twenties sharing the same fine features and wearing a large pastel-hued turban – her eldest brother, Gurdev; a middle-aged man wearing a white turban and sporting an extravagant moustache – an uncle; and a plump, moon-faced woman munching on a *ladoo* – the matchmaker. On the floor, the gifts they had brought along: a crate of apples; a box of sweets; and sections of brightly coloured silk and cotton with gold *mohra* scattered across them. Mum remembers overhearing her mother speaking tensely to her eldest brother when they returned.

'I worry the family are so different from ours. The boy's brothers, they like drinking, you can see it in their eyes, the mother-in-law – you can see she is sly, and the boy himself . . . he looks . . . simple to me. He's going to pardes, *he's marrying our daughter, but he didn't utter a word*

to us. He didn't stop playing with that radio all evening. Did you notice?'

Mum's elder brother Gurdev hadn't noticed. He had spent the second visit as he had spent the initial visit, when the marriage was arranged – having a lively conversation with my father's boozy brothers.

'Naniji,' he'd said. 'You know what I think? I think you think too much.'

Going to Britain threw things out of kilter for Mum. Having watched her three brothers get married, she'd expected a gap of six months or so between the engagement and the wedding. Instead fifteen months passed between the *kurmai* and the *biah*. She'd expected not to meet any of her in-laws until the *muklava*. Instead, one of her future sisters-in-law – another of my father's sisters – joined her at home in the village of Rurka a month before the wedding. She had been arranged in marriage to a man in England, and it was thought they should travel together. And then there was the stress and upset of travelling to Bilayat itself . . . a journey from which there was no return.

I wanted to know everything about this journey, what it felt like to go from a world where it was taboo for women to reveal ankles or arms, to a world where miniskirts were a common sight and couples kissed openly on the streets. I wanted to know what it was like to see a white man for the first time, hear Elvis for the first time, eat in a restaurant for the first time, see a plane for the first time, watch TV for the first time, realize there was poverty in Britain, as there was in India, for the first time. But not only has Mum still not done some of these things – she has never drunk alcohol, had her hair cut or been to a restaurant in Britain, for instance – the grief of leaving everything she'd ever known seems to have blotted out her memory of the journey. All I got were glimpses, snapshots: the sudden and overwhelming feeling of sickness when the moment for departure arrived; her father standing next to the bullock cart at the bus station in Jalandhar, declining to go any further (he was admitted into hospital with chest pains afterwards); the meal of rice and dhal she couldn't face in the airport; a future brother-in-law half-joking: 'I can't see her surviving the journey'; her mother insisting over and over that she wouldn't miss her family once she had a home of her own; the humiliation of having to be shown how to use the toilet on the plane; the first blast of refrigerated London air; the unexpected kindness of the translator in immigration who had seen it all before . . . 'Will you recognize your husband?'

'Did you see Dad at the airport?'

'Yes, he was there – standing at the back, with the whole family. They'd all come because his sister was coming with me, remember? But we didn't talk.'

Of course. The Punjabi aversion to public intimacy between the sexes.

'Then?'

'Then we went in different directions. Your father went back to Grays [in Essex], where he'd been living with your aunt Bero and your uncle Phuman. I went to Wolverhampton with the rest of the family. Number 26 Newport Street.'

'What was the house like?'

Again, I was hunting for detail. But all I got was: 'It was cold. Coal fires. Outside loo.'

'How many people were living there?'

'Let me see. There was your aunt Pindor and uncle Malkit, your *bibi* and *baba*, and also, Rani, your *chacha* Kashmir, Surinder, Billa, Bebe, Buboo, Kuldip . . .'

'Twelve people?'

'It was cramped. But it's amazing what you can deal with when you have to. There were some terraced houses nearby that had up to twenty people in them. There would be beds in every room, upstairs, downstairs, and sometimes men would use the beds in shifts, according to whether they worked the night or day shift at the factories.'

'Did you go out during those few weeks?'

Mum bit her lip.

I desperately wanted her to remember something, to compare her first impressions with those in a piece that was published in the *Express & Star* around the time of her arrival, in which a white female reporter called Valerie James had, in a quaint journalistic experiment that even the *Daily Mail* would balk at today, blackened herself up, donned a sari and walked around town to describe what it was like to be an Asian woman in the Black Country.

'*A small boy whistles derisively and laughs as you pass him in an empty street . . . a man turns curiously when he sees you climb into a taxi . . . At a bus stop four girls walk abreast down the pavement towards you. Chattering, they surround you for a moment . . . Workmen who call out to every female between the ages of fifteen and fifty-five are silent. But an Indian youth hisses quietly at you from a square-side seat. Brown-skinned men and women single you out in a crowd. But a white woman's glance slides uneasily away when you meet her gaze. Most people are shyly polite. Some people are hostile. Some, you find yourself noticing with gratitude, are friendly . . . An Englishman bumped into me. He didn't apologize. But two other white people, a man and a woman, hovered to help me pick up scattered parcels. White people were kindly but reserved. Service felt slower . . . in the seven short hours I spent as one, I found enough evidence of prejudice from my English compatriots to realize that an Indian girl's lot isn't an entirely pleasant one.*'

But again, no such luck.

'I don't think I went outside in those first few weeks.' Pause. 'I was in the *amanat* of the groom's family and they probably felt they had to guard me against mishaps. The men used to go to work early in the morning – your granddad and uncle Malkit worked in a foundry – your uncle Malkit worked at the Qualcast factory . . .'

'He worked there for twenty-five years, didn't he?'

'Yes. People don't know what hard work is nowadays. Your *baba* worked very hard too. He was in his sixties when he started, and worked for eight years unofficially after retirement. He was in his seventies and doing heavy foundry work. Your *bua* was pregnant with twins when I came. I stayed in the house there till our wedding.'

'Our wedding . . .' It was strange to hear the words come out of Mum's mouth. I'd never heard Mum or Dad talk about it before.

'What kind of . . . *wedding* was it?' I asked.

'Nothing like weddings are now. You know, people would get married in school halls, community centres and houses and there wouldn't be more than a little meal afterwards. Sometimes the bride and groom would be sat down with a couple of guests in someone's living room and read a passage that vaguely resembled the *lavaan* from a *gutka*, and that was it.' Mum laughed again. She laughs quite often, Mum.

'Was yours like that?'

'Not quite. We had use of the Cannock Road *gurdwara*.' Odd. We went to that temple at least once a week for decades, my two sisters were married there, I went there on every birthday, I had Punjabi lessons there, we slept nights there during *akand paths*, it was where Mum abandoned our cats, whenever she thought we had too many (the implication was that somehow it was less of a sin to abandon animals in the vicinity of a temple), I could remember it more vividly than our old house – and yet no one had ever once mentioned that it was where Mum and Dad had got married.

'And we had a priest reading the *lavaan* from a full copy of the Guru Granth Sahib.'

'Were there any photos taken?'

'No.'

Actually, there was at least one picture taken. A few months after this conversation Mum visited India and went through her deceased brother's trunk; at the bottom she found a parcel of documents, in the middle of which she found a picture of her wedding.

'Was there a *milni*?'*

'No. Who was there to do a *milni* with? None of my family were in the country. And in those days, the couple didn't walk around the Guru Granth Sahib clockwise four times like they do now.'

* A ceremony on the final day of a wedding where both families exchange blessings.

'Right.'

'They just sat there and stood up at the end.'

'Together?'

'Yes . . . And the thing is . . .' I could see from her reflection in the TV screen that she had the end of her shawl to her mouth '. . . the thing is that at the end the ceremony . . . your father didn't get up.'

'What do you mean?'

'Your father didn't get up. From the altar. He just sat there.'

'He just sat there?'

'Your uncle, your *phupre* Malkit, had to lift him up.'

Jesus. The equivalent at a white wedding would be the best man having to prompt the groom into saying 'I do'.

More omissions followed. There was no banquet, just some chapattis in the temple after the ceremony – the kind you get if you drop into any *gurdwara* on any Sunday morning. There were no *bidai* songs to mark my mother's departure to her new home. And after the besuited men had returned from sinking a few celebratory pints in the Lewisham Arms, none of the bride's brothers appeared to push the couple's car away in the direction of Grays as a sign of their love and support.

Mum said it was a relief to arrive in Essex. Although there were hardly any Asians in the town, unlike in Wolverhampton, the terraced house that was to be her home was less cramped than Newport Street – four adults and three children sharing the same space; she was grateful not to be living with the mother-in-law – like all Punjabi women, she'd been instructed to expect her husband's mother to be cruel – and my Bero *bua*, who poured mustard oil at the pillars of the door to welcome the newlyweds, and who had no family nearby, seemed pleased to have them.

On arriving, Mum was sat down in the living room and Bero began the process of relieving her of the wedding paraphernalia. First the large red veil that had been concealing her from view was removed, revealing a parting painted vermilion. Next to come off were her bangles, which had tinkled whenever she moved. She'd been stripped down to her heavy red and gold embroidered tunic by the time my father, who had all day been no more than a presence to her right, occasionally a violet shadow at her feet, strode into the room.

I tried again to imagine the scene: my mother looking as she does in her earliest picture, used in her first passport – a sparrow-thin, pale girl of sixteen or seventeen with a red *bindi* between her eyebrows, an embroidered *chuni* framing a long face with soft eyes, a heavy gold pendant hanging off a gold chain around her neck, a smaller pendant hanging off a delicate chain running down her parting, red and white ivory bangles encircling hands patterned with henna – and my father looking as he does in his early passport picture, the large brow, those sad eyes, the immaculate quiff. I asked Mum whether that was the first time she got a proper look at Dad.

'I don't know. Maybe.'

'Did he look different from what you expected?'

'—'

'You must have seen his picture by then? You know the photograph – it's in his passport.'

'—'

'You know the one. I've got a copy of it somewhere. His hair is hilarious . . .?'

A lengthy pause. On the TV a polar bear was disembowelling a seal, while beyond the patio doors, dusk was falling. In the dimming light I could make out the shape of the fir trees I had planted at the back of the garden with Chacha. It was the last thing we had done together before he passed away, and we had put them up because the kids in the house opposite would climb the apple tree at the back of their garden to hurl racist abuse at my parents as they mowed the lawn. The firs had grown quickly, and you couldn't see the apple tree any more.

'To be honest, I don't remember what he looked like,' Mum said eventually. 'All I remember is that he came up to me and slapped me across the face. Your uncle Phuman came running into the room, shouting, "What do you think you're doing?" . . . Your dad didn't say anything at first . . . But eventually he pointed at where I was sitting and said: "Look where she is sitting. That's Phuman's place on the settee. Doesn't she realize?" . . .'

11. You Got It (The Right Stuff)

The biggest cliché and most fundamental truth about madness is that, like beauty, it is all in the eye of the beholder. Something considered crazy by one bunch of people at one time might be considered normal by another bunch of people at another time, and, actually, my mother's obsession with marrying me off is a good illustration: it may seem bizarre viewed through Western eyes, especially given what she went through with her own arranged marriage, but is unremarkable within the context of Punjabi society.

Sikhs, you see, are – and there's no better word for it – crazy for matrimony. For people of my parents' generation in particular, a wedding is more than just an occasion at which two people agree to commit to one another in a spirit of mindless optimism. It is an occasion at which two families are united for ever, an expression of a mother and father's devotion to their child, an exposition of *izzat* (honour) – that most intense of Punjabi feelings – and the fulfilment of a sacred duty. The numbers tell the story: Sikhs have the second highest rate of marriage of all religious groups in Britain (59.2 per cent, after Hindus at 60.8 per cent), the lowest proportion of people who have never married (27.8 per cent)* and the average wedding apparently now costs in the region of £25,000.†

Before you even open your bejewelled invitation to the auspishous (sic) occasion of Mr Singh's matrimumy (sic) to Miss Kaur – the increased investment doesn't seem to have eradicated the problem of spelling mistakes – you know you'll soon be spending three days at a five-star hotel/private beach somewhere,

---

* Figures taken from Gurharpal Singh and Darshan Singh Tatla, *Sikhs in Britain: The Making of a Community*, c.2006.

† According to research published by Asian bridal magazine *Viya* in August 2007.

watching the groom arrive by elephant/on horseback, and being filmed belching your way through a twelve-course dinner by a camera crew whose last project was *Brokeback Mountain*. A wedding I recently attended at a swish hotel in Manchester even featured a bagpiper, who appeared in full Highland dress at the beginning of the *milni*, to give a full and hearty rendition of 'Loch Lomond'.

For a moment, I thought I was hallucinating. I'd been encouraged to drink what felt like a litre of rum the night before, and the day before that I'd driven my family across the country in a minibus, each of my nine passengers managing to find a unique way to irritate, so was feeling psychologically vulnerable. And then, noticing that everyone but me had greeted the bagpiper with the kind of nonchalance London commuters reserve for a delayed train, I thought I must have missed something. Maybe the bride or the groom had a Scottish connection? But conversations with relatives nearby revealed they hadn't. The closest thing to an explanation to transpire was that 'Bagpiper' was a popular whisky brand in the Punjab, and that the groom's family were enthusiastic drinkers.

The day continued in this surreal vein – it was as if the hotel had given the family a list of every conceivable wedding option imaginable, for every ethnicity under the sun, and the family had ticked every box – and when the couple, who had only met a few times before their bethrothal, had their first dance to 'I Will Always Love You', I couldn't help guffawing and remarking on the irony to my patient brother, who, worn down by my incessant moaning, finally snapped, exclaiming: '*Why do you have to analyse everything?!*'

He was right. I'd missed the point. Like Bollywood movies, Sikh weddings aren't meant to be analysed: they are simply exercises in escapism and showing off, a mindless, albeit heartfelt, amalgamation of influences from a variety of cultures. Not that understanding this makes them easier to endure. I find weddings, in general, onerous, for the compulsion to have 'fun', for the persistent refusal of any of the pretty girls to flirt or even acknowledge me in any way whatsoever. But Sikh weddings, with their mindlessness and extravagant length, with the way they require you to sit for hours with a bunch of men talking about the buy-to-let-market, are agonizing. So much so that I just don't attend them any more.*

Unfortunately, I had no choice in attending weddings as a child. And, if anything, weddings were even more arduous then, for they invariably meant three days of being hugged by moustachioed uncles with alcoholic breath, having to sit cross-legged in silence during impenetrable ceremonies which could go on for five hours at a time and having to share toys with tedious younger cousins while interesting elder cousins went round doing cool things like trying to derail the trains that ran on the tracks at the end of our back yard.

I was going to say that the single worst thing was being forced to dance to bhangra, a genre of music for which I'd developed no enthusiasm, despite being force-fed it for up to fourteen hours a time at the factory. But actually, there was something even worse: being forced to watch a video of myself trying to dance to bhangra a matter of days after each wedding, my family pointing and laughing at my lack of rhythm and coordination. When it is done well, watching someone perform bhangra can be mesmerizing, but when I did it, it looked as if I was being electrocuted while trying to simultaneously unscrew two light bulbs.

Maybe the weddings wouldn't have seemed so bad if there weren't so many of them. If I wasn't at one, I felt as if I was being dragged along by my mother as she prepared for another – the shopping trips began months in advance – or being forced

* Having said that, Dal, Ruky's brother, recently asked me to be best man at his wedding, a job I accepted on the grounds that (i) he is lovely and (ii) I thought it would involve little more than standing next to him for a few minutes on the morning of the third day of the wedding. Imagine my shock therefore when at 9 a.m. on the big day I was dressed in an Indian *sherwani*, with a garland of flowers around my neck, and was being asked to lead a group bhangra dance of around thirty people down a suburban street in Wolverhampton. While being filmed. So far, I have avoided watching the video . . .

to watch a video, reliving the agony in real time. And when I
dared to hope the frequency was declining, it became fashionable
for couples to have separate English-style registry office ceremonies
as well, which doubled the number of weekends lost to betrothals.
And then, just as I dared to hope I was running out of cousins
to get married, cousins I didn't realize I even had started appearing
from India as well, bearing gifts of sugar cane, asking to be shown
the whereabouts of the nearest porn shop and announcing they
wanted to be married too.

Watching these Indian cousins get married at least had a certain
Challenge Anneka, against-the-clock appeal. They were often in
England 'on holiday' or 'seeking asylum' – though sometimes they
would admit they'd entered the country illegally – and because
the one thing that would legitimize and/or extend their stay was
marriage to someone with a British passport, the prolonged and
exhausting process of arranged marriage would have to be tele-

scoped. As soon as they made it through Customs and Immigration, or as soon as they were liberated by their human trafficker of choice into an alleyway in Dudley, and before they had even got used to Western customs such as not spitting on the living room floor, arranged marriage aunties were scouring the land for potential spouses, their criteria being that the person be a British Sikh of the appropriate sex and caste and be willing to get married very quickly.

In fact, these were the *only* criteria, which meant these visitors, who often managed to combine an intense desire to stay in Britain with sustained whining about the shortcomings of the UK versus India, represented a matrimonial opportunity for those lingering in the relegation zone of the arranged marriage league table: the over-25; the obese; or the offspring of those parents who were most concerned about Westernization and wanted their children to marry Indian spouses to keep alive their traditions of religiosity, illiteracy, alcoholism, manual labour and domestic violence. Some of my relatives would eventually join this group, but when it came to arranging Puli's marriage, when she was nineteen, the family went for a British-born boy from Coventry.

It felt odd being on the other side of the fence. Until then, organizing weddings had been like voting Tory: we endured the horrendous consequences of other people doing it, but never did it ourselves. But I accepted the development as another change in a time of change: the eighties were turning into the nineties; the two Germanys were being reunified; Margaret Thatcher was on her way out; I was at secondary school; and we had by then moved out of our terraced house in the centre of Wolverhampton into a semi-detached on the outskirts, where our Pindor *bua* and Chacha had already moved to.

In the end, Mum hadn't been persuaded to move by my complaints about sleeping arrangements, or by an intensification in the infestation of cockroaches, or by the damp caused by the shoddy workmanship of the Indian builders who had 'renovated' the house, or by the increasingly violent domestic disputes of our neighbours, or by the favourable conditions in the property market, or by the fact that we were the only bit of the extended family left in Park Village, or by the brick that the white man from number 58 threw at our living room window when, after two decades, he had finally had enough of the whirring of my mother's sewing-machine. In the end, it took an inner city riot to convince her of the need to move.

As with so many defining moments in the life of my family, I missed it. I woke up on the morning of 25 May 1989, after an unexpectedly refreshing night's sleep – unexpected because I was by then making my unhappiness about sleeping arrangements felt by sleeping in a duvet on the floor of my parents' bedroom – went downstairs to fix myself a bowl of Weetabix, moved to the TV that my siblings were huddled around and slowly realized that the mob of lunatics depicted throwing petrol bombs at police officers in flame-resistant suits and riot helmets were doing so in the housing estate down the road.

'Senior policemen fear that violence associated with the sale of crack may erupt in Britain after several hundred youths in Wolverhampton rioted early yesterday morning. The riot started after West Midlands drug squad officers raided the Travellers' Rest public house in Heath Town, where cannabis and crack supplies worth £1,500 were seized and twenty people arrested.'

My immediate reaction was: what the hell is crack? And after my brother had explained, I couldn't help wondering which other mundane nouns were going to turn out to be narcotics. After 'glue' and 'crack', were 'door' and 'carpet' going to be next?

There was a surprising amount of interest in the house given it was infested by cockroaches, encircled by semi-feral cats, damp-ridden and now on the edge of a riot area. And after a number of visits to building societies, the arrangement of various bridging loans with relatives, and a great deal of breast-beating from my mother, who made it known she had only borrowed money from a bank for the first time in her life for the sake of my brother and me, we were piling our furniture into the back of the factory owner's Volkswagen van, as my mother surreptitiously abandoned

Pussy and the ironically named Lucky on a nearby industrial estate.

'No more mice, no more need for *dadnia* cats,' Mum pronounced as I wept.

The Indians can be a cruel race at times.

The arrangement of Puli's marriage was comparatively straight-forward: a family acquaintance telephoned Mum, saying she knew of a good boy from a good family who might make a good match for my sister; Mum, Dad, Chacha and Chachi went to visit the boy and his family at their home in Coventry; and then some time afterwards they returned the visit.

'We've got to move with the times,' Mum pronounced. 'We can't just marry the girl off to any old *pagal*. She must meet the boy and see if she likes him.'

I saw them arrive from the double-glazed window of the new bedroom I shared with my father, next to the new bedroom my mother now shared with my two sisters. There were five of them packed into a red Ford Orion and they made two attempts at parking on our steep drive before pulling up, rather sheepishly, against the kerb. When the rear doors were flung open, it was clear why they had struggled with the gradient: the two women on the back seat were heffalumps who had not only eaten all the pies, but all the pakoras too. The prospective groom, a round-faced youth trying to hide behind an out-of-date mullet, an over-long fringe and weekend stubble, and the prospective groom's father, a clean-shaven man wearing a sky blue turban, looked cartoonishly slight next to them. I tried to imagine the quartet as a family, watching fireworks with them at Diwali, sharing one of our two Christmas Day dinners with them, but couldn't make the mental leap.

The atmosphere in what the estate agent had puzzlingly called a 'breakfast kitchen' – what made it particularly suited to the first meal of the day? – was nervous, as my siblings and Chacha's four children swapped first impressions of the prospective groom and mimicked the fat women waddling into the house. There was a dispute about who should take the first tray of tea and biscuits into the living room, where the adults had gathered. Puli – more sombre than the rest of us, presumably because she was on the brink of being married off to a man she'd never met before – excused herself on the grounds that she'd been instructed to make an appearance at a specific time. Bindi, who was at this stage working at a branch of Safeways as a cashier – more sombre than the rest of us, presumably because she was probably beginning to realize that she would be in the same position as Puli in a year's time – excused herself on the grounds that she might be mistaken for Puli. My cousins were too young. So it was down to me or my brother, which meant it was down to me, for while Rajah had by this stage made it through his extraordinary Michael Jackson phase, and was now in the midst of a more subtle Jordan Knight from New Kids on the Block phase, studying business and finance at a college in Dudley, his other-worldliness still excused him from most domestic tasks.

The memory of walking into the living room with those cups of tea and plates of *ladoos* is a vivid one, in part because it was so unusual to see men and women of my parents' generation sitting in the same room together. Normally, when visitors arrived, the men segregated themselves into the front room, while the women drifted into the living room, just as men sat on the right at religious services at the *gurdwara* and women on the left.* But here they were all together: the men lined up in the chairs Mum had bought from an office clearance sale; the fat women on the creaking settee that was threatening to give way under their weight; my mother and Chachi sitting in front of the double-glazed patio doors behind which lay the huge lawn that had immediately replaced the cats in my affections.

The other memorable thing about the scene was the silence. Of course, I'd witnessed such social stillness before. I was regularly stunned at how little Punjabi men had to say to one another until they had consumed half a bottle of whisky each. But I'd never been in a room containing so many Punjabi women which had been so quiet. Moreover, I'd never been in a room containing so many Punjabi women, one of whom was my mother, which had been so quiet. It was actually a bit scary: like the moment in a play fight when your partner pretends a little too convincingly to have died. As I directed the tray towards the coffee table and three pairs of hands stretched out to steady it, you could almost hear the midday shadows inching across the wall.

Needless to say, when the silence was finally broken, it was Mum who broke it.

'This is our youngest boy – he is studying at the grammar school,' she said, as if there was only one grammar school in the world, as if this was why Chacha had swapped his afternoon shift for a morning one, and why I was at home and not at the factory, as I would normally have been on a Saturday. I smiled thinly and headed towards the door, only to find myself being pulled back into a seat by my always-mischievous Chacha, amused at my visible discomfort. 'You know we'd never even heard of the school, but, thanks be to God, his headmaster Mr Ball entered him for

* Second-generation couples in my family seem to have inherited the habit. Husbands and wives may now be liberated enough to visit pubs and restaurants together, but the men invariably end up necking pints at one end of the table, while the women sit together at the other end nursing glasses of orange juice, or, on very special occasions, a single glass of wine – a frustration for those who prefer conversation with the opposite sex.

the exam, and his teacher Mr Burgess gave him extra lessons, and then, thanks be to God, he passed, and then there was an interview – they even interviewed us! – and thanks be to God he passed that too. But then there was a letter saying they wanted thousands of pounds a year in fees but when something is meant to be, it is meant to be, and thanks be to God, we filled out the forms and now the *gor-ment* is paying . . .'

The fat aunties nodded, the male guests murmured between slurps of tea, and I flushed like a raspberry. My mortification was in part the mortification of any gangly pubescent – I was beginning to feel uncomfortable in my own skin. But more than that there was the knowledge that my mother's pride was misplaced. Things were going badly for me at my new school, and had been from the moment I went to buy the uniform from Beatties department store in town and Mum asked me to haggle down the price, only for the assistant to retort: 'This isn't Wolverhampton market, madam.'

Into my second year, I still felt bewildered by the school: the way the music teacher gave us a keyboard and just expected us to be able to read and write music; the way some of the kids patted the corners of their mouths at the end of their packed lunch; the way, frankly, they were so white. Until I went to Wolverhampton Grammar, I hadn't really been aware of being different. Largely because, even with my topknot, I wasn't. In my final class at Woden Primary, there were two of us in my class alone with long hair and, if anything, my classmates found my name – translating as 'god', and bearing an admittedly hilarious likeness to 'Batman' ('digadigadigadiga . . . Satman!') – more amusing than my hair. But now I was one of just a few topknots in the whole school, and my days were marked by taunts of 'Oi, turbinator' and 'Is that your packed lunch on your head?' and (with a squeeze) 'Oink oink' and (with a mimicked topknot-siren) 'Nee-naw, nee-naw'.

In this new milieu, I felt I could do nothing right. When we were asked to wrap our textbooks for protection, I did so in 1970s floral wallpaper, while the boys around me came back with

theirs expertly cellophaned. While the other kids who had packed lunches came with neatly packed sandwiches, Mum gave me omelette sandwiches and *aloo gobi parathas*, which stank out the packed lunch area so much that I sometimes ate alone outside. After several months I had managed to make only one proper friend – James Lockley, or Lock, as we called each other by surnames, who caught the bus to school from a similarly crap part of town and shared my pop music obsession.

From wanting to be the centre of attention, I became timid and speechless, my unhappiness measured out in numbers in my end-of-term reports. At the end of my first year I was sixteenth in French, fourteenth in Latin, sixteenth in History, and even in my best subject, Maths, I was seventh. At junior school, parents' evenings had been the absolute highlight of my year, as exciting as a birthday and Christmas combined. I would whip myself into a state of high excitement as Mum disappeared down the road with Puli – who went to translate – and almost shake with pleasure as Mum returned to repeat every comment with a smile and a congratulatory '*Shabaash*'. But now I couldn't stand them.

Mum's insistence that I still take the congratulatory pound coin, that she was still proud of me, made it worse.

'He wants to be an accountant when he gets older,' she continued in front of the guests, renewing the agony. 'He's always been good with numbers. But they now say computers are the thing to go into? Not that we mind. We just want him to be happy. That's all any of us want for our children, isn't it? We want our children to be happy. And for them to listen to us. That is all. Nothing more . . .'

Mercifully, we were saved from any more of this by Puli's arrival into the living room, an event which was greeted with a silence even more monasterial than the one preceding Mum's monologue. She glided around the room with a plate of *barfi*, her head downcast under a *chuni* a few tones away from the deep red of the Indian bride, not making eye contact with anyone, even the prospective groom, who was the only person in the room looking more mortified than me. I'd been to enough weddings to know this was the way brides were meant to behave: silent and coy. This timidity might once have seemed an unconvincing act, given Puli's ferociousness. But in recent years, the explosions, while they hadn't disappeared, had abated. It was almost as if she'd been hooked up to a mood thermostat, which kept her temper within certain boundaries . . . which was what had, in effect, happened.

You see, Puli had by this stage been taking antipsychotics for more than three years. I didn't know she had schizophrenia at the time, obviously, and neither, less obviously, did she. She still hadn't been told the diagnosis; and when she spent a year unemployed after failing her A-levels, she claimed the dole rather than the sickness benefit she would have been entitled to. But when we moved house she began to feel better and started applying for jobs, and ended up working at the council's poll tax office, earning what seemed like an unimaginable amount of money to me. The work seemed to do her good. Looking at her, you wouldn't have thought she was unwell. Looking at that room, you'd never have thought there were two people there suffering from the most devastating mental illness around.

Once Puli had slid out of the room, it was Chacha's turn to break the silence, taking, as he often had to, my father's role.

'I think we should . . .' He cleared his throat. 'I think we should let them have a little time by themselves.'

You might have thought from the astonished glances exchanged that he'd just suggested the boy and girl pop next door to smoke some crack.

After the visitors had departed, there was a rush for the one slab of *barfi* that hadn't been scoffed by the fat ladies and to issue verdicts on the prospective groom.

'Might have bothered to shave,' said Mum.

'It's the fashion though,' said Bindi (sniffing).

'Seems okay,' said Chacha. 'Family business. Prospects.'

'Claims he doesn't smoke or drink,' said Chachi.

'Dodgy hair,' said my brother, who had forgotten his loose perm.

I murmured my approval. Nowadays, the list of things I deem necessary for a relationship to work – a shared sense of humour and level of silliness, tolerance of one another's careers and TV habits, sexual compatibility, etc. – is almost as long as the average Sikh wedding. But at that age, having never had a girl smile at me with romantic attention, one person seemed as good as another. Not that my opinion, or anyone else's, mattered. After the meeting Mum consulted a *pandit*, who looked into his crystal ball, or his orange pyjamas or whatever it is *pandits* look into, and announced that if Puli didn't get married to this boy with an outdated mullet she wouldn't get married for years, and because Mum feared this prospect even more than she dreaded not being able to force-feed us again, the deal was struck. Owing to the superstition that an eldest daughter should never be married off at the age of nineteen, the wedding was set for exactly three days after Puli turned twenty.

In the run-up to the big weekend, I found myself in the unusual position of looking forward to a wedding. Puli's departure meant I was one step closer to having a room of my very own. My role as a brother meant I was going to get cash during the ceremony. I was going to get several days off school. And because one is supposed to look unhappy at one's sister's wedding – you are losing a member of your family – I was told that I wasn't allowed to dance, which was a bit like being told I wasn't going to be allowed to have my legs amputated with a fondue fork. Chacha teased me that I'd be upset when the day came, bet me I'd be in tears by the time it came to say goodbye, but I was convinced otherwise. It all seemed to be upsides from where I was standing.

My recollection of the first two days of the wedding isn't great: there have been so many weddings, even among my siblings, that they're all a blur of boredom and bhangra and sitting cross-legged in boiling *gurdwaras*. But a few things stick out. I remember the strange feeling of no longer being ignored by my elder cousins. My place at grammar school had given me an odd celebrity status. I would have liked to believe they were all stunned by my academic promise but, judging from the comments, it was more that they were amused by the idea of a member of the family attending private school. 'So do you speak to your teachers in Latin?' 'Do you wear a top hat?' I also remember having to share my room with a cousin for one night, and him standing semi-naked in front of my bookcase, one hand on his hip, another rearranging something in his Y-fronts, asking whether I'd really read all the books I had lined up on the shelves.

I had five books on the shelves.

He followed this up by asking whether it was 'a bit gay' for a teenage boy to have so many George Michael posters on his bedroom wall.

Gay?

What was he talking about?

I got up early on the morning of the main ceremony, to avoid the embarrassment of being seen having my hair combed by Mum – I could tie a plait, but I still couldn't get the knack of tying the knot – and popped in to see Puli after the make-up and *mehndi* artist had visited. I know it is customary to say brides look beautiful. But she really did. Mum had never allowed my sisters to use make-up. Indeed, it was only at that moment that the wobbliness started, that I began questioning the wisdom of my sister being married off to a man I'd exchanged a total of one greeting with.

'All right?' he'd asked.

'Yeah,' I'd responded.

Who was this guy who was going to be my brother-in-law? Wasn't it all a bit sudden? Who was going to do all the translating now Puli was gone? The factory owner put more effort into hiring sewing-machinists than the family had put into finding Puli a husband. I put more effort into my mix tapes.

Still, I kept it together, during the over-long ceremony, during the subsequent party at a nearby community centre, during the always-emotional departure ceremony, where I was required, along with the rest of the family, to say goodbye to Puli in the back of the car, the lens of a video camera pressed against one side of my face, and the gold embroidery of Puli's sari pressing against the other. It was only when it came for Dad to say goodbye that I lost my bet with Chacha. Not that he noticed: he was too busy trying to get my father to let go.

12. This Is A Low

Mum went to bed after telling me the story of her engagement and wedding. Late the next evening she resumed the story of her early marriage, going through everything that happened up to the point of Puli's birth in 1970, a year after the wedding. Then, on the third and fourth evenings, she finished the tale, up to the point of my birth in 1976. Several weeks later I found myself removing a 35cl bottle of Gordon's gin from a Fitness First rucksack, pouring a glug into a china teacup, and sitting down behind a laptop placed on a flatpack desk I had bought from Argos, to attempt to write a version of the story.

A woman, they say, always remembers her wedding night, and my mother is no exception.

That seemed acceptable. Clear. But should I talk about Mum as Mum? Somehow, it didn't sound right. Good journalism was impartial and neutral.

A woman, they say, always remembers her wedding night, and Jito is no exception.

Better. Another sip of neat gin. Gag reflex. Vodka next time.

After Cugi, the husband she had not yet talked to, slapped her in the living room of their new home, she retired with him to the front bedroom, which was . . .

Which was what though? Mum hadn't been able to provide much of a description. She had said the room was in a terraced house, and that there was a mattress on the floor, but she couldn't remember anything about the decor or the light. Also: was it a slap? She'd used the word '*thupar*' – meaning slap – the first time she ran through the story, but then '*muka*' – meaning punch – when she referred to it again. Not to worry, though: you can always return to these things. I would put question marks next to bits that required further probing.

After Cugi, the husband she had not yet talked to, slapped her in the living room of their new home, she retired with him to the front bedroom, where he punched her in the stomach. He growled to sleep on the double (?) mattress under the window (?) while she cleared up her own vomit . . .

Then what? Mum had gone on to a description of what happened the morning afterwards, but did anything . . . Christ. Just the idea of having to ask had me reaching for the bottle. This was turning out to be much more difficult than I expected.

The compulsion to drink alone wasn't the only unexpected consequence of listening to Mum's story. In the daze that followed I gave up on my already disintegrating social life – I felt a need to talk about what I'd learnt, but at the same time couldn't bear doing so; I decided to quit my ridiculously perfect but now part-time job – I needed it to distract me, but at the same time realized that writing my parents' story was more important; I started spending more time in Wolverhampton – another paradox, in that I wanted to get away, but felt panicky whenever I did get away; and – this was perhaps the most unexpected development – when Mum, once again in contravention of our agreement, mentioned a nice Sikh girl who was working as a teacher in Wolverhampton, I agreed to have an arranged marriage meeting.

Since graduation, I must have been on twenty or thirty such set-ups and have gone on them for all sorts of reasons: a family member was particularly insistent; I was dating someone inappropriate and having a brief meeting was a good way of keeping the family off my back; I was single, and why not? I even had a brief flirtation with a Sikh matrimonial website. But this was the first time I agreed to meet someone purely to please Mum. Having heard her story, the old saviour complex kicked back in. The more I thought about what my parents had been through, the more trivial my anxieties about love and marriage seemed, and an arranged marriage meeting a tiny thing in comparison to the sacrifices my mother had made. I wanted to lessen her grief, and told myself if I could do this by marrying a Punjabi Jat, then at least I should try.

Besides, the arranged marriage meetings I'm required to go on do not in any way resemble the horrendous tea parties my sisters had to endure. I've had a few of those, but like I said earlier, it is generally a case of blind dating with parental approval. And so, for the first time in weeks, I removed the lumberjack shirt I'd bought for £7.99 from Fosters when I was fifteen, put on a once-trendy but now frayed Paul Smith T-shirt, got Mum to wash my jeans – she returned them with a crease ironed down the middle – and headed off to meet my potential future fiancée in the Wolverhampton branch of Starbucks.

Discovering Wolverhampton had a Starbucks had been a bigger shock than discovering it had a tourist information centre. Indeed, for years, I had defined my home town by its lack of a Starbucks. The fact seemed to sum up the city's arrested development: the aggressive coffee chain, which seems to have more outlets than employees, which would open stores in the lavatories of the opposition if it could do so, couldn't, evidently, be bothered with Wolverhampton. But as with so many things to do with my past, I'd got it wrong.

My date was late, giving me plenty of time to see how Wulfrunians were taking to café culture. Judging from the conversations floating around the till, they were struggling.

Customer one: 'So y'am saying "tall" ay yower biggest size?'

Customer two: 'Can't I just have a simple coffee?'

Customer three: 'Do yow serve fish and chips?'

After fifteen minutes – still no sign of my potential future fiancée – I tired of sneering at people at the counter, got a second coffee and switched to sneering at people sitting around me. As with most branches of Starbucks, half the store was occupied by teenage girls laughing uproariously as if starring in an episode of *Friends*, but their liveliness was counterbalanced in Wolverhampton by a gaggle of Goths gathered in a corner – about eight of them, looking miserable, or trying to look miserable, in combinations of black, dark red and purple. A couple holding hands and kissing on the periphery of the group caught my attention – the girl because she was too pretty to make the angsty-consumptive-poet look succeed, and the boy because, despite his backcombed hair, black streaks of eyeliner and army surplus combat boots, he was just too cheerful-looking and too, frankly, Asian, to pass off as a proper Goth. Indeed, I think he might have been the first Asian Goth I had ever seen, and the couple, the first teenage interracial couple I had spotted openly smooching in Wolverhampton. Watching them, I remembered all the surreptitious dates I'd been on when I was a teenager, the lengths I went to to avoid being caught, and then, remembering I was on the brink of another date, began replaying all my past marriage meetings in my mind.

The fur-coated banker whom I met in a London hotel bar and who announced half an hour into our meeting – 'Hope you don't mind' – that she'd brought four friends along for moral support, and they were scattered around the bar. The ball-breaking stockbroker who revealed that at the age of thirty she'd never had a relationship of any kind: not a kiss, no hand-holding, nothing. Was she saying it because she thought it was what an Asian man would want to hear? The pretty marketing assistant who pronounced in the pub she'd agreed to meet me in that she'd never had a drink, would never have a drink, and could never be with someone who did drink, because drinking alcohol was a transgression of the Sikh faith. And then, most memorably, the solicitor from the matrimonial website, who met all my criteria – she didn't have a moustache, thought London was the best city in the world, could sustain conversation without resorting to the words 'wikid' or 'innit' or '*hunna*' every other sentence, didn't use an excessive number of emoticons or exclamation marks in emails, didn't have a disconcerting habit of comparing potential partners to her father/brothers, thought our parents' obsession with caste was ridiculous given that the gurus declared all men and women equal, felt as silly as I did when trying to work out the difference between 'wheatish' and 'wheatish medium' in the 'skin colour' section of the website application, didn't seem to be secretly in love with someone else, wanted a proper relationship before committing to living together forever in electric dreams, and who was petite and cute and clever and who actually seemed to like me, but who the next day sent me a 2,000 word – 2,000 words! – character assassination by email that literally made me cry.

Over the years I've often wondered why these meetings are so weird – more so than normal blind dates – and reluctantly concluded that part of the problem is me. According to regular unsolicited feedback from those who know me best, I have ideas above my station and routinely go for people out of my league. Also, I'm not interested in many of the things second-generation Asians tend to care about: Bollywood, bhangra, R&B, bling. However, I also think there is something intrinsic to such meetings that encourages weirdness. Existing in the grey area between a date and an arranged marriage meeting, you have to act like you're there because you want to be, even though you are compelled to be there; you have to flirt but at the same time imply no sexual intention whatsoever; you have to reveal things about yourself, without giving too much away (you can't risk damaging information getting back to your family); and because your 'date' has been chosen by someone else, and because so many British Asians are (like me), for want of a better word, schizophrenic, constantly switching between personas to fit into different worlds, you have absolutely no idea what end of the Punjabi spectrum they are coming from, and whether they mean what they say. They could be anything from a sword-wielding religious Sikh who has never cut their hair or left their house without a chaperone (or pretending to be), to a nymphomaniac alcoholic who is throwing up into your lap after an hour and demanding you move on to China Whites for a boogie. In short, the meetings are fraught with potential disaster. Which, of course, raised the question of what the hell I was doing in Starbucks on the verge of another one. Listening to Mum's story had made my head spin, I was finding it difficult even to talk to my friends, the aversion to TV had returned with such a vengeance that I now couldn't even stand *BBC Parliament* – some of those Welsh Assembly sessions can get pretty heated, I tell you – and here I was throwing myself into the most difficult and brutal aspect of life imaginable. It was like failing a driving test and then agreeing to race in the Monaco Grand Prix. But just as I glanced at my watch, and wondered whether a delay of half an hour was a sufficient excuse to cancel a date, there was a soft voice over my shoulder.

'Are you . . . ?'

I turned around . . .

. . . and she was lovely. A bit tall for my taste maybe, but a nice open face, no sign of teacher-frumpiness, big brown eyes – people always say Indians have nice eyes, but she did – sexy thin-framed spectacles, a smart black suit – back from work? – the whiff of Yves Saint Laurent Opium and, best of all, no hint of the anti-Viagra of a Wolverhampton accent.

'Sorry I'm so late. . . nightmare at school.'

'No problem.' For some reason I had pulled my mobile out of a pocket and was waving it around. 'Can I get you a drink?'

She tilted her head to one side.

'Decaftripleventinonfat3splendaextrahotstirrednofoamcaramel macchiatowithwhipcreamandextracaramel please.'

A moment's pause as I tried to diagnose whether she was joking: you can take nothing for granted in arranged marriage scenarios.

'I read somewhere it's the most complicated Starbucks order you can get.' She smiled in a way that gave a suggestion of Colgate-advert teeth. 'Americano please, fat milk.'

I came back with a coffee for her, a smoothie for me – I'd already had enough caffeine to keep a herd of bullocks awake for a week – and a muffin for . . . God knows who. After exchanging observations about our surroundings – we both agreed it wasn't fair we didn't have coffee shops to hang out in when we were teenagers, that the Goth lovers were sweet (subtext: she is cool with idea of interracial relationships, phew) – we began the task of finding out about each other, and I discovered she was the elder of two children, that she'd always wanted to be an RE teacher but now fancied becoming a property developer, that she had gone to university in Birmingham and had had a relationship there which petered out with the end of her degree, that she lived in Wolverhampton with her family but would happily move elsewhere – who wouldn't – that her dad was a bus driver, her mother a sewing-machinist, and that she thought I asked too many questions.

'Sorry, occupational hazard.'

'What about you? What do you do?'

'I'm a journalist . . . kind of between jobs at the moment though.'

'Oh. What do your parents do?'

'Mum used to be a sewing-machinist too. Retired now.'

She leant forwards. 'Whereabouts?'

'Park Village.'

'Oh yeah. I know it. Which factory was it?'

I told her. 'We lived just behind it.'

'What does your dad do?'

'Doesn't work.'

'Retired?'

'Ill.'

'Oh.'

'Hasn't worked for years.'

'Mind talking about it?'

This is the other thing about these arranged marriage pseudo-dates: you begin with the kind of discussions you would normally only have three years into a relationship. How many kids do you want? Where do you see yourself in ten years' time? Do your parents love your siblings more than they love you? Too often it's dating, robbed of the things that make dating fun: the flirtation; the attraction; the snogging; the sex. It's also another reason why I struggle to get anywhere with them. Not only is discussing big things unsexy, it is, paradoxically, unrevealing. Frankly, I don't know where I see myself in ten years' time. I don't know how many kids I want. Most of the things I look for in girlfriends are small. They have to be cheerful in the mornings. They can never attempt to make me dance in public. It helps if they don't visibly detest me. And, normally, I would at this point have turned the subject away from the subject of my family, to the handful of anecdotes I always churn out with strangers, such as the time I was sat next to George Soros and asked him what he did for a living, the time a PR rang my line at work and asked to speak to 'Satan Sinatra', my first week at university when I went around telling people my nickname was 'Blade', and how my best friend had never let me forget it. Stories which were self-deprecating but still carried vital nuggets of flattering information about myself: the Cambridge degree; the occasional brushes with power and celebrity; the interesting career.

But because this girl was warm and attractive – obviously I was far from sure if I wanted to spend the rest of my life with her, but I'm not sure I even want to spend the rest of my life with myself – and because she didn't fall into the two categories that my previous Punjabi dates had fallen into,* I made the mistake of telling the truth. Even worse: the whole truth. I told her my father and sister suffered from schizophrenia, but I didn't realize until recently. That the doctors thought Dad had the beginnings of dementia, but I wasn't sure. That I'd made a succession of terrible mistakes recently in the emotional turmoil of a break-up, chief amongst which was the decision to write a book about my parents' life, before actually knowing what the story was, that now I knew the whole story I felt like I'd been a victim of one of those elaborate undergraduate jokes in which your friends come into your room while you're

* I'm hoping that writing this in a smaller font will make it sound less misogynistic, but in my experience, second generation Punjabi women – being the product of patriarchal culture – are either depressingly servile or terrifyingly aggressive. As one of them once put it to me – or rather screamed at me – Sikh girls don't have person-alities, they have post-traumatic stress disorder. They have to fight so hard and so persistently for their independence that they become brutalized by the experience, and even when they have their freedom, they can't stop fighting.

away and turn all the furniture upside down, that somehow I'd gone from not being able to read misery memoirs to writing one, that I had no idea how I was going to write about the violence my mother had suffered at the hands of my father – it was too painful – that I found it hard to distance myself from the story, and that I felt utterly miscast, like Steven Seagal in *Pride and Prejudice*, or Judi Dench in *Police Academy*.

'*Don't move, dirtbag!*' My potential future fiancée had put her coffee down and was making a pistol shape with her hands.

'What?'

'*Don't move, dirtbag!*' She pretended to shoot me. 'Remember? It was the catchphrase of that fat woman cop in *Police Academy* . . . she was dead quiet, but then she'd suddenly lose it and punch people out . . .'

'Oh yeah.' I sipped some of my smoothie. 'There was also that guy who made those noises with his mouth . . . What was his name? Hightower?'

'No, Hightower was the big quiet guy . . .'

'How do you remember that?'

'Asian girl. Didn't get out much in the eighties. No Starbucks then either, remember?' She picked up her coffee again. 'It's cool you're writing a book, though.'

Cool? No, I said. It didn't feel cool. For, having got my mother's version of events, I now faced the worrying prospect of having to verify the details with relatives who had witnessed what happened. Why and how was the prospect of talking to my relatives worrying? Well, for myriad reasons, not least the unfortunate fact that sections of my extended family believe my mother to be a kind of witch – yes, a witch, who puts curses on people; some of my relatives weren't talking to my family any more, and of those relatives who were still in contact, even if I did get them to agree to talk, on tape, after ignoring every single invitation they had sent me for the last decade, and made an appointment to see them at a fixed time of day ('Of course we'll be home'), I knew they would arrive one, maybe two hours late ('Needed a haircut') and then, before being able to pose a single useful question, I'd have to endure a tour of their new house, a ride in their new car and be required to coo over at least 329 individual pictures of their 329 new grand-children. After this – the suggestion that we get down to the matter in hand having been ignored entirely – I would have to explain to an audience of at least eight how I'd managed to graduate from university and reach the age of thirty without having a house, a car, a wife or a career in medicine to show for it. An hour or two later, edging tentatively towards the purpose of the visit, and wanting to discuss the sensitive issues at hand in some kind of privacy, I'd attempt to get the interviewee into a room on their own, but they would insist on staying in the living room, the wide screen TV blaring in the background and random visitors adding their two pennies' worth. If I was lucky, they would then shout and bluster their way through a version of events transparently skewed by their position on old and often irrelevant family feuds, not pausing for questions, glossing over the most interesting tales, providing only a bare outline of events, making no effort to provide dates, inter-rupting their account only to guffaw at my poor Punjabi, answer mobile phone calls, or launch paeans to the superiority of the milk (ah, it was so much creamier then!), the mangoes (so juicy!) and the ghee (my God, the freshness of pure ghee!) in 1950s India.

'Sounds stressful.' My potential future fiancée had both hands around her mug, like a model in a hot chocolate advert. 'Some-times I'm glad I've got a small family. But why don't you just write the story like your mum told it? Keep it simple.'

Ha! If only it was that easy. But didn't she read the papers? Every week there seemed to be a new memoir-related scandal, where someone was crucified for getting things wrong, for claiming they'd spent six years in prison for kidnapping but had in fact only been cautioned for jumping a red light, for writing an account of getting lost in the Amazon when in fact they'd just taken a wrong turn in a safari park. And the problem was that my mother's account was full of gaps and inconsistencies. Not major inconsistencies. The kind of inconsistencies you get if you come from an oral culture, if you haven't had novels and Radio 4 to condition you into remembering and talking about things in a certain way. The kind of inconsistencies you get when you are discussing very painful things that happened a long time ago. Besides, if I was going to pen a journalistic account of my parents' story, I would have to obey some of the basic rules of journalism, including those on sourcing, which state that it is important to get two, or three, independent sources for each story, always to ask yourself why your source has chosen to tell you something, and to seek to disprove what you've been told, even if it takes time.

'Blimey.'

I'd finally moved from the subject of the book to a set of more general anxieties, including the post-romantic stress I suffered after breaking up with Laura, and my inability to make relationships work longer than three or four months, and my worry that all the stress I was currently under would result in the loopings of my mind accelerating out of control, forcing me to succumb to schizophrenia too, when I noticed she'd wrapped the strap of her handbag around her index finger, was looking over my shoulder, and that the remains of the muffin I had been prodding while talking were scattered across the table between us, washing around in the remnants of my preceding cups of coffee, looking like . . . well, like a physical manifestation of my emotional diarrhoea.

As much as arranged marriage meetings differ from conventional dates, there are certain rules that apply to both. It's important to pay your date compliments, for instance. To dress well. To talk more about the other person than yourself. To not go on about your exes. To be happy and upbeat. To not drink too much. To pay. And the only commandments I'd managed to obey were the not-drinking and the paying. I asked if she wanted another coffee and she said no, she ought to be heading off – lots of marking to be done – but thanks very much for the coffee, it had been lovely to chat, she just had to pop to the loo before going, but I shouldn't wait, she'd be in touch, and yes – handshake – it would be lovely to repeat the experience over a proper drink soon.

The remorse I felt on the walk home was savage. By the time I got to the end of my parents' street I'd concluded that suicide was the only option. But then I saw the local off-licence and had another idea: alcohol. And so – because Mum hates there being booze of any kind in the house – I found myself smuggling alcohol into my bedroom for the first time since I was seventeen. Thus fortified, I began trying to write Mum and Dad's story.

The following morning Jito prepared Cugi's breakfast – a paratha with yoghurt – and packed his lunch into a tiffin box – carrot and potato (?) sabzi packed with chapattis. As he left for work at a local timber yard/concrete factory (?), he instructed her not to, under any circumstances, leave the bedroom while he was away. She wasn't to have contact with anyone at any time, not even with the children of the household. Jito did as she was told, beginning her morning by making the bed, emptying the contents of her red (?) suitcase into the solitary (?) wardrobe standing at the end of the room (?), straightening the cracked (?) wall mirror, putting up a picture/calendar (?) of Guru Teg Bahadar/ Guru Nanak/Guru Gobind on the windowsill and using her fingers to pick out debris from the brown (?) carpet (????????).

Christ, what was wrong with me? People wrote about their families all the time. But I couldn't get beyond the first page. I slammed my laptop shut – though not so loud as to wake my parents, who were in bed already, though it was just eight – and had a few more glugs of neat gin.

It was not until this time of my life that I began to understand the appeal of alcoholism. Previously, I'd watched, with varying degrees of puzzlement, several relatives drink themselves to death,* and wondered how they could stand the hangovers and the effect

* 'A particularly distinctive feature of British Sikh society today is the high rate of alcoholism among males. Consumption of alcohol has always been high among Sikhs, with the per capita rate among Sikhs of Punjab among the highest in the world, but recent studies have shown a growing epidemic. Consumption rates are higher than in any other ethnic minority and in the white community; Sikhs from Punjab seem to be prone to high levels of consumption; in one study 80 per cent of men of Asian origin who died from alcohol-related liver disease were judged to be of Sikh origin. Alcohol-related problems are rarely discussed ...' Gurharpal Singh and Darshan Singh Tatla, *Sikhs in Britain: The Making of a Community.*

the drinking had on their relationships. But finally I got it. You drink and you keep on drinking not because you enjoy the alcohol and don't mind the hangovers: you drink because you feel better drunk than you do when you're sober. It's not about where alcohol takes you, it's about what alcohol takes you away from.

But I couldn't even seem to do alcoholism right: that evening, rather than taking me out of myself, the drink dragged me deeper into myself. Walking around the room, my head spinning with contraband gin, everything I looked at seemed to tell me I was a twat. Here was the Homer Simpson radio my brother had bought me for a birthday, but which I hadn't taken to London because I had a deluxe Roberts model in my bathroom. Here was a wall clock my sister Puli had bought me when I got my flat – it had probably cost her a good portion of a weekly benefits cheque – but which I left in Wolves because I had my eye on something trendier. Here was the plaque Bindi had made for me when I graduated – 'To Sathnam; Congratulations on passing your exams, graduated on 26ᵗʰ June 1998' – but which I didn't take because I thought my London friends might consider it gloating.

The view out of the window didn't offer much consolation either. I'd spent large chunks of time staring out of that window when we first moved into the house. At Prosser Street all I could see from my bedroom window was a railway track and the tops of some factories, but suddenly, with the new house on the foot of a hill called the Beacon, I had panoramic views of Wolver-hampton. I was mesmerized, not just at the breadth and depth of the view – you could see for tens of miles across the Midlands – but by the foreground too. We had only moved to a different part of town, but it felt like a different world. Here people kept dogs on leashes, rather than letting them roam the streets, had broadsheet newspapers delivered every day and washed their new cars on Sunday mornings. But no matter how hard I tried, I couldn't recapture that feeling of awe. All I felt was irritation at the sight of our front lawn. I used to spend hours getting the edges perfect and the stripes just right. I wanted it to be indistinguishable from the lawns of our white neighbours. But in my absence, not only had most of our white neighbours moved, and the surrounding lawns been hacked, the edges of ours had been cut away unevenly and someone had made a hole in the middle and plonked a bush in it. It was a mess.

13. Devil's Haircut

After spending all of 1989 and most of 1990 considering the matter, I realized I needed professional help. But not having ever entered a hair salon before, the professional help I required lay beyond a canyon of ignorance. What, for instance, was the difference between a 'barber' and a 'hairdresser'? What, for that matter, was the difference between a 'hairdresser' and a 'hair stylist'? Come to think of it, what was the difference between a 'salon' and a 'parlour', how come some 'hairdressers' charged £5 for a cut and blow-dry, while others charged £15 for the same thing, did you pay more, the more hair you had, and what was with this 'unisex' business? – the word seemed to imply one-sex only, like uni-cycle implied one wheel only, but I was sure I'd seen both men and women through the window of the 'unisex' salon on the Dovedale Road.

Looking for clues – and this being an age before the internet – I started browsing hair and beauty magazines in the Mander Centre branch of W. H. Smith after school, standing in the corner opposite – this being an age before the internet – the permanent gaggle of schoolboys foraging for pictures of naked women in photography magazines. Unfortunately, while the titles contained plenty of tips for girls wanting to jazz up their highlights, few articles were of much use to a teenage Sikh boy seeking his first snip. Even a piece headlined: 'Tips to Increase Chances of a Good Haircut' turned out to be a disappointment.

Tip one. Hang out! Visit a salon, listen to the banter, see how the atmosphere makes you feel!

I knew exactly how the atmosphere would make me feel: nervous. And if I was going to go through the trauma of appearing in a salon with a topknot gleaming on my head, I might as well go the whole hog and have a haircut.

Tip two. Ask around! If you see someone with a cool hairstyle, enquire where they had it done! That'll give you somewhere to check out!

My brother had a great haircut – he had made it through his Jordan-Knight-from-New-Kids-on-the-Block phase, and now that he worked at a local accountancy firm, had a sensible hairstyle that for once wasn't inspired by a celebrity – but even to mention a haircut to him was to risk him telling my mother, which was to risk her killing me or herself, or both of us, in outrage.

I abandoned the magazine and went home to spend the evening doing what I did most evenings at that time: flicking alternately through textbooks, the underwear spreads in the Kays catalogue and the hairdresser and barber sections of local phone directories. And it was while flicking through the Yellow Pages that I noticed something that I'd somehow overlooked the last 342 times I'd gone through it: 'mobile hairdressers'. It sounded promising. And the next evening I went to the phone box on a nearby main road – you can never be too careful with Mum – and, ankle-deep in discarded copies of the *Wolverhampton Chronicle*, called the number at the bottom of the advert which said:

Hair & Beauty by Vicky
Fully Qualified – 15 years exp
Eve & Wknd Appts Available
Wedding Day Hair & Make Up

Vicky answered straight away. I'd expected a light, friendly, girly voice, but instead got a raddled, almost masculine Black Country growl. The stresses of mobile hairdressing had clearly taken their toll.

'Yeah?'

'Hello,' I responded, originally. My voice was all over the place. Calling a sex line would have been less stressful. 'I was wondering whether you . . . [cough] . . . I was wondering whether you could explain how you . . . eeeuuuh . . . sorry . . . could you tell me how you work?'

'Oi'yam a mobile hairdresser.'

'Right.'

'Which means oi'yam mobile . . . and oi'yam a hairdresser.'

'Yes. But I rather wondered . . .' Jesus, my brother was right: my posh school was beginning to make me sound like Trevor McDonald. I tried to sound more Black Country. 'Do yow cut . . . or dress . . . hair in . . . a van?'

'Eh?'

'DO YOU CUT HAIR IN A VAN?'

'A van?'

'I thought . . . [cough] you might work like those . . . mobile fish and chip vans?'

'Oi ain't got a van. Oi go into people's houses. Usually old or disabled folk and what have yow . . .'

'What do you do about the hair . . . the hair mess?'

'I've a plastic sheet . . . Hold on.' Shuffling on the line, and then the voice re-emerging even more growly. 'How old am yow?'

'Fourteen. Do you charge more the longer the hair is?'

'How long is yow hair?'

'From my knees to my head.'

'Y'am a fourteen-year-old bloke with hair from yow *knees* to yow *head*?' Laughter on the line. 'Is yow Jeremy Beadle or wot?'

'The other way round, I mean. From my head to my knees. But it's in a topknot most of the time. Could you come over on a Sunday morning, when my Mum and Dad are at the templ . . .'

Click.

Buzz.

Shit.

I was going to have to go to a hair salon.

After a little more procrastination, a little more anxiety and

– this was perverse, given the sacrilegious nature of what I was planning – a little more praying, the possibilities were whittled down to two options: 'Ranjit, Hairstylist' on the Dudley Road; or 'Stylistics' in the town centre. Over the next month, I staked them out like a bank robber planning a heist: timetables were timetabled; dry runs were dry run; escape routes were escape routed. Eventually, I settled on 'Ranjit, Hairstylist' on the Dudley Road, on the grounds that a bunch of Indian barbers were less likely to be freaked out by a fourteen-year-old boy with hair beyond his bum than a salon full of glamorous blonde hairdressers. I scrawled an 'H' for haircut in the Friday section of my home-work diary. I would go in the evening, after school.

I suppose I should explain at this point what it was that finally led to the not insignificant decision to cut my hair, defy my mother, and begin a process of alienation from my family and culture which would lead to me dating an English girl and eventually having to come back home to plug the gap that had opened up between what I had been and what I'd become. And there's certainly no shortage of excuses to proffer. I could mention, for instance, how my Sikh faith had been diluted by years of compulsory Christian worship at school. I could highlight the haphazard nature of my instruction in Sikhism: all that Punjabi classes on Saturday mornings had taught me was how to write 'the camel went to the well' in Punjabi script; and while Mum was forever providing moral guidance, she'd provided a random set of rules – don't look at girls, don't eat meat or egg products on Sundays and Tuesdays – rather than a coherent belief system. Not least, I could point out that the theological thinking behind the notion of long hair seemed as woolly as the beard threatening to erupt from my chin: some Sikhs said having *kes* was a necessary way of showing respect for the God-given form; some said it was a necessary expression of love for the Guru (like a married person would wear a wedding ring); some linked it to intelligence, health and spirituality; some said Guru Gobind Singh made the keeping of unshorn hair manda-tory to give Sikhs a binding identity; while others argued that long hair wasn't actually necessary to be a Sikh.

I could mention all these things. But I wouldn't be telling the truth. You see, there was no crisis of faith, or philosophical dark night of the soul, behind my decision. If there was any theological or intellectual dimension to it at all, it comprised little more than thinking: Dad and Rajah cut their hair, and they haven't been struck down by lightning yet, have they? And maybe: God can't be that impressed by my topknot, I'm doing crap at school. Basically, I wanted to get rid of my long hair because: (i) I was fed up of being teased about my topknot; (ii) I hated the way my topknot restricted my freedom – I still couldn't leave the house until Mum had combed my hair; and (iii) I LOATHED the way it made me look. It wasn't so bad when I was little. People would say I looked like a girl, but I was an over-sensitive ponce of a child and felt like a girl a lot of the time anyway. But puberty changed things: brillo pads sprouted everywhere, on my top lip, between my eyebrows, all over the place. Suddenly, I couldn't stand the sight of myself in photos and mirrors. If we had visitors, I'd shrink away to my bedroom. Being within 400 yards of a pretty girl gave me an instant fever of 44 degrees. I felt like a combination of the Elephant Man and the psoriatic arthropath in Dennis Potter's *Singing Detective*.

Trying to think of ways to get rid of my hair, without having Mum freak out, became a chief intellectual preoccupation. Maybe I could have an 'accident' with the vibrating clippers I used in the factory to trim threads off blouses, or persuade my GP to say I needed to get rid of my hair for health reasons? Frankly, I considered everything,* up to and including contracting a mild, curable cancer – a spot of chemotherapy would have done the job – but in the end, on seeing the horrendous results of a photo

---

* Or at least I thought I'd thought of everything, until I picked up a newspaper recently and read about a fifteen-year-old Sikh boy in Scotland who cut his own hair, and then tried to cover up the act by punching himself in the face, writing racist remarks over his body and pretending he'd been the victim of a brutal race attack at the hands of four white males. It was a brilliant plan, and would've worked perfectly if his parents hadn't reported the attack to the police, if the police hadn't assigned dozens of officers

I had to have taken for a new passport, a picture in which I thought I looked like Rocky, the boy with a massive facial skull deformity in *Mask*, the Cher movie, my unhappiness simply outweighed the anxiety I felt about my mother's possible reaction and I decided to have it snipped off.

On the momentous day in question, events stiffened my resolve. Mum, who was running late for work, moaned unsparingly as she combed my hair, tied it into a plait and knotted the plait into a bun. '*Balle*, son, when you going to learn how to do your hair yourself? Your cousin Harminder started tying his own *ghuti* at the age of ten and now does his own turban too. I've been up since six, my back hurts, I'm late for work and here I am having to comb your hair as well. Will I be doing this when you are married with children? You should be looking after us, not the other way around . . .' At school, there was the usual teasing and sarcasm and low-grade wit: one boy threw a blackboard rubber at my topknot during lunch; and when the Latin master asked the boy behind me why he wasn't noting down the declensions from the board, he said it was because 'Sanghera's head is in the way, sir.' I bolted out of school at 4 p.m. to catch the number 510 bus, which got me into the town centre in time for the 4.20 number 558 bus down to the Dudley Road.

I can remember more about what followed than I can recall of what happened yesterday, or even this afternoon. It was pouring with rain: so much so that the windows of the bus got steamed up and I missed my stop and ended up walking, getting soaked through my single-breasted school blazer, my V-necked pullover, my long charcoal grey trousers and my plain shirt. It was dark: prematurely dark. Winter was setting in and the clocks had just

---

to the case (who then visited several local high schools, questioned 120 people, set up a dedicated text service and email address for people to contact), if 200 Sikhs hadn't held a vigil in the city, and if a top Sikh religious institution, the Siromani Gurdwara Prabandhak Committee, hadn't then raised the matter with the prime minister of India. Eventually, presumably out of guilt, the boy fessed up. The police, presumably out of embarrassment, didn't press charges for wasting police time.

been turned back. And standing in front of the barber's door was surreal and unnerving, not unlike returning to a piece of writing after a month or two: all I could see were mistakes and omissions. Among the things I had somehow missed on my recces was a sign in the window indicating that the shop closed at 5.30, the proximity of the salon to the Sikh temple across the road, and a poster of Hare Krishna on the wall. The closing time was a worry: I had no idea how long it would take to cut my hair and wondered whether I'd left it too late. The Sikh temple was an anxiety too: the priests, and possibly members of my family, might witness the sacrilegious act. But the Hare Krishna poster was the most serious oversight, for it meant that Ranjit was a Hindu.

With hindsight, it might have been even worse if the barber was Sikh, but at the time, the revelation felt catastrophic, for it added an entirely unwelcome, symbolic edge to what I was about to do. My understanding of Indian politics wasn't particularly sophisticated, but I knew that after two Sikh bodyguards had shot the Indian Prime Minister Indira Gandhi, Sikhs and Hindus didn't get along. In fact, they had a recent history of chopping one another to pieces. And I knew that one of the things that often happened when Hindus attacked Sikhs was that they cut off their hair. If I'd also known then what I know now, that the turban was a symbol of the Sikh community's struggle to be accepted in Britain, that it was a Sikh bus driver's struggle to be allowed to wear a turban that in part inspired Enoch Powell's 'Rivers of Blood' Speech, I doubt I would have had the courage to open the door.

Inside, the three men waiting to be seen, and the two men in the leather seats being seen to, and the two barbers, one of whom was presumably Ranjit himself, turned to look at me as I entered, directly, in the eye, in the way that English people never do. In the moment, I felt the oddest sensation – the sensation that I was starring in a movie of my own life. Not a good movie. An independent production that didn't get beyond non-broadcast pilot stage. But a movie nevertheless. I tried to avoid their gaze – a difficult task with the wall-to-wall mirrors

– sat down on the felt bench next to the door and tried to get my bearings.

The barber shop was basically a converted terraced house: two seats in the front room; behind the wall, another two unoccupied seats in the living room; sixteen appliances plugged into just two sockets via a serpentine combination of extensions and adapters; near the door, a payphone, with business cards advertising Asian building firms and lawyers and estate agents pasted around it; a board emblazoned with the pun 'a cut above the rest'; another board emblazoned with prices – hair £4, beard £8; a calendar on the wall advertising ASIA AIR TRAVEL; and hair. Lots of hair. Everywhere.

Of course, I had expected it. But not so much of it on the floors and hanging in the air. And not so much of it being removed from so many different parts of customers' bodies. One man was having the back of his neck shaved. Another had asked the barber to remove the hair in his ears – *and he was doing it.* Having been indoctrinated about the evils of cutting hair by Mum – those almost daily lectures about the holiness of long hair and stories about how witches would try to cast spells on you by cutting your locks – and having grown up watching my brother kick and scream whenever the time came to visit the barber's* – the disgust I felt was intense.

I had an audience of eight – evidently the closing time was, like all Indian deadlines, flexible – when the fatter of the two barbers, who may or may not have been Ranjit himself, indicated it was my turn by spinning the chair in my direction and wiping it clean with a white cloth. I moved towards him with the trepidation of someone about to undergo heart surgery, handed over my blazer, placed my rucksack on the floor and put my arms through the giant black bib held up for me. After sitting me down he pumped the metal bar under the leather seat, bringing my topknot to his cutting level and, making eye

* I realize now that this was because the barber would always give him a bowl cut, torture for someone with an innate sense of style like my brother. But at the time his behaviour deepened the association between cutting hair and voodoo, death and sin.

contact in the mirror, asked: 'Your dad know you doing this?'

'Yeah,' I said, thinking it was my mother he should be worried about.

And then he hacked up some phlegm into a tissue.

Reassured about my family's non-violent intentions, the barber plucked the hanky off my topknot, revealing the bun beneath. Despite the day's assaults, it was still recognizably one of my mother's better creations – intricate, swirling, vaguely reminiscent of Princess Leah's vertical buns in *Star Wars*. He unravelled the knot and let the plait hang down the side of my face. For years, having my hair undone in public had been my ultimate nightmare – I worried about it more than I worried about my mother discovering my collection of page 3s, or my English teacher discovering that the poems I wrote for creative writing exercises contained plagiarized Stevie Wonder lyrics. But oddly, sitting there, the silhouette of my head resembling that of a giant cherry, I didn't feel any embarrassment at all. If anything, I wanted to savour the moment.

My barber's hairy hand – maybe it needed a shave – hovered over the paraphernalia laid on the shelf in front of us: clippers, driers and razors spread out like instruments before an operation. Just as I was committing the moment to memory – click – he picked the biggest, cleanest pair of scissors and in a blink – snip – more than 5,000 days of hair growth fell to the floor like a dead crow. I'd like to say the room gasped. Or that I literally felt the weight of the world lift from my shoulders. But no one blinked and I felt no different. They say that amputees sometimes continue to feel their limbs when they've gone: maybe it is the same for Sikhs with their hair. The barber retrieved the plait from the floor and waved it in my direction. Images of the 1984 Anti-Sikh riots in India snapped through my head like genocide flashcards. Iron rods. Knives. Clubs. Kerosene.

'You need this?'

'Um.'

He put it into a Mahal Supermarket carrier bag anyway.

'Your mum will want it.'

'Oh.'

I watched him put the carrier bag next to my rucksack. And then he began spraying the back of my head as if it were a sunflower.

'How you want?'

'Anything but what you've got,' I wanted to say. I didn't know a great deal about hairstyles but I knew that the orange highlights in his hair were at least a decade out of date, if they had ever been in fashion at all. But instead, being prepared for the question – one of the magazine tips had been 'Bring a picture! It's not true stylists don't like you to bring a photo!' – I reached for my trouser pocket and pulled out the sleeve of the cassette single of 'Freedom '90' by George Michael – in retrospect, a bad choice for several reasons, not least because it was a moody shot, taken in semi-darkness. The barber looked at it for a nanosecond, squinted at my reflection, hacked up some more phlegm and remarked: 'Pushed back and grade 3 then?'

'Yeah,' I said, having no idea what grade 3 was. I thought numbered grades were what you got for playing the flute.

There followed a frenzy of clipping and cutting and spraying and tugging and combing during which I tried to obey the magazine tip to 'Stay still! Once your cut is under way, quit wriggling and follow the stylist's instructions, or you'll magnify the chance of a mistake!' And after five or ten minutes I looked nothing like George Michael on the sleeve of the cassette single of 'Freedom '90'. Instead, there seemed to be four styles fighting for dominance: Amitabh Bachchan's bouffant vs. Victoria Principal's bob vs. Johnny Rotten's mohican vs. my old topknot. Any one of them could have won.

'Is that much length okay?' he asked, pointing at a point on a comb.

'Yeaugh.' He may as well have been asking me for my opinion on Danish monetary policy.

The frenzy of clipping resumed, and then about five minutes after the moment at which I thought things were beginning to look acceptable, he suddenly and inexplicably stopped, picked up a canister of something and a tub of something else and asked: 'Spray or gel?'

'Yes, please.'

'No. SPRAY . . .' He waved the canister in my direction. 'Or GEL.' The tub looked like it contained wallpaper paste.

'Gel?'

A minute later he was waving a mirror behind the back of my head and asking: *'Teek taak?'*

Of all his questions, this one seemed the most preposterous. What would he do if I said the haircut wasn't *teek taak*? He could hardly put all the hair back. And given that I'd never seen the back of my head and never would, what did I have to compare it with? As it happened, from all the angles I wasn't sure if it was a case of *teek taak* at all – Amitabh Bachchan's bouffant had definitely won out, but there was a bit of Johnny Rotten in there still. But grateful that at least he hadn't shaved SIKH SCUM into the back of my head, I murmured in gratitude, and after undoing the overall that had protected my soggy school uniform from the hair storm, the barber brushed my shoulders with what looked like a minature mop and handed me a tissue, which I used to blow my nose.

'No, that's to wipe hair.'

I lifted the snotty tissue towards my virginal bouffant.

'No! For this . . .' He held me steady by the shoulder as he forcibly rubbed tiny hair clippings from my face, in the way that Mum used to remove dribble from my chin when I was three.

Walking towards the door and still trying to avoid eye contact with the waiting customers, I put my hand into my pocket and pulled out the £4 I'd counted out days earlier. He put the cash into a safety deposit box and stepped back to admire his handi-work.

'You look okay. Normal.'

The old me prickled at the implication: was he suggesting that topknots were abnormal? But, in truth, normal was the look I was after. That was the point.

'Thanks.'

Outside, at the bus stop, I experienced a strange inversion of the phenomenon known to afflict owners of new cars, when they suddenly notice that half the country seems to be driving the same model. Everywhere I looked I saw turbans – green, blue, white, black, orange – and beards in every shape and size imaginable – shaggy, fluffy, dishevelled, sprouting. It was too much after my act of sacrilege, so, given that the rain was easing, I decided to walk home, catching my reflection in car windows and trying to get used to the new shadow my head cast on the oily pavements.

I walked the long way back, thinking the extra half hour was exactly the time I needed to come up with the right words for Mum, when months of thinking about it hadn't. But by the time my house came into view I realized I still had no idea what to say. As I approached the door, I found myself wishing for still more time, thinking that if I could just get to my bedroom without being spotted, I could sit there, with a towel covering my head if necessary, until the right words came. As (bad) luck would have it, when I entered through the back door the entire family was passing through the kitchen. Rajah, back from work, was swigging orange juice from a carton. Dad was standing over the grill – making himself a sausage sandwich for tea. Mum, back from work at the factory, was kneading some dough. Bindi, back from her supermarket job, was washing up. I caught a reflection of myself in the glass of the kitchen cabinet before anyone caught a glimpse of me, and flinched. My hair was wild. It seemed to be wanting to return to its preceding condition, like a regenerating worm. There was a pause before the responses came.

Rajah said: 'Bloody hell, you look like Doogie Howser.'

Bindi sniffed and said: 'Bloimey.'

Dad smiled.

Mum, meanwhile, did a double take and. . .

In the years beforehand I'd put thousands of boy hours into worrying how Mum might react. On bad days I thought she might strangle me with my disembodied plait. On good days I thought she might drag me from the house, using my disembodied plait as a leash, abandoning me like Pussy and Lucky on an industrial estate. But in all my worrying, it never once occurred to me what would in fact happen: that she would put her hand to her mouth, walk up to me and then pull me, quietly, towards her.

I still don't understand why she was cool about it. Asking her about it recently, she claimed that she knew I was being bullied, and that she had never been keen on long hair: giving me a topknot had been Chachi's idea, and she didn't care either way. But that's not how I remember things. She put incredible pressure on me to keep my hair long. And while I'd like to believe she was relaxed about it because she is a highly intelligent woman, who will love me unconditionally, regardless of what I do, I can't help suspecting it was due in part to the fact that she had other things to worry about. You see, by the time I had my hair cut, it was becoming clear that Puli's marriage to the mulleted boy from Coventry was coming to an end.

14. Two Rooms at the End of the World

I'll concede that I probably shouldn't have fretted quite as much as I did about having my hair cut, and, as it turned out, I could have worried a little less about the task of corroborating Mum's story with relatives. I should have known that if there's one thing I can rely on with my family, it is narrative, and that eventually a scenario would arise that would give me an excuse to interview relevant members of the extended family in reasonably natural circumstances. Though when the opportunity arose – in the form of a complaint from Mum that no one seemed willing to take her to visit an ageing and distant relative dying in a hospital in Grays – I almost missed it, as it cropped up in the middle of one of her monologues, camouflaged between complaints about the quality of lentils nowadays and her arthritis. She had moved on to the more general topic of price inflation in supermarkets by the time I cottoned on.

Hold on, did she say *Grays*?

Hold on, Grays was where Mum and Dad began their marriage, living with my Bero *bua* (one of my father's elder sisters) and my Phuman *phupre* (her husband).

Hold on, Grays was where my uncle and aunt *still* lived.

The idea of using the hospital visit as an excuse to pop in to talk to my uncle and aunt about what happened in 1969 wasn't without problems. Would they think it strange that I hadn't talked to them in a decade but was now suddenly appearing with a million questions and a dictaphone? Would Mum mind if I asked her to stay in a separate room while I talked to them? But in many ways it was an ideal solution. Bero *bua* and Phuman *phupre* were still in regular contact with our family. I was very fond of them and they had been very generous to me in the past – I lived with them for several months during one of my university holidays, doing a summer job in London.* Their children all got married relatively late, so I wouldn't be treated like a freak in an arranged marriage museum, and taking Mum to visit the elderly relative provided a reasonable cover for my sudden appearance.

A week later I was having a predictable argument with Mum about how many carrier bags of food we should take on the 153-mile journey – I suggested no more than one, given that we would be spending the night at my well-stocked flat in London before returning to the Midlands, but Mum ended up taking six – and a less predictable argument about the car I had chosen to hire.

'I'm not getting into that,' she remarked sharply when she spotted the innocuous blue Ford Focus.

'What's wrong with it?'

'Those.' She pointed at the leather seats.

Mum hasn't always been a vegetarian – at Prosser Street she ate everything but beef, like the rest of us. But when she retired, she took a religious vow, started carrying a ceremonial dagger, and gave up consuming flesh. Over the years the vegetarianism has become increasingly strict. She has given up cooking meat curries for my father. Started demanding that the Christmas turkey isn't roasted in the house – last year I had to cook it at my brother's house in Dudley, and then drive it to my parents before lunch. And now she won't eat any food that has been touched by someone who has not washed after eating meat, and even objects to leather.

'Mum, what do you think your shoes are made of?'

She looked down at her sandals and then back at me. 'They're made of rubber.'

I took a close look. And they were. Christ. 'So you want me to change the car? You know it's going to cost me another £50 . . .'

---

* I think they assumed I was doing something serious and swish in the City, but I was in fact working at a cable channel based in Canary Wharf called Live TV, where my responsibilities included working on the self-explanatory programme *Topless Darts*, and dressing up as the station mascot – 'News Bunny' – to act out the news in hand and ear signals as it was read out by a news reader on the hour.

It did the trick. 'Okay then. But next time, no leather seats.'

The subsequent four-hour car journey was hard on the nerves. Having persuaded her to sit in the front seat – like royalty, Mum instinctively heads for the back – she grabbed the door handle and wouldn't let go for the first forty miles, and even then only did so to begin praying for our lives. And then she would only quit praying for our lives to begin complaining about the heating (it triggers migraines), my sense of direction (even though she cannot read road signs), my taste in music (in good company there), and, when I'd switched off Prefab Sprout in favour of Radio 4, requested a running translation of the afternoon play. It was truly a delight to see Grays come into view.

Though Grays, situated on the apex of a sharp bend in the Thames, twenty miles from London, fifteen miles from Southend-on-Sea, doesn't really 'come into view'. Most towns and cities have some emblem that lodges them in your mind. Blackpool has its tower. Wolverhampton has its Man on the Horse. But Grays has nothing. All that can be said about it is that it is a collection of anonymous housing estates near some objects of vague utility: the Dartford Crossing, the M25 and the Lakeside shopping centre. The lack of definition extends to its name. When we were kids our parents, struggling with the pronunciation, vacillated between 'Greer-s' (Puli once stunned her primary school classmates by announcing she'd spent some of her summer holiday in 'Greece') and 'London', but the modern road signs didn't seem much more sure, oscillating between 'Grays Thurrock' and 'Grays'.

Being so featureless, we got lost as soon as we arrived, and I ended up having to call my aunt to meet us on the forecourt of a petrol station, the closest thing the town has to a landmark. She arrived almost as soon as I'd hung up, looking as tall and hand-some as I remembered her – my father's sisters are a testament to what not drinking and not having schizophrenia can do for your health – and surprised me by greeting me with an English 'Hello', before revealing she'd been taking English lessons at a local community centre. 'You can't live in a country for thirty years without learning the language,' she pronounced before speeding off to the hospital in her runaround, instructing us to follow.

In our Ford Focus, it was my turn to nag Mum. Why couldn't she learn to drive like my aunt? Learn to speak English? It would change her life. But there were just the same old excuses: 'I could never drive – I'm just not mentally alert enough'; 'I'm too old'; 'I'm too ill'. I know Mum is unwell, but the fact that she has been making out she is on her deathbed for the last thirty years makes me wonder whether she protests too much. I wish I could find a way to persuade her that her life isn't over.

Unfortunately, in the hospital, it was evident that our distant relative – Mum had repeatedly explained how we were related, but I still didn't understand – really was on her deathbed. I would say she looked much frailer than when I saw her last, but I last saw her eighteen years ago, when she must have been around eighty, and she looked pretty frail then. Nevertheless, despite her failing eyesight, and faltering hearing, she recognized my mother after only a little hesitation; they embraced and she managed to ask about each one of my mother's children and grandchildren by name. When she got to me, my mother instructed me to move closer and accept a blessing. With my head placed under her hand, I was thinking how great it was that the elderly were so respected in Punjabi culture, having one of those actually quite common moments when I felt proud to be Indian, when she put her crinkled mouth to my ear and wheezed: 'Why haven't you got married yet? Find a wife and make your mother happy.'

Someone once told me that one of the last things that goes when you're dying is your ability to recognize faces: but with Punjabi women, it must be the impulse to nag about marriage. Sadly, she passed away a few days later.

On the other side of town my uncle Phuman greeted us with bare feet and a smile. Walking into the house bought back a flood of childhood memories. Apart from a trip to India when I was four, a fantastic day-trip to Weston-super-Mare when I was nine, and a correspondingly depressing day trip to Portsmouth when

I was ten – we expected a beach, but ended up walking around warships – Grays was the only place we ever went 'on holiday' as a family. And it was seeing our cousins in their home, with their stereos in their rooms, posters of hot chicks on their walls, white friends popping over to play and say hi whenever they liked, that made me realize for the first time that maybe our family wasn't very relaxed.

As I wolfed down chapattis and chicken curry, and as Mum nibbled at the vegetarian option of chapattis and lentil curry, my uncle and aunt brought us up to date on their family news, and as I took my dishes to the kitchen, my aunt surprised me again by asking how the book was going. It turned out a cousin had read something about me on the internet. I've put so much effort into making sure my London and family lives are separated that it comes as a surprise when the two cross. After I'd moaned unspecifically about the agony of the task, and revealed what the book was about – the bit about my parents anyway – and asked if my uncle and aunt would mind talking about what happened in the late sixties, it was Mum's turn to surprise me: she suggested I take my uncle and aunt to their front room, while she slept off her migraine. Either she was genuinely under the weather, or understood the importance in journalism of getting independent accounts, or she simply didn't want to go through the story of her early marriage again. If it was the final thing, I knew the feeling.

In the front room I took a chair opposite my uncle and aunt, who sat down on the long sofa. Looking at them – I'd never seen them sitting next to one another before – I noticed for the first time that my uncle was considerably shorter than my aunt, and then began arranging the stationery I had bought along on the glass table between us – dictaphone, chronology, photographs. I put my A4 pad on my lap. I had written down seventy-two numbered questions on the first page, all related to the bits of Mum's story that I needed corroborating: one thing I've learnt about interviews is that it's important to get all the questions on one side of paper so that you don't draw attention to the artificialness of the process by flicking through pages during conversation. But looking at them, I couldn't decide on one to begin with. Meanwhile, my normal openers – the devastating 'how are you?', the penetrating 'run me through a typical day in your life' – weren't suitable. In the end, in halting, flailing Punjabi – I could hear my brother collapsing in laughter if he ever heard the tape – I began by saying I wanted them to run through the story – the *kahani* – of what happened when first my father came to live with them in 1968, a year before my mother joined him.

'Do you want the full story?' asked my uncle.

'Yes, please.'

And so he began with the full story, starting by explaining how he ended up in the UK, an extraordinary tale which involved a stay in Singapore, a flight to Britain, a stint at a wool factory in Bradford, a stint working in a pie (or did he say tie?) factory in

212

Huddersfield, a drunken fallout with a close relative in Gravesend, a return to India where he and my aunt were – get this – attacked by a bomb, or a grenade, while sitting at home, and an eventual return to England. And here you have the difference between Indian and Western narrative methods. Not only is there more drama, but while the Western way is linear – X happened, then Y happened, and, as a consequence, there was Z – the Indian method is roundabout and circular: there was X, and Q and D, and did I mention M? But after all the meandering, you usually end up in the same place, the point, which in this case was my uncle's decision to settle down with his young wife, my father's sister, and his young children in the south-east, where there was plentiful work in the paper mills and cement works. My father joined them in January 1968, more than a year before he was married, and my uncle got him a job where he worked, at Thermalite, a building materials company.

'Was Dad well when he arrived?'

'Yes. He used to play *kabaddi* and football and did weightlifting. He was really strong. *Jwaan*. We would work ten hours a day, five, six, sometimes seven days a week, but we played hard too – would drink two or three pints a night normally, five or six at the weekend. Your father ate loads as well. He would eat half a packet of butter with each meal. And I remember he had a really big and heavy topknot. Really thick hair.'

The only bit of this description that wasn't remarkable to me was the stuff about the butter. You could rewrite the National Health Service's guidelines on healthy eating, replacing the word 'vegetables' with 'ghee', 'fruit' with 'red meat' and 'water' with 'beer', and you'd have a sense of what is considered healthy eating by Punjabi men. I remember once watching my twenty-stone grandfather melt an entire slab of Anchor in a saucepan of boiled milk and drink the concoction before bed. But every other detail was mesmerizing. Work and football and drinking might be normal things most dads do, but I've never seen my father do much of any of them. I remember him once coming home smelling of booze – I must have been around seven – and Mum berating him for it. At the time I thought she was being harsh – other dads went to the pub all the time, why couldn't ours? But I understand now she was just looking out for him: alcohol and antipsychotics don't mix. As for work, I have a few memories of Dad digging the vegetable patch at Prosser Street, and nowadays he can occasionally be persuaded to push the lawnmower while Mum holds the extension cord. But I've never seen him do any other work. Meanwhile I had assumed the weightlifting was one of Dad's delusions. It was amazing to think he actually did it.* *Thrilling* to think that at one point he might have led a normal life.

But as desperately as I wanted to believe it, something niggled at me about my uncle's description: the topknot. Dad had never mentioned he had one, and I knew from his passport photo that he didn't have long hair when he came to Britain. Was my uncle sure about the long hair?

'Oh yes.' My aunt nodded next to him. 'He had a lot of hair. He used to wash his hair in *lasee*. He had his topknot cut off here in Britain.'

'But in his passport photograph – in his first passport – he has short hair.'

'Really?'

'So, are you sure?'

My uncle shrugged. 'Maybe he cut his hair in India then . . .'

If this had been an interview for a newspaper, I would have made an almighty fuss about this. Encounters with public figures are so controlled by public relations officials, so slick and dull and unrevealing, that the slightest slip becomes a big deal. But having been humbled by the enormous gaps and inconsistencies in my own memory, I overlooked the remark without qualification, gave my uncle total benefit of the doubt. These events happened a long time ago and this was possibly the first time he had discussed them. I simply repeated the question.

'Was Dad really completely well in 1968?'

* My brother remembers a conversation with our late Chacha in which he talked about how he would go to the gym with my father, and how my father once won a powerlifting contest.

'Yes.'

'No unusual behaviour?'

'Nothing happened that year.'

'He didn't get into any fights?'

'No, he didn't fight with anyone.'

At this point my aunt pushed the plate of Bombay mix on the table away from her, as if she'd suddenly lost her appetite, though she hadn't actually touched it, and said: 'Let me tell you something.'

I groaned inwardly. Whenever Mum used this phrase it tended to be followed by some bleak admission that had me instantly gasping for a stiff drink. It's the rhetorical equivalent of the jab before the knockout punch, the 'We need to talk' before the 'You're dumped'.

'Some time during that first year with us, the family decided to send for your mother to come to Britain. For that we had to fill out a *rahdari*. You know what a *rahdari* is?'

'A permit?'

'Yes, a permit. We had to make an application, and your dad had to sponsor it. We went to Wolverhampton to fill it out. During that visit we were all sitting in your uncle Malkit's house in Newport Street one evening. The men were drinking glasses of whisky and everyone was eating and your dad . . . suddenly . . . for no reason . . . smashed one of the glasses.'

'He dropped it?'

'No, he smashed it. With his bare hand. The glass was sitting on the table and he whacked it with his bare hand. With his palm. Like this.' She slapped the table, making the tea in my cup leap over the brim into the saucer. 'That's when I first saw signs of how . . . angry he could be . . .'

My uncle blinked. 'I wasn't there that day. Your aunt came back and told me about it.'

My aunt continued. 'Then there was the time we had to go to pick your mum up from the airport . . .' The chronology on the table reminded me of the date: 16 March 1969, a cold day across the whole country, according to *The Times*. 'Your father and your uncle were working on shifts: your uncle was on nights and your father on days. I woke your dad up at 4 a.m. and said: "Phuman is about to come back and we're leaving at six." He got up and came down to the kitchen for breakfast. I was pouring some tea when he came up close and . . . pushed me . . .' My uncle shuffled next to my aunt on the sofa. '. . .Pushed me so hard that I fell on the floor. When I got up I asked him why he'd done it. But he didn't answer. And when your uncle came back from work, he confronted him about it. Your father's response was: "I didn't do it, she must have fallen by herself." I said he was lying and asked if he was going to carry on like this when his wife joined him. If he was, I didn't want him to live with us any more. He replied: "If I did push you, I'm sorry. I made a mistake." After that he didn't touch me again, but he would stare at me. He had this stare. These terrible bloodshot eyes. It was like he wanted to eat me.' Pools of moisture in her eyes. 'I was terrified. But I thought he'd improve when your mum came.'

This is an important point, and while it doesn't excuse what happened, it needs to be stressed: the Indian obsession with marriage extends to believing it can cure mental illness. In a recent study from North India, nearly 18 per cent of male students and 50 per cent of female students surveyed believed that mental illness could be cured by marriage.* This may even explain my mother's eagerness to get Puli married off so quickly, when she knew she was ill.

'He didn't get better though, did he?'

My uncle, looking at some point over my shoulder, spoke after an interval.

'Your mother didn't say a word. And then he hit her.'

'You're talking about when you all came back from the wedding in Wolverhampton?'

'On the wedding night he . . .'

'Shhhhh,' my aunt interjected. 'Leave it there. Let's just say life was hard for your mother.'

* D. Bhugra, 'Indian teenagers' attitudes to mental illness', *British Journal of Clinical and Social Psychiatry*, 1993, 9.

'What were you about to say?' I didn't want to hear but needed to hear.

'Couples didn't have honeymoons then,' my uncle continued. 'They stayed at home. On that night he . . . When I woke up, I saw your mother's face and what he'd done to her . . . I went and said to him, "Aren't you ashamed? She has just come from India, has no family here and look what you've done." He apologized and promised he wouldn't do it again.'

My aunt nodded mournfully. 'Your mother told me in the morning what he'd done. She said she didn't want to stay in Grays, wanted to go to Bibi's in Wolverhampton, to be with the family. I said I would put her on the train. But when Cugi heard, he cried and said if Jito went to Wolverhampton, he wanted to go to Wolverhampton too. That was the thing about him – he treated Jito terribly but didn't want to be away from her either. We had a talk and agreed that if he was good to Jito, then they could stay. They had no space for them in Wolverhampton anyway. But then . . .'

My uncle finished my aunt's sentence: '. . . then he started acting strange . . . again.'

'How?'

My aunt responded. 'Well, son, whatever happened, happened . . . Things were hard for some time. Your mother was so strong. And then everything came to a head one bank holiday . . .'

A braver, less involved journalist would, at this point, have pressed for more information. Indeed, a semi-brave journalist had written down the pertinent questions in the A4 pad sitting on my lap. Were most of Mum's injuries scratches or bruises? Did they remember anything about the time Dad took Mum for a walk by the river, and began kicking her on the street, before they even got there? Did they know my father eventually told my mother she couldn't leave the bedroom while he was at work, even to use the toilet? That he would check the bucket in the corner of the room at the end of the day, to make sure she had complied? A braver, less involved journalist would have asked all these questions, but my aunt was in tears, my uncle's eyes were brimming with tears, I was struggling, and there was still so much more to get through, not least the bank holiday incident.

My uncle told the story, which tallied almost exactly with Mum's version. The whole family, except for my grandparents, had come down for a break on a bank holiday weekend, and as the guests arrived, the women began cooking in the kitchen, with Mum baking chapattis and placing them in metallic trays that had already been filled with servings of meat and *sabzi*. The children ferried the trays into the front room, where the men sat nursing tumblers of whisky, and once they had eaten, the children were served, and once the children had eaten, the young women served themselves, eating quietly, with their heads veiled, on the living room floor.

After the tension of the preceding weeks Phuman and Bero must have felt like they were breathing pure oxygen. But then my father suddenly lashed out. Recollections diverge on who he lashed out at first: Mum says it was at Phuman; Phuman says it was at my uncle Malkit; my uncle Malkit would later remember that my father lashed out at my aunt Bero; but there is consensus on what happened as a result: Dad was bundled into a room upstairs, and the door locked, in the hope he would calm down. He didn't calm down: he kicked the door down.

'That's when I went and got the police,' recalled my uncle.

'Did you call them?'

'No, I went and got them. We didn't have phones then. I went to the police station and they came to the house with dogs. They came and took him away.'

'The police?'

'Yes, the police. We went to bed, but a couple of hours later, the police let him go. They said he was drunk, and that he would be okay now, these things happen.'

'What happened then?'

Another divergence in accounts here. My aunt Bero says they took my father back in immediately. My mother, meanwhile, says he knocked on the door – he wasn't screaming or ranting any more – but the family refused to let him back in. Defying warnings that she would surely be killed, Mum said she joined him outside, where he was sprawled across the pavement. She helped him up, and they began walking, wordlessly and aimlessly, around Grays. At some point they ended up on the bank of the river and Mum remembers crying. Not the silent howls of the preceding weeks, always trying not to disturb the other people in the house. But loud, guttural sobs. Behind her, Dad, his head between bandaged hands, wept too.

Of the many disturbing images in my mother's account, this one, of my young parents, both of them still teenagers, sobbing on the bank of the faithful river flowing past from the oldest and greatest of the world's river ports towards the ends of the earth, is the one I found most troubling. They walked around town until the street lights began giving out to the dawn and when they returned to the house, it was arranged for them to move into a rented room in a house nearby: 11 Grange Road.

My aunt's justification for the decision was that 'I thought he was arguing because of me and thought they may get on better alone.' There may have been truth in that, but I can't help suspecting that she and her husband had simply got to the point that all families eventually reach when they have schizophrenia in the family. They couldn't cope any more. As Torrey puts it in *Surviving Schizophrenia*: 'a family within which the patient has been assaultive or violent is particularly poignant and lives in a special circle of hell. Its members are often afraid of the patient yet at the same time feel sorry for him/her. The ambivalence inevitably felt by the family members is formidable; fear and love, avoidance and attraction, rest uneasily side by side.'

During the following weeks, my uncle and aunt didn't see much of my parents. Mum says my father went round to their house and said he wanted to permanently sever all contact. But my uncle continued to witness his behaviour at work and socially. 'He would swear at people, get into fights. He would throw glasses at people in the pub, grab friends by the arm and try to wrestle with them. When he got sacked I got him another job at a wood factory – where they made doors – but he got sacked from there too. Everyone was scared of him. He could have killed someone.'

He very nearly did kill someone: my mother. My parents' landlady was so worried by the incessant beatings that she came over to my uncle's house to beg them to do something. But it must have been hard, when my father had told them to stay away. My aunt did what she could and asked her mother in Wolver-hampton to come and intervene. My grandmother did so, but unfortunately, her help, according to Mum, consisted of little more than a sudden appearance on her doorstep and the confident declaration that my parents' problems were the handwork of malevolent forces – maybe someone had put a curse on her son or put something unscrupulous in his food. The only course of action, she said, was to have prayers said in India. And as prayers didn't come for free, she asked for some cash. Mum remembers handing over £150 of the £500 that Dad had saved since he came to Britain. And then my grandmother left. That was it. God knows what happened to the money: maybe it was actually spent on prayers in India, but most likely it was used by my father's elder brothers in Bilga, who had by this stage settled into a life of alcohol and drug abuse and wife battery that they would remain committed to until they reached their respective premature deaths.

But then, one night, my mother was beaten so badly that she left her room in the rented house in the middle of the night and appeared on my aunt's doorstep, asking to be sent to safety in Wolverhampton, to the house in Park Village where my grandparents and my Pindor *bua*, another of my father's sisters, lived.

'She came very early in the morning,' my aunt remembered. 'It was 4 a.m., Cugi was asleep. The kids were asleep. Your *phupre* got up and said he wouldn't go to work, would stay with the kids, while I dropped her off. I took her on the train to Euston and then put her on the train to Wolverhampton, telling her which stop to get off at. I think it must have been the fourth or fifth stop. When I returned, Cugi was here, shouting and storming around the house, asking where Jito had gone. I said I didn't know. After searching the house, he demanded we phone Bibi, to ask if Jito had turned up in Wolverhampton. But when we got through, Bibi told him Jito wasn't in Wolverhampton. Which was the truth: she hadn't arrived at the station at the time she was meant to. Your Pindor *bua* had come back alone. But he was convinced she was there and got a taxi to Wolverhampton.'

'A taxi?'

'Yes, for £25. It was a lot of money then. He put all his stuff into the car and went. And that was it. Your parents didn't come back to live in Grays after that.'

The statement hung in the air between us. Rain beat against the windowpane. I'd asked maybe a quarter of the questions I meant to, but I shut my pad nevertheless, telling myself I would come back and ask them at some other point. The time-counter on the dictaphone said an hour had passed, but it didn't feel that long. Eventually my uncle spoke.

'Towards the end, some people – his friends – started saying he'd gone mad.'

My aunt flinched. 'Who said that?'

'Some of the boys we used to hang out with.'

'Well, I've never said that.' She sounded affronted. 'And I never would.'

Even after all the revelations, this one took me aback. Despite having had to live with such trauma, not only did my uncle and aunt still not have the diagnosis of schizophrenia, they still didn't realize my father had a mental illness. I felt a deep well of pity for them and for my father and mother, brief astonishment at the incredible ability of families to not discuss things, and then a powerful surge of anger at the multiculturalists out there who argue that immigrants shouldn't be forced to learn English. This is the consequence of not understanding English. It means ethnic communities can't educate themselves, don't understand what is happening even when the most extreme things occur.

'They were right, though,' I said eventually. 'Something had gone wrong with his mind. He'd fallen ill . . . with a disease called schizophrenia.'

'What kind of disease is that?' asked my aunt.

I closed my A4 pad and for some reason became suddenly aware of my legs, like I hadn't noticed I had them before. When I crossed them, it seemed effeminate. Spread open, the posture seemed too aggressive. I settled for closing them back together in front of me.

'It's called schizophrenia. It affects 1 out of every 100 people around the world.'

'I've never heard of it.'

'I didn't know Dad had it until recently.'

'Does it affect young people?'

'It tends to.'

'You know, sometimes you could almost see his anger building up. He would boil away and then explode.'

'My sister Puli has the same illness.'

'I had no idea.'

'Nor did I until recently.'

As my aunt nodded in disbelief, my uncle spoke. 'His friends left him one by one. He would swear at them, pick fights. Everyone was scared of him.'

My aunt said: 'We didn't know what was happening. I thought maybe your mum had done something . . .'

'Something?'

'Your grandmother started saying that she must have done something to him.'

'Black magic?'

'Yes.'

So that's where the witch thing began. Not only was Mum married off to a violent, mentally ill man, but she was then blamed for his violent mental illness. I loved my grandmother: she was so sprightly and funny when we were growing up, and didn't understand why Mum was so wary of her. But now it made sense.

'Indians always need to blame someone,' I said. 'It's just a disease, like Chacha's leukaemia was just a disease, like the cancer that killed Lock, my best friend at school, just after he left university, was just a disease, like the diseases that will probably kill us are just diseases. Just bad luck. Just *really* bad luck. Sometimes bad things happen for no reason . . .' I stopped when I thought I heard someone raising their voice in another part of the house. But it was just my echo.

My uncle looked stunned. 'So all that time, it was an illness?'

I ended the interview as awkwardly as I started it, by saying thank you, forgetting that Punjabis don't really say thank you, as it is regarded as a kind of payment and hence insulting.

'What do you mean?' asked my uncle. 'We weren't doing anything . . . we just talked.'

'I meant, I'm grateful that you talked to me about this.'

'So is this what you do for work? Talk to people?'

'Yes.'

'And then you write a story?'

'Yes.'

'And you get paid for that?'

'Sometimes.'

'And then it appears on TV?'

As we drove away, it occurred to me that we could stop off at the houses my parents had lived in, walk along the riverbank they had ended up on, maybe even see the football field that Dad used to play on – to verify and flesh out some of the details of the two accounts I now had. But we didn't. We drove in silence towards my flat in London, which I'd prepared for Mum by removing all the alcohol and all the things that might have betrayed the fact that I'd ever had a girlfriend: the tampons in the bathroom cabinet; the surplus toothbrushes; the earrings in my bedside cabinet; the photographs on the walls. It can take you by surprise, sometimes, the number of ways in which people leave marks upon your life.

15. I Remember That

A cocktail of fear and excitement ran through my veins as I walked through the school gates without a topknot for the first time. I went straight to reception to sign the late register – half wanting, half dreading bumping into someone I knew – and remember scrawling 'broken down bus' in the slot reserved for excuses. But this can't have been true. It seems more likely I was late because I'd spent too long getting ready in front of my bedroom mirror, trying with the aid of my brother's gel and mousse, my mother's moisturizer and jasmine oil, to get my hair right, not realizing it was normal for a style to lose its salon-look within minutes and that most boys settled for a dab of spit. It was ironic that one of the reasons I'd wanted to get rid of my long hair was the hassle of maintenance.

My German set, shivering in a Portakabin as some part of the school received a makeover of its own, swivelled around as I entered. Jaws dropped, classmates did double-takes and for a millisecond I was a transformed Sandy in *Grease*. At breaktime, my form gathered around as if I was an exhibit in a motor show, staring, asking for the name of my stylist and attempting to ruffle my hair, only to realize it could no more be ruffled than a lump of granite. It was surreal. I'd wanted to blend in, to no longer stick out and face mockery, but now I stuck out for different reasons and was *actually being admired*. It continued being surreal for some time: a boy in my chemistry set asked me my name; a boy who fancied himself as the class Lothario asked if I had any sisters; a bus driver hesitated to let me on to his double decker because he didn't believe I was the topknotted kid with the crap moustache on my bus pass photo; I was invited to my first ever house party; and, most thrillingly, having not even established meaningful eye contact with a girl before, I

225

was felt up by two members of the opposite sex within the matter of a few weeks.

Though the first of these molestations probably doesn't count, as it was a sanctioned element of the school curriculum, occurring one afternoon during a 'PSHE' lesson. The subject – the initials standing for 'Personal, Social and Health Education' – had been introduced on to the syllabus under the eye of a liberal new headmaster who had surveyed the boys in the school (there were only girls in the sixth form) and concluded, astutely, that while we were heading for some of the best exam results in the country, we had the emotional intelligence of doilies. And, if memory serves, one of the first lessons in this new subject, presided over by a not entirely unattractive female member of staff, was structured around the foreign concept of 'trust' and involved a role-play exercise in which we were asked to pair off and then take turns to close our eyes and fall backwards into the arms of our partner, 'trusting' them to catch us.

Anyone who has witnessed teenage boys interact won't be surprised to hear that the classroom was quickly filled with the sound of skulls cracking against floor. Of course we didn't trust each other. That was the point of being an adolescent boy. *Durrr.* However, those of us who survived were punished with an exercise perhaps even more unsuited to our sex and age: we were asked to pair off again, to close our eyes again and this time *let our partners feel our faces with their hands.*

This kind of crap might wash with middle managers on bonding weekends, but we reacted as if we'd been asked to sodomize each other. I can't remember whether anyone went along with it – somehow I doubt it – but I do remember the teacher attempting to demonstrate what was required by picking me out and using me as a guinea pig. It was the first time a woman I wasn't related to had ever touched my face, and was not entirely unthrilling.

The second molestation occurred in a slightly more conventional venue: in the garage of a friend's house, at that house party I'd been invited to. In a sequence of events I still replay in my mind three or four times a day, the prettiest girl in the house – a Kylie lookalike according to the host – strode into the room, surveyed the quivering specimens before her, walked up to me, told me I had pretty eyes (*what?*), suggested we retire somewhere private (the garage), and then . . . snogged me. And I mean precisely what I say: *she* snogged *me*. I made very little contribution. I'd watched a thousand kisses on screen, and thought I'd know what to do if hell actually froze over and a member of the opposite sex allowed me to touch them, but it quickly became apparent that watching Madonna tonguing a black saint in the 'Like a Prayer' video had no more prepared me for the task than watching *Back to the Future* had taught me how to time-travel. Wolverhampton Kylie would've got a bigger kick out of kissing the Flymo at our feet. Still, for me it was the most erotically charged ten minutes of my life. I told myself to get used to things like this happening all the time. But nothing quite so wonderfully uncomplicated ever happened again.

Forcing myself to look at pictures from this period, it's a puzzle why my haircut elicited such a reaction. I was a strange-looking child. The CFCs from the hair products had turned me an odd magnolia colour, and there was something worryingly Engelbert

Humperdinck about my bouffant. Meanwhile, my face was permanently lacerated. No one had taught me how to shave, and as I still regarded the act as shameful somehow, I surreptitiously and guiltily ran my father's brutal steel razor over my acne and bumfluff, using soap rather than shaving foam as lubrication, assuming it was normal to lose a pint of blood during the process.

The only explanation I can conjure up is that what happened was a demonstration of the role that confidence plays in attraction. The excitement I felt at no longer feeling hemmed into myself, of being able to relax, must have been palpable. Bus journeys that were previously dreaded, for the sweet wrappers and paper balls hurled at my topknot, became opportunities for flirtation with members of the Girls' High. Points of difference that had previously caused anxiety became opportunities – I started, for instance, *asking* Mum to pack *aloo gobi parathas* in my lunchbox, because Matthew Davies would buy them from me and I could use the cash to buy chips. I went from running away home at end of school, to chairing the fundraising committee, helping set up a school council and a debating society. And I realized that what I had seen as the intellectual superiority of my peers was in some cases just expensive schooling. Their prep schools had given them a head start, but with Mum insisting I give up the factory to concentrate on preparing for my GCSEs, I found I could, with hard work, not only excel again, but even have energy spare to cultivate the air of effortless superiority so prized by the English private school system: working like crazy at home, and acting up in class, pretending it all came easily.

Before my haircut, my behaviour at school was as unadventurous as my taste in music. I was never one of those who set fire to the gas taps during chemistry or who drove the history master half mad by humming throughout his lessons. But suddenly, I was. And given that I was by this stage translating my own school reports to Mum, and could intercept letters of complaint from the school to my parents, and given that, unlike many of my contemporaries, I didn't have the guilt of my parents paying thousands of pounds for my education, I found I could go further than most. My report for the Michaelmas term of 1992 bears witness to just how much of a pain in the arse I'd become. Maths: 'Sathnam has generally produced work of a good standard this term and his test results have been most satisfactory. However, I'm a little unhappy with his attitude and behaviour in class.' Physics: 'His work has been very good 'as usual but I've not detected any special effort to do well. I still find his behaviour a little immature.' Form teacher: 'I'm astonished that he still finds it necessary to misbehave in class.'

The transformation at school found an echo in my social life. I didn't suddenly become part of the big group who did poppers at lunchtime and drank in the remarkable number of pubs that served underage drinkers in school uniform around Wolverhampton. In many respects, I was still puritanical and, like anyone who has ever been been bullied, the experience had left me with a fear of groups. But I developed several new friendships, the most important and revelatory of which was with a boy called David Radburn.

It was revelatory in part because until Dave, all my friendships, such as with Lock, were based on having things in common. But Dave and I were from different planets. He was Conservative in his politics. He was a Wolverhampton Wanderers fan. And when he first spoke to me it was to mock me for the George Michael picture I had plastered on the inside of my history folder (God knows why I hadn't been castigated for this earlier). During the subsequent argument he revealed that his favourite band were, of all things . . . *Dire Straits*.

It was also revelatory because Dave was the first white friend I had who seemed to want to visit me at home – as it was an academic school, my mother implicitly trusted any friends I made, and didn't mind them staying over – and because Dave was the first white friend I had who invited me to stay with his family. Moreover, he was the first white friend I had who invited me to stay *in the mansion he shared with his family in the Staffordshire countryside, and the holiday home he shared with his family in Yorkshire.*

And it was during these stays that I learned numerous important lessons about life, including: bread doesn't always come sliced; some people have curtains with *linings*; boiled eggs don't have to be hard-boiled; there are people out there who allow their children wine with their evening meal; there are radio stations out there that don't play music; and (this was the biggest shock) there are actually real people out there who behave the same way in front of their parents as they do in front of their friends. I remember Phil, Dave's dad, a newspaper publisher, taking us out to a Chinese restaurant in Stafford and asking, when he saw me flailing around, if I'd ever used chopsticks before. I didn't dare mention I'd not actually been to a restaurant before.

I was reminded of what a culture shock it was recently when a friend, talking about how all families are weird in some way or another, used the analogy of going to the toilet. Raising a family was like wiping your bum after going to the loo, he argued: a private act, conducted behind closed doors, which you cannot do 'normally' because you have no way of knowing what 'normal' is. I liked the analogy, not only because I am scatalogical, but because for me the shock of discovering families could be so different, via Dave, was epitomized by his family loo. I'd got over the shock of discovering that English families didn't have water bottles in their bathrooms, like Punjabis, some years earlier. But Dave's family had dried flowers in their bathroom – DRIED FLOWERS. And BOOKS. Even Lock was astounded when I told him. Doubtless, Dave was equally stunned by some of the bizarre customs in my household.

Looking back at what I've written, I worry I'm being hyperbolic. Did things really change so completely? Did my old personality and insecurities vanish into the Wolverhampton canal along with my disembodied plait?* Well, I have compressed events – these

* Apparently, it is traditional to dispose of a cut topknot in natural running water, the parcel packed with sugar. But as Wolverhampton is a long way from the nearest bit of sea or river, we settled for a canal, wrongly assuming that the water flowed. Most likely, my disembodied plait is still languishing at the bottom of the Broad Street locks.

changes took place over a year or two – and the old urge to hide under a table didn't disappear, it would re-emerge, as it still does, at the oddest times, like a draught under a door. Otherwise, yes, things were like this. However, as my personal life began gliding along like a Sunseeker yacht cruising the Caribbean, my home life began to increasingly resemble a North Sea trawler in a force ten gale.

By this stage, all my siblings had been through the marriage mill at least once. Bindi had been married off to a bright and handsome turbaned boy from India, with whom she already had a baby boy. My brother had married his sweetheart Ruky, a beautiful, happy girl from down the road, and one of the best things that has ever happened to our family. Meanwhile Puli was back at home, her marriage having failed. It transpired that her mullet-haired husband was in love with an unsuitable girl – whose existence he had revealed to Puli on their honeymoon – and he'd only gone through the arranged marriage to please his father. In the event the betrothal lasted eleven months and for the final six months of those he didn't speak to Puli. Despite this, it took him actually running away from his parents' house for the families to accept that the marriage wasn't going to work.

You might have thought my mother's delight at Bindi's marriage, and Rajah's marriage, in particular, might have outweighed her anxieties about Puli's divorce. After all, my brother had got engaged as soon as Mum had discovered he was dating; his wife was the right religion, caste, age, skin colour and height, displayed many traditional homely virtues, and was happy to move in with us. But it wasn't. She took the breakdown of Puli's marriage badly, as personally as she'd taken the arrangement, and my chief memory of the aftermath is of her sitting on the settee in the living room raging and wailing a monologue in front of various visitors that went along the lines of: 'My God what sins and crimes did I commit in my previous life that I be given a kismet like this dear lord why was I born why does God make me suffer so . . .'

In contrast, Puli seemed to take it well, carrying herself like someone who'd been in a road accident but survived. After the

initial shock, I thought I saw relief and then determination to make the most of her second chance. She quit her job at the council and got a part-time job in a chemist's. She took up a range of alternative therapies, became vegetarian, cut her hair and had it styled. She enrolled on a women's studies course at Wolverhampton University and developed a tendency to make proclamations that went along the lines of: 'All my life I've been doing things for other people looking after them doing things to please them but now I want to be my own person in my own right and I'm no longer afraid of doing what I want to do . . .'

These declarations, which sometimes came in response to requests such as 'Like some tea?', or in the middle of *Brookside*, made me cringe sometimes, but I never considered them odd. And neither did I consider it odd that she would stand at the front door for five or ten minutes every night, checking and re-checking that it had been locked, that she would sometimes call home from work to check whether she'd left a window open or left the iron on, that she and Mum would argue bitterly in the bedroom they now shared, almost every night. The arguments actually made sense. Mum had by this stage started talking about another marriage and Puli was refusing to entertain the possibility.

I didn't understand why Mum was in such a rush to get Puli

married off again. But then I didn't really understand anything. I didn't understand that Puli had taken herself off the medication that had kept her stable since 1986, for the schizophrenia she still didn't realize she had. I didn't understand that Puli's sleeplessness, irritability and vagueness were the signs of an impending schizophrenic relapse. I didn't understand that my mother's sobs following the arguments weren't those of self-pity, but a result of the fear of witnessing yet another mental breakdown, and the beginning of a depression that she would eventually have to be medicated for. And I didn't understand that in her urge to get Puli married off, she was, in a strange but very Indian way, trying to save her.

All I felt was a profound sense of emotional claustrophobia and the universal teenage urge to get out of the house. And I got the perfect opportunity when to my surprise, and to the surprise of more popular pupils whose support was catastrophically fragmented, and to the surprise of the staff who wrote violent notes objecting, I was elected by my school year to be head boy. The job didn't, on paper, involve a great deal: I had to mutter 'Dismiss by rows' at the end of school assemblies to indicate it was time for everyone to shuffle off to lessons, and got to hand out detentions if kids were particularly rude to prefects. But I managed to make it almost a full-time job, and as the role changed my relationship with teachers, who suddenly seemed to notice I was a human being with actual thoughts and feelings, I got the chance to develop several close friendships with staff, most importantly and permanently with my English teacher and tutor, Robin Roberts, who lived half an hour away with her boyfriend, Steve, and whose house I began visiting whenever I could.

No other period of my life is more difficult to unpick than what followed. And no other period makes me question my ignorance of the schizophrenia running in my family. Did I choose not to know? There are things both Dave and Robin say I told them that I can't, even with their descriptions, remember happening. And it makes no sense why the gap between Puli's account and my memory is so oceanic, when I saw more of her than any other member of the family. Most evenings I was locked away in my bedroom working, or away at Robin's or Dave's, so I didn't see much of Rajah and Ruky and Mum, who were away at work. But I was at home most afternoons after school, and Puli was there with me and Dad, as I had my turkey burger sandwiches and watched telly. There was even one time when I watched a video of Mel Gibson's *Hamlet* with her. The play was an A-level set text and I'd got the film out because I was having problems getting into it. One of the essay titles? 'Was Hamlet mad? Discuss.'

Every time I excavate, the narrative comes out differently. But here is an attempt.

I remember walking into Puli's room one of those afternoons and finding her in the middle of a yoga exercise. She was dressed in a tracksuit, her knees drawn up to her head, her hands under her knees, and with her spine rounded was swinging back and forth, like a human rocking chair. I tiptoed out, thinking nothing more of what I saw. She'd been doing yoga for some time, at home and also, once a week, at the Dudley Health Centre. But I might have given it more consideration if I'd come back a few hours later. Puli tells me now that in the early stages of her breakdown she would sometimes stay in that position rocking back and forth, back and forth, for up to four hours at a time.

I remember mowing the lawn (gardening was a way of escaping the claustrophobia of the house), opening the wheelie-bin to throw away the cuttings and finding a photo album full of Puli's wedding pictures. Some of them had been scratched and defaced. As with the yoga, I thought nothing much of it. Mum had disposed of the wedding videos in an act of anger weeks before. If anything, I was surprised Puli hadn't thrown them out sooner. I tipped the cuttings over them, slammed the bin shut and didn't worry about the discovery. But if I'd dug deeper into the bin, Puli tells me now I would have found something to worry about:

she had thrown her family photo albums away too. And some of those photos had been scratched and defaced as well.

I remember another time, talking to Puli in her bedroom: I'd popped into her room to show her some of my poetry. I still liked maths, but Robin had made me realize that my predilection for pop lyrics could be extended into literature, and I fancied myself as the Asian Seamus Heaney. But as I handed over my latest awful composition – thank God I didn't circulate the work further – I noticed her twitching and looking agitated, so I asked if she was okay. 'My boss hates me,' she said. Her pupils seemed to have contracted. 'The bitch is always talking about me behind my back.' It wasn't an extreme expletive, nowhere near as offensive as the insults I bandied about at school, but still, it was the first time I had heard any of my siblings swear. We never swore at home. 'It's all in your head,' I said, rushing out of the room, not realizing how right I was. 'Try not to worry about it.'

I remember the arguments between Puli and Mum becoming so bad that Mum began sleeping downstairs, in the living room. My father was already sleeping downstairs by this stage, in the front room, because he was having difficulty sleeping, which gave me difficulty sleeping, which distracted me from studying. I remember feeling guilty that my parents had both been reduced to sleeping on impromptu mattresses in their own home. The guilt intensified when I tiptoed downstairs one night, to sneak away some of the whisky left over from my brother's wedding, and heard Mum crying, alone. I wanted to ask what was wrong, but couldn't risk her smelling the booze on my breath.

I remember having my first and last and only argument with Dad. As part of my Dave-influenced gentrification, I had begun using the monotone of Radio 4 to mask the racket of crashing pans from the kitchen, the R 'n' B pulsating from my brother's bedroom, and the fights raging around the house. But I noticed, increasingly, that on the rare occasions I left my bedroom, my father would be walking down the stairs, or just entering the bathroom, or standing on the landing. Eventually, I realized he was lurking outside my door. I didn't wonder why he was doing it, just knew it made me uncomfortable, and things came to a head one morning when I went to have a bath and returned to my bedroom to find Dad sitting on my bed, one ear to the radio, like the HMV dog. Irritated, confused and adolescent, I screamed at him to get out and – not knowing what I was saying – accused him of being as mad as Hari, the nutter who used to walk around Park Village with a ghetto-blaster on his shoulder. I remember the flash of anger in his eyes and his plea afterwards. 'But Hari . . . Hari is . . . *mad*.' I felt afterwards like I'd kicked a kitten in the face, and thinking about it now, it feels even worse because I understand that he was experiencing auditory hallucinations, as his own mental health condition was exacerbated by the stress of what was happening to Puli. 'Unfortunately he has been suffering from sleeplessness,' explains a letter in his medical notes. 'His elder daughter is also suffering from vague and bizarre symptoms, suggestive of acute stress reaction and depressive illness. She has been under consideration for assessment under the Mental Health Act 1983. However, this domestic upheaval has not helped Mr Sanghera . . .'

I remember Puli sitting making notes in the living room as I watched *Neighbours*. She always seemed to be making notes. I assumed they were related to her studies. But they were more than that. 'When I started writing, I couldn't stop,' she remembers. 'It was the same with other things. If I did yoga, I couldn't stop. If I started laughing, I would keep on laughing. If I started crying, I would keep on crying. Once I started writing, I would get carried away and start writing all this stuff about witches, how I felt they were possessing me, about how I could melt witches with hot water. That's how ill I was. It's painful to think I handed in some of that stuff to the tutors. I take such pride in my public behaviour, and yet . . . I actually did that.'

*

I don't remember Puli locking herself in the bathroom and threatening suicide, though I must have known it happened as Robin says I mentioned it to her.

I don't remember doctors coming to see Puli, but they did. 'One of them came when I chucked all my belongings out of the bedroom,' she says. 'He asked me what I was doing and I said I was clearing things out because I felt so well, because I'd come off my medication and was feeling so good about life, that getting rid of the stuff was like getting rid of bad memories. He listened to me and gave me a piece of paper saying I was okay. And then when the other doctors came, I showed it to them. I really did believe I was fine, but I was actually getting worse and worse. It got so bad that at one point I ran in front of a bus. I thought that if I was hit on the head, if I had a blackout, then that would sort out what was wrong in my head, and I would wake up normal. The driver managed to stop before he hit me. But I can still remember the way he looked at me, afterwards, just before I ran off.'

I don't remember Puli barricading herself in her room, but I remember there being a lot of commotion in the house one day and my brother asking whether I had somewhere to be for the rest of the day. As it happened, I did have somewhere to be. I had a date, with a girl called Amanda: she was in my English set and from Bridgnorth and wanted to study English at university like I did. She met me off the bus, gave me a volume of W. B. Yeats's poetry, and after wandering around town, we kissed. My technique wasn't passive any more: if anything, I'd gone too far the other way and it must have looked like I was trying to give the poor girl mouth-to-mouth resuscitation. She ended things before they had really begun soon afterwards, with a gentleness beyond her years: it was less like being dumped than being put to sleep before an operation. I heard later, through the grapevine, that she considered me 'a little intense'.

*

By the time I came back home – I think I spent an evening at Dave's after seeing Amanda – Puli had gone. I don't remember being in the house when the police and ambulance came. All I recall is coming home late in the evening, with Dave – we'd been for a drink in a pub near my house, and he was staying over because he couldn't drive home – and Mum telling me in our darkened hallway that Puli had been taken away. I remember hugging her, and crying in my bedroom. I remember Dave's kindness in not looking embarrassed as I did so. And of the six weeks Puli subsequently spent in hospital, I remember visiting only once, and of that visit I recall nothing of what Puli looked like, of what she said, of what I said, only the shaking and slobbering of the patients around us. Somewhere in the back of my mind, I put it down to a nervous breakdown.

But Puli remembers events differently. It was one of the things she asked to write, rather than talk about. *'You were in the house when the police and the ambulance came,'* her letter began. *'Initially I refused to co-operate, tried to convince everyone I wasn't ill. But then I heard someone breaking down in tears downstairs. At the time, I thought it was Dad. But later, when I came back home from hospital, Mum told me it had been Rajah. It was hearing those sobs that made me accept I was going to have to go to hospital. I suddenly felt exhausted and started to doubt myself. You were there at the time. I'll never forget the look on your face, when the police came, and I was going on and on, spouting out all the nonsense that came into my head. You looked disgusted. And it took me by surprise.*

'And I remember you visiting me in hospital. You came with Dad and Rajah. I was surprised when a nurse said I had visitors – I had been feeling isolated and had not expected or even wanted visitors. I walked up the corridor in a kind of daydream. And there you all were, walking towards me, from the opposite end of the corridor.

'Seeing your faces . . . I think that was the only time during my hospital stay I felt positive emotion, almost delight. It was a special moment for me. You all looked so handsome, even Dad. It was like I hadn't seen you in years. I was glad at that moment that I had family

and wasn't alone in the world. As you saw me, you quickened your pace and hugged me. It was the most genuine, true-hearted hug I had ever had. It was just what I needed. Then Rajah hugged me. And then Dad hugged me too, which meant a lot, because I know hugs aren't always easy for Dad.'

16. Summer of '69

I returned from Essex determined to maintain the momentum. No longer was I going to get hung up on what to write and how to write it – that was something to worry about later; the drinking had to stop – at least, the daytime drinking had to reduce; and I had to focus like a panther on the task at hand, namely, gathering all the corroborating evidence I could find. Besides, verifying the next bit of Mum's account was going to be a relative breeze. She'd told me that doctors were involved with my father almost as soon as he arrived in Wolverhampton in his £25 taxi cab. Doctors always take notes. And every patient has a right to see a copy of their medical records under the Data Protection Act of 1998.

After permitting myself only the briefest wobble about the ethics of viewing them – on the one hand, my father did not understand the significance of the request, on the other my mother, in her legal capacity as his carer, was keen on me deciphering the notes* – Mum submitted a request with Dr Dutta, the eldest of three Indian-trained GPs who look after my parents (the other two being his wife and son-in-law). He took £15 for photocopying fees, as he was entitled to, said the notes would shortly arrive in the post, and we began waiting.

The adjective in the preceding paragraph that should have alerted me to the anguish that followed was 'Indian'. As anyone who has visited the subcontinent will know, Indians tend not to so much follow regulations as acknowledge them with a noncommittal yes/no headroll, before ultimately resisting them, and this is what happened with my mother's request. After a couple of weeks, a follow-up query from Mum produced the claim that

---

* Besides, I was making up the rules as I went along.

the file was large and taking longer than expected to photocopy. And then, some time after that, the youngest of the doctors, Dr Dutta's son-in-law, took her aside as she waited to see a doctor on another matter, and bombarded her with paranoid questions. Why do you want to see the notes? Why does your son want to write a book about you? Does he *know* what your husband did to you in your early marriage? Why can't he write about something more cheerful?

It really did take all the willpower in the world to resist storming down to the surgery to stab the doctors through their respective skulls with a garden fork. The single worst thing about being illiterate is the way people can deny you your rights. But I tried to keep calm, reminding myself of what Dr Patel had said, that continuity of care is important for people with my father's condition, of what my mother had said about the eldest of the male doctors – he had been supportive throughout the mayhem of her early marriage – and telling myself there could be any number of prosaic reasons for their procrastination, short of them trying to cover something up. Maybe they'd not had a request to view medical records before. Maybe they'd been put on edge by the word 'journalist' – it puts me on edge sometimes and I am one. And you need only glance at a Bollywood movie to see why they might be perplexed by the idea of a book about Mum and Dad. The misery memoir is very much a first world phenomenon. In India, you only need to glance out of your window to feel grateful for your lot.

But when weeks threatened to turn into months, I lost my patience and visited the surgery with Dad, where I found myself discussing the request with Dr Dutta's wife, Mrs Dr Dutta, if you like, who I'd last seen when I was ten and having trouble with eczema. Resisting the urge to roll up my sleeves or remove my trousers, I launched into an unexpectedly controlled speech about how everyone had the right to view a copy of their medical records under the Data Protection Act of 1998, how my mother in her capacity as my father's carer, and I, in my capacity as a son and translator, wanted to view my father's records, and how they were obliged to present them within forty days in a format we would understand.

Mrs Dr Dutta looked taken aback. But not as taken aback as I must have looked when she responded by saying we could see my father's medical notes, as it was our legal right to do so, but the practice could only supply us with records going back to *the mid-nineties*. The explanation provided for this was that my father had briefly been under the care of another doctor during the nineties, and that this doctor hadn't, apparently, forwarded his older notes, an extraordinary claim because one of the excuses proffered for the delay was that there were so many notes – going back all the way to 1969 – that it was taking ages to copy them.

Somehow I managed not to explode, and through teeth clenched so tightly they were at risk of being ground to flour, I repeated the request, saying we wanted to see all the notes they could find, as it was our legal right to do so, and that I would be contacting my father's previous GP about the older notes. I did so immediately, roaring to the other side of town in a taxi with my father, where I sat flicking through copies of *Bella* magazine for an hour as the surgery staff searched for any sign of the files under the various misspellings of his name – Jaggit Singh, Jagitt Singh, Jangit Sangera, Jagit Singh Sanghara, etc. – and various dates of birth, until, as expected, they confirmed they didn't have them and, as expected, added they were confident they had been forwarded.

Back in London I wrote a letter to the GP I'd met, forcing myself to be more polite than I felt, thanking her for the care and attention with which she and her family had looked after my parents over the decades, explaining I'd visited the surgery of my dad's previous GP, and that they'd told me they had forwarded his full set of notes, going back decades, to her practice when my father switched back to their care in the mid-nineties. I added that I'd expected this was the case, given what her husband had told my mother, that we wanted the surgery staff to have a thorough search through the files, and that we looked forward to seeing a full set of photocopies soon. My mother eventually heard back from the practice manager, who sent an application form, which I filled out and returned with a cheque for £50 and a note repeating our desire to see the FULL set of records.

Christ.

Finally, after a couple more prods, and well after the forty-day period within which doctors are supposed to provide them, a brown parcel landed on my parents' doorstep with a promisingly heavy thud. Naturally, the first thing I did when flicking through the sheaf of double-sided photocopies, with Mum sitting next to me, was look at the dates. Were there any documents pre-dating the mid-nineties? Yes: letters and notes from hospitals and GPs from the nineties, eighties, seventies and sixties. Relief, mingled with resentment at having been lied to.

What was their problem?

The next thing was to try to find the earliest notes, related to my father's first few months in Wolverhampton in 1969, when he moved in with my mother at my aunt's house in Park Village. In another of those episodes almost too difficult to contemplate, Mum had got lost on her way to Wolverhampton – it was the first time she had travelled in Britain on her own, and she was badly injured – disembarking at Birmingham instead of Wolverhampton. She had been put back on a train by a helpful Indian, but got lost again in Wolverhampton, where my aunt Pindor, the eldest of my father's sisters, had understandably given up waiting. Mum eventually arrived half a day after she was meant to, and as a doctor was called to attend to her, my father arrived in his taxi. In a story since confirmed by my uncle Malkit, my Pindor *bua*'s husband, he greeted my father at the front door wielding an axe, saying that if he showed any hint of the violence he'd displayed in Grays towards his wife or to anyone else – this was the first time they had seen him since the chaos of that bank holiday – he would be given a taste of his own medicine.

Apparently, my father had been registered with Dr Dutta that very same day, as he tended to my mother, and having seen my own very full and detailed medical notes, I was hoping for something along the lines of:

10/5/69	Patient age 19 years, 13 stone. Arrived England January 1968. Labourer in Essex. Wife, also registered, showing signs of violent abuse. Living at sister's house in Park Village. Withdrawn.
20/5/69	No violence. Seeking work. Indications of depression.
24/06/69	Moved out of sister's house with wife, due to overcrowding: living in rented room nearby.
3/7/69	Fractures wife's nose at home during sister's wedding. Aggression alternating with catatonia, and emotional flattening, severe apathy, indications of paranoia: claims wife is having affair. Indication of auditory hallucinations. Acute depression.

Something along those lines would have been enough to corroborate Mum's story, to give me enough to pen a journalistic account of what happened. But, not for the first time, I was confusing my experiences with my parents'. My medical notes were lengthy, detailed, coherent typewritten documents, because I was on private health, and because I was a literate hypochondriac, who demanded to know what was going on. But my father was an illiterate mentally ill immigrant who didn't know what was happening to him, in a family of illiterate immigrants, who didn't know what was happening to him, dealing with an NHS doctor who was himself an Indian immigrant. Correspondingly, the doctors' notes for the period consisted of nothing more than:

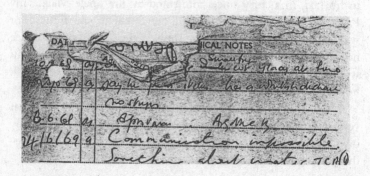

After a great deal of squinting, all I managed to decipher were the phrases 'Paracetamol' and 'AC mental troubles' – no shit – 'Small cut' and 'Communication impossible . . . something about water'. At this stage I wrote another letter to the surgery, this time to Mr Dr Dutta, saying it would be useful if he could decipher his notes, and that I would pay him for his time if necessary, but received no reply – and still have received no reply, but remembering I was a panther focusing on the task at hand, I moved on to the next bit of the story, my father's first hospitalization, which was at least covered by a typewritten letter.

WOLVERHAMPTON HOSPITAL MANAGEMENT COMMITTEE

JREW/KP/K17958

NEW CROSS HOSPITAL
WOLVERHAMPTON
TELEPHONE NO. 732255

21st July 1969

WOLVERHAMPTON.

Dear Dr.

Jagg^t
Jugelecler Singh
26 Newport Street, Wolverhampton.

The abovenamed was admitted to the Psychiatric Unit at this hospital on 11.7.69 in a state of depression. A course of electroplexy was started without delay, but after only two treatments he insisted on discharging himself from hospital, though I would have preferred him to remain a little longer, as he had only had two treatments at the time.

He was advised to continue to take Tofranil mgms 25, 2 t.d.s, Mandrax 1 nocte, Perandran mgms 5 t.d.s. and Valium mgms 5 t.d.s., and was given a week's supply of these tablets when he was discharged.

He agreed to come for electroplexy on an out patient basis at this hospital.

Yours sincerely,

Consultant Psychiatrist

245

This may have been neat and legible but in many ways it was even more impenetrable than the murky photocopied squiggles that preceded it. The dates tallied with the dates Mum had indicated and it described a hospitalization, which must have been the hospitalization Mum discussed, but that was the point at which the details ceased corresponding. Mum had told me that the hospital was in Stafford and this letter came from a hospital in Wolverhampton. The address cited in the letter was my aunt's address, whereas Mum said she and my father were living in a rented room at 15 Prosser Street by this time. Most confusingly, the tone of the account of my father's breakdown in the letter – as much as there is one – didn't in any way relate to the tone of Mum's story.

According to Mum, my father's violence had become so extreme that my aunt Pindor had insisted that her parents – my grandparents – rent a room in the same house to keep an eye on him. And on one of their first nights together Dad was being so aggressive that my grandmother insisted on sleeping in their bed, to keep them apart. But even this didn't help: according to Mum, my father reached over his mother – she can't have been much of a buffer – and attempted to strangle Mum with her own *chuni*. It was at this point that my grandfather, in his sixties now, ran into the room and pinned him down, allowing Bibi to take my mother downstairs to safety.

With Dad still showing no signs of calming down – Mum said he kept on saying: 'You're going to be dead by twelve tomorrow, just you wait and see' – my grandfather spent the night on the stairs, to make sure he didn't come down after my mother. In the morning, with no sign of his anger abating, and the landlady threatening to throw everyone out of the house before somebody was killed, Baba broke the habit of a lifetime, said he wouldn't go to work and called Dr Dutta. On arriving the doctor apparently immediately called the police. The police, for reasons my mother does not understand, refused to restrain him. According to Mum, they had to be called twice more that day before they agreed to take Dad away – and then only did so when, with a

246

crowd of people watching my mother being taken to safety at another house, my father lunged at her in front of them.

However, this letter made my father sound like Robbie Williams checking into the Priory after a disappointing set of album sales. There wasn't even a hint of a forced committal: it sounded as if he had volunteered to come into hospital. Indeed, so large was the gap between the accounts that I began to wonder whether there might have been some confusion with identities. The spelling mistake – Jugclecler Singh – was spectacular, even by my family's illiterate standards.

But discussing the letter with Mum, and delving further into the notes, explanations began to surface. Subsequent letters revealed that while the letters came from Wolverhampton, 'the Psychiatric Unit' referred to in the letter was indeed in Stafford. Mum explained that my grandfather was the only member of the family who went with Dad when he was taken away, which might explain the massive spelling error (my grandfather didn't speak or write English), the mistake with the address (having just moved he most likely hadn't had time to memorize the new address), and maybe was the reason why the violence wasn't mentioned. The language problem, combined with his inevitable confusion and shame over what had happened, perhaps explained why he didn't convey the extent of my father's breakdown to the doctors. You would think the GP would have done, but then, judging from his notes, Dr Dutta was hardly loquacious, and, remember, this was the doctor who, sixteen years later, didn't tell Puli she had schizophrenia when he diagnosed her.

But these possible explanations only gave way to more questions. What did the psychiatrist mean in the letter by 'state of depression'? Wasn't Valium used to treat anxiety disorders? Wasn't Tofranil – internet search – an antidepressant? Slowly, the horrible reality of what had happened sank in: Dad had been misdiagnosed. Not only had he been misdiagnosed, but he had been mistakenly given 'electroplexy' – ECT – as a result.

It was a very good job I'd read around the subject by this stage. Otherwise I would have surely struggled to control my anger. The stalling from the GPs had made me tetchy and suspicious, and, on the face of it, a misdiagnosis doesn't have worse consequences than ECT. From its negative portrayal in *One Flew Over the Cuckoo's Nest*, to U2's anti-ECT anthem 'The Electric Co', few medical procedures have a worse popular perception than ECT. And the last thing a paranoid schizophrenic needs is to be forcibly electrocuted.

However, the discovery didn't make me angry at all. Sad, but not angry. Why? In part it was because I knew that while many psychiatrists think ECT does not help treat schizophrenia, there are some, including the great E. Fuller Torrey, who think it has a modest role to play. Also, while the initials ECT bring to mind an array of horrific images of people being cruelly electrocuted against their will, it is unlikely my father would have been given it unmodified: it is generally administered under anaesthesia and with muscle relaxants.

Any potential outrage was further tempered by the understanding that even the very best psychiatrists struggle to diagnose schizophrenia. In *Schizophrenia: Understanding and Coping with the Illness,* Dr John Cutting admits that over a period of four years he was referred some fifty psychotic patients by colleagues, to give a second opinion, and that in no less than twenty of these, the diagnosis turned out wrong. 'I myself am continually making mistakes on the basis of one interview,' he admits. Furthermore, it was highly likely that when my father was assessed, he was in a highly depressed state. Schizophrenia and depression go hand in hand. Though my father sometimes does a good impression of one now, there aren't many happy schizophrenics out there.

But the main reason I didn't immediately get on the phone to a medical negligence lawyer, or travel to the doctors' surgery with mallet in hand, was that I was distracted by another detail in the letter, a detail which provided an answer to the question that had been troubling me most since Mum had given me her account. The question was this: why did my mother stay with my father?

She had told me that in the weeks after the hospitalization, the formidable machinery of Punjabi honour had finally cranked into gear. Several men from her family village in India had appeared, saying they'd heard about what had happened and that they wanted to pay for her to be sent back to India. A telegram had arrived from her father, saying he wanted her sent home and that he would pay the fare. There was also a conference of my father's relatives, where several of my uncles offered to pay to send her back to India, if only for a break. They would do everything they could to make the marriage work afterwards, they said, adding in a typically melodramatic, typically Punjabi flourish, that they would all leave their wives, my father's sisters, if the family didn't honour the marriage. (It says so much about the role of women in Punjabi society that even at this stage the implication was that Mum was fortunate to have a husband.) People were falling over each other to help, Mum must have been terrified, desperate to see her family, she was still only eighteen or nineteen, had only been married for four months, but still she refused to go. Why?

Of course I understood that Mum's approach to relationships was different from mine. Over the years I've split up with girlfriends, and been split up with, for myriad reasons: because they were not bookish enough; because they lived on the wrong side of London; because they smelt funny; because, how could I forget, I had a fear of confronting my mother about wanting to be with an unsuitable girl. But I knew Mum was brought up in a patriarchal society, where a woman's place was in the home, and where splitting up and divorce were taboo. I also understood that she had different expectations from marriage, expectations I hear her articulating now whenever my sisters have marital crises and call for advice. 'In one's life one must fulfil one's duty,' she will intone, standing at the phone in the hallway in her sandals. 'Your kismet is your kismet. What is going to happen is going to happen.' Unfortunately, 'everything' means everything up to and including domestic violence, which, alongside alcoholism, is the scourge of my community. Thankfully, I have never seen my father hit my mother, but domestic violence was a fact of life in other families as I grew up – there were Punjabi men on Prosser Street who would beat their wives in their back yards.

I also understood that my mother loved my father. The love between them may not be of the romantic comedy variety, the type I aspire to, but having watched my mother take care of him, seen her cook his every meal, wash his clothes, ride his moods, I have always accepted it as a fact of life. In her accounts of the violence at the start of the marriage, Mum always qualified her descriptions by saying things like: 'You've got to understand that I've never hated your father. Every time he hit me, he would cry afterwards and say: "I'm sorry, I'll stop, I'm sorry, I'll stop. Please don't leave me."' In other words, even though she didn't have the vocabulary or the medical know-how, she knew his behaviour was due to an illness. She knew he couldn't help it.

But despite all this, I still didn't entirely understand why Mum didn't go back to India, if only for a break. It was clear she was exhausted, there was nothing to be lost from having a break, she must have been grief-stricken with homesickness, and she must have known Dad would take a long time to get better. Even by her exacting moral standards, it didn't make sense. But when I transcribed the dates mentioned in the letter on to the chronology section of my 1800 x 1200mm professional dry-wipe magnetic whiteboard, I was struck by a possibility, a possibility that had me returning to the tape recordings of my mother's account of what had happened during my father's hospitalization.

'I used to go and see him at the hospital with the family in Stafford,' she said. 'It was a secure unit, like a prison really. But I would wait outside. Even then, everyone in the family was frightened he might try to attack me. During one of those early visits I remember being taken in to see his consultant. He asked so many questions and kept on saying he couldn't believe how little I knew about marriage and life. I didn't know anything.

'And then, after a week or so, the doctors said I should try to meet your dad again, to see how he reacted. They had six or seven people in front of me, members of the family lining the way, just in case he tried to attack me. I walked up to him really slowly. I think the family had told him I had gone back to India, so it took him a while to work out it was me. And when he did, he didn't get angry at all, he just cried. I don't think I've ever seen anyone cry that much before.

'After that I worked out how to get to the hospital myself. We used to get £6 a week in benefits: £2 would go to your Bibi, for groceries; £2 would go on rent and there would be £2 left, which I would use to buy bus tickets and fruit for your dad. I went whenever I could. But then, one day, your father, he just appeared at the door. Yes. At the front door of the house where we were renting rooms. This was a few weeks into his hospital stay. He'd escaped somehow and had walked all the way from Stafford. It must be nearly twenty miles. He must have found his way to the house just by asking people.

'He looked so delighted to be back home and kept on saying: "I was worried you had gone back to India." But everyone in the house was panicking. They must have thought he was going to kill me, after what *had happened. But again, he wasn't angry, he just looked relieved and he took me upstairs quietly. I don't know if someone in the house called them, or whether the hospital did, but the police came to get him almost immediately. He was crying when they took him back. He didn't want to go.'*

Again, so many questions. Mum made it sound like Dad had escaped from prison, whereas the letter made it sound like my father had checked out from hospital, in the way you might check out of a spa out of sheer boredom. Mum said he was dragged back to hospital by the police, but the letter suggests he didn't even go back to hospital. There is no mention in the letter, or in my father's medical notes, of any interviews at any point with my mother. Could something have been removed? I don't know. I still cannot explain these things. But my mother's comments – 'the consultant couldn't believe how little I knew about marriage and life', 'your father took me upstairs' – and the nine and a half calendar months between the escape or discharge, whatever you want to call it, and my sister Puli's birth, explained why she stuck with my father. There's only one thing more unacceptable than a divorced woman in the Punjab: a single mother.

17. Stay (Faraway, So Close)

The family gathered to watch me open the letter: Bindi, staying over with her two baby boys, leaning against the radiator; Rajah's bicep bulging like a cushion against the banister; Ruky, smiling serenely on the stairs; Puli, flat and quiet, next to me by the telephone; Mum muttering '*Waheguru, waheguru*' under the picture of the Golden Temple; and Dad lurking in the living room doorway, so he could return to Channel 4 as quickly as possible.

I ran a finger over the white envelope, lingering over the college coat of arms in the corner, and everyone, except Dad, leaned forward as I flipped it over.

'Only one sheet of paper inside,' I said, tugging at the flap and feeling like Charlie Bucket looking for the fifth Gold Ticket. 'They would have sent forms if I'd got in.'

Mum broke off from praying. 'What did he say?'

My brother translated.

Dad shouted out from the back. 'What did he say?' There was panic in his voice. Anything out of the ordinary – a Jehovah's Witness, an English voice on the telephone – makes him jumpy.

'Nothing for you to worry about,' Mum retorted, before turning to me. 'Just open the *chithi*, will you? What will happen will happen, nothing will change your kismet.'

If that's the case, I thought, then why are you praying? But as this wasn't the right time for theological debate – there's never a right time for theological debate at home – I unfurled the letter and squinted at the text.

Thank you for coming to Cambridge for interviews in November. We were glad to have the opportunity to meet you . . .

Shit. The classic introduction to every rejection letter. I'd been writing to local newspapers for some time now, asking for work experience or opportunities to write and they all began like this. Thanks for your letter and sample article. BUT it was derivative. BUT the prose was overwrought. BUT we don't have space for 2,000 words on why Atzec Camera were better than A-ha.

But, there was no 'BUT' this time.

'So?' My brother's expectant face.

'Um.' I felt tiny.

'Yeah?'

'Er.'

'Yeah?'

'Yeah.'

'What do you mean Yeah?' He slapped me on the back. 'You mean YEAH!'

Through the hugs and blessings that followed, I heard Puli saying, 'I knew you'd do it,' my mother weeping and Bindi asking Ruky: 'So where is Oxbridge anyway?' The telephone rang before the news that I was going to inspect the wonder of Mr Wonka's chocolate factory had sunk in. It was Robin offering congratulations and asking whether I'd read the letter in full. I thought she meant: tell me what it says. But what she meant was: I know what it says, but do you understand? In my confusion, I read it out to her, the words passing through my brain undigested. *Matriculation offer. Pass two A-levels. The condition that you remain at school until next summer . . .*

There was a lengthy interval before the penny dropped.

'So I just need to get two E grades to get in?'

'Yes. But you're not going to give up, are you?'

'I just have to turn up and sign my name on the exam papers really?'

'Yes. But you're not going to give up, are you?'

'Two E grades, you say?'

I promised Robin I wouldn't give up, and became even more determined when I discovered that the college had called school to ask whether I'd be more motivated by a 'three A offer', or a

'2E' offer. Robin, knowing I was an emotional cripple, and had no chance of making the three As I had been optimistically predicted, had made a case for the easy offer, and I knew that if I gave up and lowered the school's overall exam grades as a result, she'd be held responsible. But when it came down to a choice between memorizing bits of Ferdinand Mount's *The British Constitution* and my other commitment – feeling crap – there was no contest. I gave up on school work and took up crying, full-time.

I'm reluctant to call it depression because the word is overused and because when you have mental illness in your family it's uncomfortable to admit you might be susceptible yourself. But it was the unhappiest I have ever been – even the trauma of the last few months seems like one long cocktail in the Lanesborough compared to those grim months. What was behind it? Well, I think it was in part your normal teenage Samuel Beckett blues, in part, with the pressure of work removed, a delayed reaction to the chaos of the preceding year, but mostly, it was guilt.

Of course, on the face of it, everyone was chuffed. Some of my cousins had gone to university by this stage, but no one in the family had been to Oxbridge and Mum played the role of the proud mother with aplomb – she was on the phone for the rest of the day telling anyone who would listen that her son was going to 'Kerm-bridge'. Meanwhile, my brother was more than just pleased for me. In the hallway that morning I saw something new in his eyes: determination. He'd drifted at school, but would soon be taking evening classes, enrolling at university, earning a degree, part-time, and then an MBA, his career taking off in parallel.

But the family response was more complicated than that. Behind Puli's smile, for instance, there was disappointment. She'd been a straight A student once: struggling through her illness to study for her O-levels and A-levels. But while teachers had talked about university, Mum had talked about husbands. After her marriage ended she had enrolled on a course at Wolverhampton University, but again illness had stopped her in her tracks.

And then there were my parents. As much as Mum twirled chillies around my head to fend off the *nazar* apparently coming my way, there was something in the precise way in which she quoted me to visitors ('It's the best university for his chosen subject') and something in her questions ('You say this college is much better than any in the Midlands?') that betrayed her feelings. I was abandoning her. Worse than that, my brother and I were both abandoning her. It was clear by this stage that Rajah and Ruky were going to have to, at some stage, move out. They needed their own space. And with Puli now saying she wanted to get married, it meant that after everything, my parents were going to be living alone. Their ultimate nightmare. It was left to Dad, with his emotional directness, to articulate their anxiety. He walked into my bedroom on the morning of the letter and asked:

'Isn't there a school . . .' Any educational establishment is a school for Dad '. . . a school you could attend in Wolverhampton?'

'*Dedi.*' I tried to force out a laugh. 'I'll be coming back all the time. Twice a month . . . or . . .' The commitment was already being diluted '. . . once a month at least. And I'll be here every Christmas and Easter and in the summer too.'

Mingled with the guilt was confusion at what had happened. On one level it was clear. I'd got a government-assisted place at an academic school where everyone was expected to apply for university. I'd done better than expected in my GCSEs. My enthusiasm for pop lyrics had developed into an enthusiasm for English Literature. I'd gone along with a teacher's suggestion I apply for Cambridge. I'd visited on an Open Day, I'd admired the lawns, my brother had loaned me his best blazer for the interview – 'You want to lend my jacket?' – I'd made a mental note not to get confused between 'borrow' and 'lend' in the interview, a softly-spoken tutor with an inability to make eye contact had asked me to discuss a Shakespearean sonnet I'd seen before, and when he asked why I wanted to read English, I'd quoted what C. S. Lewis had said about how we read to know we are not alone, adding that without art and literature and music, life would be utterly meaningless, a list of random and fucking painful events, and he had made a note about me on a form. A common enough grammar school tale.

But what had happened to my other ambitions? When did I stop wanting to work in a bank? Wasn't I still keen on maths? After all, I'd taken the subject for A-level alongside English and Politics. When had doing something I enjoyed replaced the need to make money and look after my parents? When did leaving home become part of the plan? My sisters would leave when they were old enough to have arranged marriages, but my brother and I were always going to be around. That's how our family had always worked: my father and Chacha looked after their mother and father, and my brother and I would look after ours. I could see that I'd got from A to B, but couldn't see why I'd done it.

This sense of disconnection remained as winter defrosted into spring and spring bloomed into summer. Sometimes I went to school, sometimes I didn't, and no one particularly cared either way. Sometimes I spent evenings at home, sometimes I stayed at Robin's or Dave's and no one particularly cared either way. I stopped socializing: my classmates were understandably whipping themselves into a frenzy as exams approached, and began the task of trying to fulfil their three, four and five A-grade offers with universities across the country; and I couldn't stand being treated like a lottery winner when I felt like death. I recoiled from family life too, sitting locked away in my bedroom listening to the Counting Crows, or reading Evelyn Waugh and occasionally trying to revise.

In the end I gave up preparing for exams and volunteered to paint the house. I did this for the same reason I volunteer to make the Christmas lunch every year: it is a way you can ask to be left alone, without being rude. Shut the door. Do not disturb. I'm busy doing something useful. Swaying on the tops of ladders, with blistered hands, I didn't feel so bad. I turned up to exams with flecks of paint in my hair, and made my way through questions with the aid of half-remembered essays and what I'd read in *The Times* that morning. On the last day of school I showed up, as tradition dictated, to sign the shirts of classmates I'd known for seven years, and to have my shirt signed in return. The only message I remember is: 'Don't kill yourself Sang'. It was no great loss when Mum stuck the shirt in the wash.

I visited the most prestigious temping agency in Wolverhampton the same day, and the day after I started as a laundry assistant at the hospital where I'd been born, where my sister had been committed, and where, unbeknownst to me, my father had been committed too. On paper, it was the worst job in the world, as it required standing at a conveyor belt for eight hours a day, next to three monosyllabic, bitter colleagues, sorting hospital sheets smothered in shit, pus, vomit and hunks of post-operative flesh. As it was high summer, some of this flesh would be partially decomposed by the time it arrived, and occasionally surgeons would leave scalpels in the bags, which, if they cut you in any way, would result in emergency tests for fatal diseases. But I didn't mind it. It was £4.50 an hour, better than the job I'd had at Burger King a couple of summers before, and the silence at the conveyor belt was golden.

Though I did eventually strike up an unlikely friendship with one of my embittered and monosyllabic colleagues: unlikely because, judging from the leaflets lying around the back seat of his Astra, he was a BNP sympathizer; and doubly unlikely because we bonded over his assertion one morning, made in response to something on the radio, that 'Billie Jean' was the finest pop song ever recorded. I suppose I could have used the admission to tackle his bigotry: to point out, for instance, that Michael Jackson was, at one point at least, black, and that the video 'Billie Jean' was not only a brilliant, hypnotic piece of choreography but culturally significant for the way it helped break down the race barrier on MTV. But I didn't. I simply used the remark as an excuse to enliven my conveyor belt hours with pop-related banter, discussing whether the Beatles were overrated, whether *Face Value* by Phil Collins was underrated, and arguing about who did the better version of 'The Look of Love': Dusty Springfield or Deacon

Blue.* This is about as principled as I get. Were I in charge of the Western World's War on Terror, I'd be issuing immunity to any terrorist demonstrating a passing knowledge of the Fine Young Cannibals' back catalogue.

I went to collect my A-level results one Thursday morning, before the start of the afternoon shift. By the time I'd arrived, everyone was celebrating or commiserating in the pub down the road, and the school corridors had never felt so empty. I looked up Dave's result first – all As. He was off to Cambridge too. Lock, who had ambitions to play drums in a rock band, was off to Lancaster. I didn't need to search for my name in the list: my grades stuck out among the battery size achievements of my former classmates: 'CAC'. I would have felt bad if the school hadn't already sent out a press release hailing the best set of results in its history and if Robin wasn't by this stage talking about quitting her job to follow her boyfriend to Italy, where she would take up a post as an English language teacher.

I made the mistake of responding when I got into work and my BNP friend asked me how I'd done.

'Bit shit.'

'Whatya get?'

'Two Cs . . .' I should have left it there. 'And an . . . A.'

Judging from his hooting, you'd have thought I'd just confessed to having spent a weekend shooting on Papa's estate in Norfolk. 'One got twoh Cs and an Ah grade in one's A-levels. Smashing! Orf to Oxford aaare we?'

'Cambridge actually.'

Our pop banter tailed off after that.

At home, the event of the summer was Puli's wedding. She'd been fixed up with a boy from India, hungry for a wife and a passport. I knew what I thought this time, but when I asked if she really wanted to get married, she said she did. She wanted to get on with her life, she said. Move on. Be normal. Which sounded fair enough. The wedding was meant to be a small affair, no party,

---

* Dusty Springfield, of course. The single most beautiful love song ever recorded.

259

a meal at the temple, but Punjabis are incapable of doing anything with any kind of subtlety, and soon an aunt in Grays was inviting a sister-in-law who was 'on holiday' from India, who was mentioning it to an uncle in Chandigarh, who was calling his brother-in-law in Wolverhampton, telling him to make sure he popped over to pay his respects – family is family, after all – and Mum was saying that, on reflection, we should probably invite the family who lived next door to us on Springfield Road (they had been so good over the business with the blackcurrants) and before we knew it, a crowd of what felt like 300 people was waving goodbye as Puli was driven off to her new life a mile away.

We all cried again, but Mum didn't stop, as she switched from the task of preparing my sister's trousseau to preparing my trousseau for university. It grew like a hillock on the bed my father would soon return to. Duvets; pillows; jars of Bombay mix; blankets; pictures of the Gurus; boxes of Weetabix and Shredded Wheat and Cornflakes; steel tins of sugar and spices, boxes of paracetamol; cups; saucers; plates; soup/cereal bowls; boxes of long-life milk (just in case); packets of Maryland Cookies; Penguin bars; prayer books I couldn't read; spoons; dinner knives; dinner forks; teaspoons; dessertspoons; dessert knives; dessert forks; serving spoons; a toaster, two sets of salt and pepper mills; a cheese grater; socks; Y-fronts; a saucepan . . .

I objected to the saucepan.

'Mum, I'll be eating in the canteen.'

'But you'll need a saucepan to make yourself tea.'

'I'll get a kettle.'

'A kettle?'

'Yes. Electric. Kettle.'

'You're going to have *gora* tea? You can't live on *gora* tea. There's no . . .' Her eyes were rolling. 'There's no *takat* in it.'

'There are millions of people in the country who make their tea by boiling water in kettles, and they are fine.'

'But you *like* Indian tea.'

'I like English tea.'

'Since when?'

'Since I started . . .' I couldn't actually remember '. . . working at the laundry.'

'You'll be saying you prefer that water the *goras* pass off as milk next.' Mum was still having gold-capped milk bottles delivered.

'Semi-skimmed milk is healthier, especially as Indians have a predisposition to heart disease.'

'Pah! Your grandfather lived to ninety and he ate a packet of butter a day.'

'*Mum.*'

'Look – I've bought it now, it's brand new. And it comes with your mother's love.' I knew what was coming next: she'd employed the same argument for the apron and the kitchen gloves. 'You should never deny a gift from your mother.'

The emotional tension intensified. Whenever a visitor popped over, Mum, mentioning the hillock, would say: 'It's like packing off a daughter in marriage.' Which, of course, translated: 'It's like losing a son.' I began having nightmares about the departure scene: my mother standing in the doorway, pressing money she couldn't afford into my hand; my father in tears; both running after the departing car, their feet splashing in the rain, screaming for it to stop.

It was a relief therefore when my parents accepted my brother's suggestion that they go to India for a holiday. He pointed out the facts: he and his wife could look after the house while they were away; he would help pay the fare; I was going to be away at college; the weather in India was lovely in September; their daughters were married; my mother was no longer working (the years of sewing had taken their toll on her back and shoulders, and she had retired out of ill health); and they hadn't been to India for more than fifteen years. And so Mum started packing, for the third time that summer.

They left early one morning, and in the end the only tears shed were my brother's. In my self-absorption, I'd not considered how he felt about things. He was married, had a swish job at an investment centre in Birmingham, was a rock for my parents and suddenly seemed so grown up. But still, he was only twenty-two, and the longest he had ever spent away from home was his honeymoon fortnight. The silence that descended upon the house when Mum and Dad left was deeper even than the one that had claimed the school corridors. It was as if some pandemic had claimed us all.

On my way back home after my last day at the laundry, I decided to take a trip down memory lane, or, more specifically, down Prosser Street, which was only a quarter of an hour from the hospital. It was a surprise to find the houses had all shrunk in size and that the alleyways we used to tear down had been gated shut, and a shock to find that Mrs Burgess's shop had been closed and boarded up. Somehow, I'd always expected it to be there. I stood on the corner, dismayed, remembering her funny expressions – someone with no hair had a head 'like a bladder of lard', posh people were 'all fur coat and no knickers' – and realized I'd never said goodbye. Was she still alive?

The plan was to go and see what had happened to our house, but when I looked down the street – somehow the houses that had been renovated in the eighties looked more in need of modernizing than those left untouched – I saw Chacha teaching me to ride a bike on the pavement, Baba heaving his extraordi-

nary frame out of our front door, six of his grandchildren scampering around him, Bindi coming back from work, smart and proud in her Safeway uniform, Rajah setting off to town in a white blazer with the sleeves rolled up (a look inspired by a Glenn Madeiros performance on *Top of the Pops*), my father taking me to school, Pussy and Lucky sunning themselves on a window ledge, Puli carrying home the bread and butter pudding she'd made in Home Economics, my cousin Nicki running down the street having been caught washing a kitten in a toilet, my cousins Pumi and Gurdeep playing hopscotch, Chachi hoovering the inside of Chacha's Cortina, Bibi off to the *gurdwara*, my mother beating a rug clean on a doorstep . . . and suddenly it seemed a better idea to catch a bus home.

The next day Robin and Steve drove me to Cambridge. They gasped when they saw the amount of stuff waiting to be loaded into the car, but didn't object when I said I wanted to take everything. Steve drove, Robin sat in the front, and I sat in the back, a box at my feet, a box on my lap and the handle of a saucepan digging into my ribs whenever we took a right turn.

18. Unfinished Sympathy

Mr Jonathan Robinson
Office Manager, Crown Court
Wolverhampton Combined Crown and County Court
Pipers Row
Wolverhampton
West Midlands
WV1 3LQ

Dear Mr Robinson,

My name is Sathnam Sanghera and I'm writing to request information related to a case that was heard by Wolverhampton Crown Court in the mid-seventies. I'm currently working on a family memoir which will need to mention the legal proceedings, and on a recent visit to your offices, I was advised that you were the best person to contact about accessing the relevant records in your archive. It was suggested I write to you, enclosing 'as much detail about the case as possible'. So, here, as requested, is the long story.

The case concerns my father, Jagjit Singh Sanghera, who is now aged fifty-six. At the time of prosecution in 1975 he was aged twenty-five, five years younger than I am now, a resident of the Park Village in Wolverhampton, and had been diagnosed with schizophrenia for more than five years. I am reluctant to ask him about what happened because he is still ill and I do not wish to distress him, and while my mother has been able to provide me a detailed account of what happened, she cannot recall the exact timings, the name of the lawyer eventually hired to represent my father, and, as she doesn't speak or write English, hasn't been able to provide precise details of the charges and plea entered: basic information I need to confirm before I set pen to paper.

You're not the first person I've tried to get this basic information from, Mr Robinson. I've submitted several subject access requests under the 1998 Data Protection Act with the West Midlands police force, using various spellings and misspellings of my father's name, but received letters back saying they can't help. I've written to the chief executive of the hospital where my father was treated following his period in custody, and received no reply. My family have requested to view my father's medical records, again under the Data Protection Act of 1998, but, for reasons I do not understand, the notes contain no reference to the incident that led to his arrest or to his subsequent treatment, and his GP, also for reasons I do not understand, has not responded to a request to discuss his recollection of events. Meanwhile, when I figured out that when my mother referred to Dad's time in 'Weesum Prison', she meant Winson Green in Birmingham, I wrote to the governor, asking whether the prison might have records of who was held in custody in the seventies and what for. A man from his office rang a few days later – some enthusiasm, at last, I thought – but only to say they couldn't help. They didn't have information going that far back, he said. Did he know of any way of getting hold of such information? No. Could he suggest the name of anyone who maybe worked at the prison in . . . Click. A dead line.

To be honest, this lack of helpfulness has come as a surprise, Mr Robinson. Before I started this project, I worked as a newspaper feature writer, and I very rarely had problems getting background information. I only had to mention the name of the artist, politician or entrepreneur I was writing about and suddenly young women called Lucy from PR departments across London were leaving voicemail messages mispronouncing my name and suggesting they supply the information required over lunch at Claridges. But with this, nothing. Perhaps this is what it is like not having the back-up of a major media organization? Or perhaps I am doing something wrong? Should I hand-write my requests? Or use a different grade of paper?

Frankly, I would have given up if I could, Mr Robinson. But

I can't. There's another letter waiting to be written, already years overdue, on which my own future depends, but I can't start that until I've laid out my parents' story on paper. Which is why I have recently resorted to spending days at the Wolverhampton Local Archive, flicking through copies of the *Express & Star*, around the dates I know my father was hospitalized in the seventies, on the off-chance that one of those committals was the result of the incident for which he was arrested, and on the off-chance that the local paper might have covered it. I have also asked a professional researcher to help me get the names and addresses of prison officers who worked at Winson Green in the mid-seventies, in the hope they might be able to suggest a way forward.

I was about to call one of these names when, sifting blankly through my mother's records, a thin and impenetrable file of Punjabi papers related to my father's land in India, I finally had a much overdue flicker of good luck when the following scrap of paper fell out:

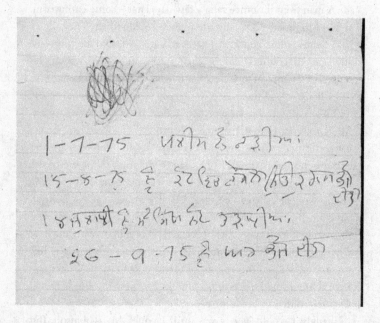

Although I spent most Saturday mornings of my early youth attending Punjabi school, I'm afraid I couldn't decipher my mother's handwriting, but I could see there were four dates – 1/7/75; 15/8/75; 18th something; 26/9/75 – and when I showed them to my mother, after a period of prolonged squinting, she said the dates were, according to her notes, when my father was 'caught by the police' ('*Police ne pharhiya*'), sent to court ('*nu court vich* [illegible word] *faisla karan bhej ditta*'), admitted to hospital (a guess, as this note was indecipherable), and sent home ('*nu ghar bhej ditta*'). She couldn't recall why she'd written the dates down, or how her previous estimate of the incident was out by some two whole years, but it didn't matter: finally I had some hard information, and I immediately caught the number 558 bus from my parents' house to the Wolverhampton Local Archive. On entering I once again noticed a poster advertising a 'family history course', and hoped that the tagline – 'Every family has a history and we've got a bit of yours' – might at last prove true.

At the microfiche reader, sitting between amateur genealogists who actually do this kind of thing for fun, I began by sifting through copies of the *Express & Star* around the first of those four dates, looking for a story that might mention my father: not the easiest task in the world, owing to the *Express & Star*'s refusal then – as now – to organize its news stories into sections. As you probably know, on one page you can get everything from a story about the Middle East, to a story about a local election campaign, to a tale about an abnormally large carrot grown by a boy in Pendeford, and you have to read it all, just in case you miss what you're looking for.

There was nothing of any relevance in the 30 June edition of the paper. And nothing of any relevance in the 1 July edition of the paper. But then, at the bottom of the third page of the Wednesday 2 July edition, next to a story about an annual garden party at the grammar school I eventually attended, and underneath a story about a woman appearing at the Edinburgh Sheriff Court being charged with murdering her two sons, there it was:

ACCUSED OF HARMING GIRL

A Wolverhampton man was remanded in custody for
a week by the town's stipendiary magistrate today
accused of inflicting grievous bodily harm on a 14-
year-old girl.

He is Jagjit Sanghera, aged 25, of Prosser Street.

I barely took a breath before loading the next reel. This time
the story leapt out from the pages of the Friday 15 August 1975
edition. It was set above a story about a Belgian being remanded
for attempting to murder a detective inspector and next to a story
about 'Europe's biggest international balloon contest':

MAN HIT GIRL, 14, ON NECK AND FACE

A 14-year-old girl was struck in the face and throttled
as she walked to school, Wolverhampton Crown Court
was told today.

As she was reeling back dazed from the blow, Jit
Singh Sanghera tried to strangle her.

He admitted unlawfully wounding the girl, and was
ordered by the court to New Cross Hospital, Wolverhampton, for treatment.

The court was told the girl was walking to school
along Prestwood Road, Wolverhampton, with two
friends.

Suddenly Sanghera, aged 25, of Prosser Street,
Wolverhampton, attacked her and then ran off.

The girl had a fractured nose bone and bruising on
her neck.

Sanghera told police: 'Some of the children had
been calling me names. She was laughing and I thought
she was laughing at me.'

I don't think I've ever thought and felt so many different things
at the same time as I did when I first read that story, Mr Robinson.

There was pity for the girl – that poor, poor girl; pity for my father – even after five years of treatment he was still seriously ill; pity for my mother – this was the kind of violence she had endured for years; weary amusement at the misspelling of my father's name as 'Jit' – which brought my running total of official misspellings of his name to eight; and the disorientation of having to tally my view of my father as a gentle and kind giant, with a man capable of horrific violence. Of course, I'd gone through a form of this when my mother had given me her version of events, but somehow it was different having it confirmed in English, in writing, in a newspaper I had begun my journalism career on, in a level of detail my father's medical records didn't go into – bizarrely, there is not a single reference to violence in his medical notes, beyond one letter from a psychiatrist which refers to 'episodes of apathy, unreasonable anger and suicidal thoughts'.

Mixed in this maelstrom of emotions was puzzlement. Why had my father spent six weeks in custody in a prison described by one official report at the time as 'a human dustbin' when he was a diagnosed paranoid schizophrenic? Surely he should have been submitted for hospital treatment straight away, rather than locked up? Did the family not arrange for a lawyer to represent him to make this simple point? My mother had mentioned that there had been an opportunity to get Dad out on bail when he was arrested, and that several members of the family were willing to arrange it, but apparently my grandmother, my father's mother, had refused to let them get involved, saying prison would teach her third son a lesson, that she didn't want any other members of the family to suffer if he transgressed bail conditions.

I don't know what your views are on people who offend while mentally ill, Mr Robinson. Given they probably account for the majority of your business – according to the Office for National Statistics, around 5 per cent of men in the general population have two or more mental disorders, compared to 72 per cent in prison – I wouldn't blame you for having harsh views. I used to be part of the lock-'em-up-and-throw-away-the-key brigade. But I've changed my mind. Jail is no place for the mentally ill. It's certainly no place for people with paranoid schizophrenia. Prisoners are required to follow rules, but how do you follow rules when your brain is malfunctioning? And judging from my mother's account of her visits, it sounds like my father's brain malfunction was worsening. She says he would spend the whole of every prison visit crying. One day he appeared with a wound on his forehead, saying he'd got it from banging his head against the wall of his cell. Could it have been he wasn't even getting the medication he had previously been prescribed?

Anyway, now that I had the court dates, I could go to Wolverhampton Crown Court, look up the records related to the case, find the name of the lawyer who eventually represented my father, and, if he was still alive, get some answers to these questions. And, after making copies of the two news stories, I headed off across the town centre to your offices on Pipers Row. Though I didn't go straight there – I went for a walk around the city centre first, and as I walked, and walked, and walked, I realized that the news stories, the confirmation of the dates, had fundamentally altered the way I viewed my parents' early marriage.

I don't know if you're a pop music fan, Mr Robinson. Even if you're not, you've probably heard of George Michael, and when my mother first told me what had happened, a few months ago, I thought of a line from 'Careless Whisper'. No, not the bit about guilty feet having no rhythm. The bit about there being no comfort in the truth . . . all you find is pain. The narrative just seemed to be a shapeless series of painful events. A list really. Accounts of family lives blighted by schizophrenia tend to be like this: because the drama is being propelled by an illness, there are no lessons learnt, no patterns, just random events. Often the painful narrative keeps lurching forward bleakly until the medication starts working or someone – usually the sufferer – dies. But now, with the dates of Dad's arrest confirmed, I thought not of the bleak line from 'Careless Whisper', but of an expression my mother would utter whenever I got over-excited as a child. 'SSSShhhhhh,' she would hush. 'Stop laughing so much. You'll only cry twice as much later.'

I grew up resenting the phrase, thinking it epitomized something rather joyless, if not at the heart of Punjabi culture, then at the heart of our family life. Mum is never more anxious than at a celebration, or on receiving good news, hovering around with red chillies to frighten away evil spirits, telling us to remember to thank God for our good fortune. I hate that I've inherited the attitude: sometimes I can feel the end of good things before I've even had a chance to enjoy them. But finally I understood why she was so fond of the saying: that's how life was for her. Whenever she laughed, she cried twice as much later.

Things, for instance, were looking up after the first time my father was hospitalized in 1969, following a violent mental breakdown when he was around nineteen. He'd been misdiagnosed, with depression, rather than schizophrenia, but was being treated for schizophrenia a matter of months later – it's unclear how or why this diagnosis was suddenly made – and soon after this my sister Puli was born. Even though there is a preference for boys among Punjabis – a son continues the family line and takes care of parents in old age, whereas a daughter joins another household – Puli was a sweet baby and the household, which included my father's parents and two of his siblings, was full of cooing and laughter for the first time since my parents had got married. He recovered enough to get a job at a local brickmaker's and when the family began discussing the possibility of buying a house of their own, rather than renting, my parents were able to pitch in for a share.

But then things went twice as wrong as they had gone right. My father had another violent breakdown when my mother was pregnant for the second time. Mum recalls him throwing a tray of hot food at her during supper. She ran out of the house, to a neighbour who had a telephone, and called the police. According to his medical notes, he was sectioned in January 1971. He clearly needed the treatment, but my mother's act of self-preservation further soured her relations with her mother-in-law: having previously accused her of making my father ill with black magic, she now accused her of sending him off to hospital for no reason.

The atmosphere soured further when my sister Bindi was born. She was just as adorable as Puli, but because there is a view in Punjabi households that a woman, in order to fulfil her marriage contract, has to produce male children – perversely, despite the abuse she'd endured, there was still a view that she had yet to earn her place in the family – my mother became the subject of bickering and mockery.

Nevertheless, things slowly began to improve again after my father was discharged from hospital. He got another job, and while he was still violent towards my mother (one of Puli's first memories is of Dad throwing china at Mum), and still had a habit of losing jobs (he lost one after threatening to attack a supervisor with a shovel), he got new jobs just as quickly, his sturdy physique making him naturally suited to manual labour, and eventually Mum, by concealing his employment and medical history, persuaded an Indian neighbour to give him a chance at Goodyear's, one of the best-paying factories in town.

She describes seeing his first wage packet – for £40 – as the first truly happy moment of her married life. It was twice what he'd ever earned before and Mum remembers using the money that started coming in to buy a sewing-machine, with which she began earning a little money on the side, and when her brother-in-law - my uncle, or '*chacha*' – was arranged in marriage and began talking about buying another house for his bride and his parents, four doors away, my parents were able to buy the family out of their share in the house.

This was a big moment. For Punjabis, a house and a family are intricately connected, a fact reflected in the language: the Punjabi word for house, '*ghar*', also refers to the domestic unit that lives in the house. There followed an even bigger moment: my brother was born. And what a boy too: from the beginning, the kind of infant who had uncles and aunties crossing the *langar* hall of the *gurdwara* to chuck his chin. After everything that had happened, I imagine my mother could barely believe her luck. After everything that had happened, I imagine my mother had never been so terrified.

True enough, for every one drop of happy, there were two drops of sad. A few months after my brother's birth, my father got into another fight with a colleague at work and was fired from Goodyear's. On 16 July 1973 he registered at the employment exchange, and this time demonstrated no desire to get another job. He sat around, overate, his weight ballooned, he developed diabetes, and my grandfather despaired. Dad's behaviour must have seemed obscene for a man who was still doing heavy manual labour after the official age of retirement. But what he saw as laziness and greediness was in fact a new manifestation of his illness. And in December 1973 my father was admitted to hospital yet again. A letter from a psychiatrist at the time explains that 'He'd been behaving strangely at home, wandering out into the road, spending most of his time in bed and overeating. He'd been referred for a course of ECT but the anaesthetist cancelled this because he was grossly obese. At this time he was displaying no bizarre behaviour but remained extremely lethargic and appeared to be hallucinating. He attended the day care unit five days a week and remained very reluctant to do any work. There was also a considerable language problem. The patient himself said that he felt better, but failed to show any great improvement.'

During this period my father's daily routine consisted of waking up late, walking to the local off-licence for a can of beer – Mum knew he shouldn't be drinking on his medication, but he would get money from relatives if she tried to stop him – and drinking it while walking around the streets. When he got to the local greengrocer's, he would always buy a banana and always eat it while standing on a specific street corner at a specific time. Often he would return home with complaints that the children walking past to and from school at lunchtime would tease him. 'Fatso, eating bananas,' he said they sang. 'Fatso, eating bananas.' Mum would tell him to ignore them, or, better still, not to stand there on the same spot doing the same thing every day, but Dad refused to disrupt his routine – he almost seemed drawn to the confrontation. Then he began complaining about one particular girl. She had it in for him, he said. She swore at him, he said. She needed to be taught a lesson. Could these insults have just been voices in his head? Regardless, they were very real to him because then . . .

Another of my sister Puli's early memories is of sitting crosslegged in the front room, playing with a doll, when the police came to arrest him. On reflection, it may not have been a case of one shot of happy, two shots of sad, by this point. The ratio may have been even more punishing. And to find out once and for all just how punishing, I headed off in the direction of the offices of the Crown Court on Pipers Row.

The sight of your offices took me by surprise, Mr Robinson. I watched the building go up in the nineties, with its reflective glass and cream stone, and went past it on the way to school for years, but somehow managed not to notice how smart it is. Admittedly, placing a cream building next to a bus station and overlooking Wolverhampton's busiest roundabout probably wasn't the wisest move. It could do with a wash. But otherwise it's great. I've been banging on about what a dump Wolverhampton is for years, but started to realize recently that it's actually not as bad as I remember. There are some nice buildings, some nice places to eat, a few coffee shops, and even the racial tension isn't as bad as before – you see interracial couples walking around town unselfconsciously, and there are even some Asian Goths.

Unfortunately, this good humour didn't last on entering. After leaving my dictaphone with security at reception, as requested, I went upstairs to your reception area, where I gave a short version of my parents' long story to a slim, friendly young woman at the front desk, who listened intently before referring me to a less slim, less friendly, and less young colleague, with the charm of a used dishcloth, who listened to my story until I got to the phrase '1975', at which point she raised her hand and remarked: 'I'm afraid we can't help yow' – Wolverhampton Crown Court has only existed since 1990.'

I opened my Fitness First rucksack – free when you join! – and showed her the newspaper cutting. 'It is from 1975 and refers specifically to Wolverhampton Crown Court.'

Her eyes passed over the photocopy before she half-turned and barked at an invisible colleague behind her: 'Oi'm roight, aren't I? The Crown Court didn't exist before 1990?' She gazed back at me. 'Most likely, if there are any records, they will be at the Magistrates' Court on North Street.'

'The Magistrates' Court?'

'Or they might be kept at the Dudley Crown Court.'

At this point I glanced down at my shirt and jacket and wondered whether there was something about my demeanour making this woman want to redefine the term 'unhelpful'. Admittedly, I could have looked smarter – my lumberjack shirt didn't go with my blazer, and there was a curry stain on my jeans – but I didn't look like a vagrant either.

'I'm sorry, I don't understand. Why would records for Wolverhampton Crown Court be kept at the Dudley Crown Court?'

'Well . . .'

'Look, it has taken ages getting to this point. Are you sure you don't have any records here? I'll be happy to go through them myself if necessary. I don't mind.'

'Yow wo' be able to do that.'

'Why?'

'Just bec . . .'

'Could I talk to someone in charge? Your manager?'

'He ay around.'

'Give me his name, and I'll write to him.'

'Send yower letter to the Crown Court.'

'Could I have a name, please? I know the letter will just get lost otherwise.'

'Address it to the office manager.'

'Does the office manager have a name?'

'Robinson.'

'Does Robinson have a first name?'

'Jonathan Robinson.'

'Thanks. And what should I write in this letter?'

'Write enclosing as much informayshun about the case as yow can. Yow will need to enclose a certificate of conviction and a case number.'

I don't know what was more preposterous: the idea that people get given certificates for conviction, or the fact that you have to produce basic information in order to get basic information.

'But that's the whole point. I don't have that information. That's the kind of simple stuff I am looking for.'

'I'm afraid it's going to be almost impossible for us to help yow.'

Of all the enervating conversations I've had recently, Mr Robinson, I think this chat took the biscuit. I left your office thinking I should find a hardware store, and return with a club to deliver 4,500 blows to the back of your colleague's charmless head. But I've had time to calm down since, and as spirit-crushing as the encounter was at the time, on reflection it was actually quite useful, because it has made me accept a few things about my predicament.

I have realized, for instance, that your colleague was actually right: it *is* going to be almost impossible to gather the evidence I'm looking for. There is no single reason for it: I'm not asking the wrong questions, or submitting my requests on the wrong type of paper. The problem is that there is an array of obstacles, ranging from the fact that my parents come from an oral culture (which means little written evidence exists), to the fact that they do not speak English (which means that any written evidence that did come into existence as a result of dealings with British authorities tends to be full of holes), to the fact that my father is an illiterate, uneducated, unemployed mentally ill Asian man (which means that officials who might be able to share written evidence with me can't be bothered to). You see, I have reluctantly and bitterly concluded that unlike the entrepreneurs, politicians and writers I used to interview for newspapers, my father doesn't matter in the eyes of society: he is not worth producing background information on.

The conversation has also helped me accept that my plan to write my parents' story as a piece of journalism is unrealistic. Not only because of the lack of corroborating evidence – so many family memoirs seem to rely on authors finding a cache of letters in an attic, but what do you do if your family don't have any letters? – and because there is too much narrative to try to corroborate, and because people don't want to give me the evidence, but because such an account would require me to present the evidence neutrally and dispassionately, and I can't do that. Moreover, I don't want to do that – I don't want these things not to upset me any more, and I don't want to doubt my mother's account any more – and it doesn't matter that I can't. My education – I did a degree in English Literature – and my career have instilled into me a view that there are two ways of writing about the world: through fiction, 'literature', where you can be ambiguous about things in artistic terms, and journalism, where you deal in truth and provable facts. But I realize now that this is a narrow view: something doesn't have to appear in the pages of a newspaper or between the covers of a novel to be true.

And perhaps the most important thing I've come to understand since visiting your offices, Mr Robinson, is that my efforts to reconstruct my parents' story have become unhealthy. Not only because I have let the search for evidence coagulate my life – it's important to know where you've come from, to unearth secrets, but it's also important to know when to let secrets go – but because my efforts have been disproportionately focused on the bad things that happened to my parents. I've been doing this because trauma and tragedy make a better story. But in life happiness is just as important, if not more so. And my parents' story, after my father's period in custody and subsequent treatment, did have a kind of happy ending. At least, the cycle of double tears was broken.

My mother tells me that after one of her prison visits, a Sikh prison guard approached her and asked why my father was always in tears. She gave him a short version of the story, and the prison guard pointed out the obvious, that he shouldn't be in prison, he should be receiving treatment in hospital, and he gave her the name and number of a Muslim lawyer in Birmingham who might, he said, be able to help. Mum visited this lawyer with my uncle Malkit, paid for his advice with the money she had earned from sewing whenever she wasn't looking after her three children or visiting my father in prison, and the lawyer got him out of jail and into hospital.

Dad never worked again and has little insight into what happened, but that hospitalization was the last he endured; he was never violent ever again – quite the opposite. Mum got him to give up drink, which was what was probably triggering his breakdowns, got him to lose weight, and then, in 1976, I was born. The years that followed weren't easy: my father continued to suffer from milder symptoms of the disease, and then, a decade later, my sister Puli fell ill with the same illness, but throughout, our parents loved us, Mum worked hard to raise the four of us and give us a happy life, and succeeded to such a degree that I spent my youth lost in a fug of pop music, and I didn't even realize my father had schizophrenia until my mid-twenties. In other words, she saved my father, she saved her children, and for that I do not need to gather any corroborating evidence, because my entire life, my entire record collection, is a testament to the fact.

So, on reflection, I've changed my mind, Mr Robinson. I'm not going to write my parents' story in the way I intended. And I don't need any information about those legal proceedings from you. Of course, you could send it anyway. But, let's face it, it's not likely, is it? Not only do I suspect you don't give a toss, but I've just done a little research and not only discovered several references to cases heard by Wolverhampton Crown Court before 1990 – your colleague didn't know what she was talking about – but I have also been unable to find a single reference to you, giving me the sneaky suspicion that you don't actually exist.

So this, in summary, is a letter to someone who might be a

19. It Ain't Over 'Til It's Over

You can shut the door on the past, but no matter how much you try to beat the present into submission, it keeps coming back at you, like those comedy birthday candles that refuse to be blown out, or, in the case of my family narrative, like the interminable drip, drip of Chinese water torture. No sooner had I packed away my 1800 x 1200mm professional dry-wipe magnetic whiteboard than it all kicked off again, this time with my sister Puli.

As with many of my family relationships, for reasons I have already banged on about at length, and the additional reason that my mother has systematically tried to shield me from potentially stressful aspects of her life ('I didn't want you to worry . . .'), I had let my relationship with my eldest sister drift. Weeks could pass without us talking, the lowest point being when she rang to tell me she had returned from a two-month trip to India, only for me to realize I hadn't even known she'd gone. But the task of reconstructing the family story brought us back into contact.

I was about to say that the fact we now talk most days was the most straightforwardly positive consequence of my time back at home, but few things about our family life are simple, and the re-established closeness has come pickled in guilt. First, there has been the guilt of simply having had so much better luck: we are members of the same family, bookends of the same set of siblings, but looking at our lives, you'd think we'd been born to different families on different continents. Whereas Puli had not lived up to her academic promise, for instance, I had outlived mine. While I had been permitted – albeit with intense emotional pressure – to procrastinate on the issue of marriage, Puli had married twice. While I had escaped many of the restrictions of Punjabi culture, by marrying an Indian with even more traditional ideas than our mother she had been dragged back into its worst aspects.

Most critically, while I had been spared mental illness, she had been afflicted with schizophrenia.

Then there has been the guilt of my past behaviour. In truth, I had deliberately and repeatedly abandoned my sister. I was aware, for instance, that her husband had once hit her, and that she had ended up back at my parents', as a consequence. Mum had only told me about it afterwards ('I didn't want you to worry . . .'), but even when I found out I didn't ask Puli about it. I told myself it was too late to do anything, that everything was fine now anyway, but the truth was that I didn't know how to handle it and I didn't want to puncture my dysfunctionally happy world with such stress and trauma.

However, getting a second chance, I promised myself, and my sister, that if she ever needed help again, I'd be there. She only had to call. Not that she did: she is fiercely self-reliant and my parents are always around to help anyway. But I kept on insisting, complaining that she struggled with things she didn't need to struggle with, and eventually she did it, she rang. I was in the reading room of a library in London when the phone went, and though I was at the time letting private numbers go straight to voicemail – to take an anonymous call was to risk having an unexpected conversation, and I wasn't ready for that kind of stress yet – for some reason I popped out of the reading room to answer it.

'Sorry for calling.' Puli always apologizes for calling.

'You all right?' I was whispering, to avoid disturbing the readers next door.

'Yes.' I could tell from her voice she wasn't. 'Actually, I went to see the psychiatrist today and during the consultation he said something that worried me.' She was reading from preparatory notes.

'What did he say?'

'I've been having these dizzy spells and headaches and muscle spasms . . .'

'Muscle spasms?'

'He sent me to have a brain scan a couple of weeks ago.'

'You didn't tell me.'

'Didn't want you to worry. And the doctor said the symptoms might just be side-effects of my medication.'

'Okay.' My heart was racing. 'And what did the results say?'

'The radiologist found . . .' The sound of a page being turned '. . . "a suspected tumour on the pituitary gland". Is that serious, do you think?'

I turned to face the wall I was leaning against, and struck my forehead on it. If our family had a coat of arms, it would need to feature an emergency siren, a broken heart, a hospital bed, an ECT machine and a bottle of pills.

'It depends,' I eventually managed to say. 'I had a lots of scans when I had my weird brain thing and sometimes what the doctors say can sound unnecessarily worrying.'

'He's sending me to see an endocrinologist.'

'Right.'

'And a neurologist.'

'Right.'

'I hope you don't mind me calling but I wanted to tell someone.'

'Mind? I'm glad you called. When is this appointment, with the endo . . .'

'Endocrinologist. They said they'd send it in the post.'

'In the post?' On private health I had an appointment with a neurologist within a day of my scare, but maybe this was normal on the NHS. 'Did he give an indication of how long it might be?'

'I should have asked, but it was quite a lot to take in . . .'

'Of course. Do you want me to call him and find out?'

'Can you?'

'I'll call him and find out how serious he thinks it is.'

'Okay, thanks.'

'Try not to worry. I'll go with you to the appointments.'

'You don't need . . .'

'Look, I insist.'

'Okay, that would be a help. One more thing.'

The extremity of my right eyelid flickered. 'Yeah?'

'I went to see *Snow White* yesterday with the kids.'

'*Snow White*?'

'The panto in Wolverhampton.'

'Oh . . . good.'

'The kids loved it and I found some bits of it funny.'

'That's great . . .'

I wondered, when I hung up, why she seemed so relaxed, and continued to be struck by her calmness in the weeks that followed, as I kicked bins and hyperventilated in hospital corridors. But I should have understood why: even a possible brain tumour isn't as bad as schizophrenia. In the course of my reading, I've come across a great many analogies that try to convey what it is like to have the illness: a telephone switchboard making faulty connections; a train gradually slipping off the tracks; an orchestra without a conductor; an engine without fuel. But none of these analogies, for me, convey the devastating effect the illness has not only on the sufferer but on everyone who knows and loves the sufferer. It isn't just a telephone switchboard making faulty connections, it's a telephone switchboard for the emergency services making faulty connections. It isn't just a train going off the tracks, it's a train carrying chemical waste going off the tracks. There are lots of horrendous diseases out there, that rob you of your dignity and bodily functions, that kill you, but to have one that robs you of your sense of self, makes you frightened of your own mind, those who you love frightened of you . . . There is little worse.

I'll save us all the precise details of the weeks of agony that followed, but, needless to say, it all began again: frustrating dealings with the NHS; a series of consultants, one more punchable than the next; the simultaneous desire to be there and to run away; the suspicion that some people just don't matter; the feeling of being overwhelmed by too much narrative; the intense wish that I had more money to make my sister's life easier, if only on a practical level. However, in the end, she had the tests, it was established that the tumour was tiny, and while it needed to be monitored, her symptoms were most likely side-effects caused by her medication, which might have to be changed.

I don't think I've ever felt as relieved as I did after the final appointment. I wanted to hire a Rolls-Royce, buy a crate of Cristal, and bathe in the contents while being driven at illegal speeds down the Stafford Road. But, instead, my sister and I settled for a celebratory cup of tea in the terraced house she shares with her husband – who has given up market-trading for taxi-driving – and two young daughters in Blakenhall, the area around the Dudley Road.

The size and inner city location of the house aren't the only things that remind me of the house we grew up in. The furniture, decor and layout are identical too, right down to the display cupboard in the front room. Though while ours was full of crystal glass – given to us by relatives who ran a taxi firm and received it as loyalty gifts from Esso – Puli's is full of photographs, of her two daughters and the four of us brothers and sisters when we were younger. Between the pictures, ornamental clocks, all set half an hour fast, a fact that always reminds me of a documentary I saw about Prince Albert Edward, who apparently devised the idea of 'Sandringham Time' for his estate, advancing all the clocks by thirty minutes to make the most of the winter daylight hours for his passion for shooting. Though the reason for Blakenhall Time is slightly less frivolous: the drugs Puli takes for her condition make her tired, late for things. Putting the clocks forward is a way of tricking herself into being on time.

I chinked my mug against hers when she came in with the tea.

'Congratulations!'

Puli smiled and laughed a laugh that reminded me of *gulab jamans* at Diwali and fairy cakes on Saturday afternoons.

'Sorry if I was a bit panicky through some of that. I could probably do with some of your medication . . .'

'Ha.' Puli kicked off her shoes, revealing bare feet. 'When I went for that CT scan I was talking to the nurse and said, "I'm worried I won't be able to look after my children if I get ill."

She just stared at me like I was . . . well . . .' It's weird how so many everyday expressions in the English language are related to insanity. 'I think she couldn't believe that I didn't see myself as ill. I take a list of medication that high, but I don't see myself as ill. I don't think she could believe I was functioning.'

'I don't know how you manage sometimes.'

'Probably looks easier than it is. One of the odd things is how much it changes. Last month I felt so good that I was thinking about getting a part-time job. But then recently even the house-work, and making the family dinner, seemed too difficult.'

'You have had all these problems recently, though.'

'True. And at least I'm not as bad as Dad. It's like that book said . . .' Puli is an E. Fuller Torrey fan too. '. . . I have a lot of the positive indicators for the illness, whereas Dad has a lot of the bad ones. Also, I'm lucky in that I've had an education, whereas Dad hasn't. And with that education, I've done work on myself – my own beliefs and faith – and that has helped me. Helps the kids are great too.'

I can vouch for my two nieces. Whenever I think of them now, I recall their behaviour during a recent weekend they spent with me in London, specifically a moment during our first day, when, after we had been to the London Eye, and before we had got to Buckingham Palace, it seemed they were struggling to keep up with me and Mum. When I asked if they were okay, they both said they were tired, but looking at their mother, I spotted the real problem: Puli was struggling to keep up, but they didn't want her to feel bad. And sure enough, when my sister admitted she needed to rest, and I arranged for a taxi to take her back to my flat, they sprang back to life and we spent the next three hours on the tourist trail. I suppose this is another thing about Puli's life that reminds me of the past. Her daughters' eagerness to please – it comes as no surprise that her eldest is top of her class in almost every subject – reminds me of how we used to be. In so many ways, schizophrenia continues to shape our family.

Puli put down her tea and asked, 'Do you mind if I say something?' If I had a penny for every skipped heartbeat . . . 'There's something I've been meaning to say.' She pulled out a sheet of A4 from underneath the table. It was covered in her handwriting, in three different ink colours. 'You remember when you started your book, you said if I wanted anything taken out or included, you would do it?'

Of course I remembered. And the surprising thing was that Puli barely asked for anything to be removed. When she called in tears after reading the first thing I sent, I thought I would have to give up on the idea of writing about our childhood. But it turned out she had not been upset about the things written about her, but by reading about me and Bindi transcribing the lyrics to 'Club Tropicana'. It had made her realize that while we were having fun, she was lost to her illness. So much of her childhood had been stolen from her.

'There's one thing I'd like you to mention . . .'

'Of course . . .'

'I've written it down . . . because . . .'

'I understand. I find it easier to say things in writing too.'

She began reading from her notes, laid out on her lap. 'You see, as a kid I always worked hard and was always busy. If I wasn't doing homework, I'd be doing housework for Mum, or cooking or doing *budria* or running errands like collecting medicines for Dad from the nearest chemist – it was a mile away. I never stopped, I was always doing something, but as I started to get ill, I started to slow down. And once I was on medication, I did less and less, began to sleep more, even in the day . . .' She turned the page over '. . . sometimes. And maybe because people didn't know I was ill or maybe they wanted to put me in my place, because Mum used to boast about me, they would often suggest I was being lazy. They would say things like: "Aren't you working? What do you do all day?" And that's all I want to say really. I'm not lazy.' I could see that she had written the following words in capital letters. 'I have never been lazy. I've had knock-backs and needed to take it easy sometimes but I've always tried to do something with my life . . .' The ink switched from red to blue. 'I have never stopped having goals. To be honest, especially a few years back, when the kids were small, I started achieving positive results. But the criticism continues and there is always someone, somewhere, by phone or at family gatherings, who will turn and say, "You still not working?" Sometimes the concern is genuine, but it's also cruel . . .'

I interrupted. 'Thing is, Puli, a lot of the family don't know you are ill. You're a victim of your success, in that way. People think you're fine.'

'Maybe that's true.' She folded over her notes and tucked them between the pillow and arm of her chair. 'It's still painful though. I've actually worked very hard, fighting against the symptoms and the side-effects of the pills, at the same time as cooking for my husband at three or four in the morning so he has hot meals to take to work, when he was on the markets . . . it can be so frustrating . . . sometimes I punch pillows in the living room to get rid of the frustration.'

'It must be so difficult.'

She placed both hands, palms down, on her lap. 'Anyway, another thing that Torrey book said was that people can reach their fifties and sixties and then the illness can just go, for no reason.'

'Did it say that?' I took a biscuit. 'It's a strange illness. Another weird thing is how it tends to strike people at a specific age, whereas many other mental illnesses, like depression, can strike at any time.'

'I think I would have got stronger if I hadn't got ill. I had enough strength with my education, to get out of the trap. I would have gone to university, escaped, but then the illness got me again. I can't help thinking my life could have gone a different way.'

'It could have . . .' The guilt.

'And I can't help wondering why it happened, what it was that triggered it.' She scratched the back of her hand, leaving red marks that quickly faded back to brown. 'Why did two people in our family have to get it? But then I suppose bad things happen to people all the time, and I should count my blessings. At least the kids are healthy and, you know, at least I don't have a brain tumour.'

Laughter in the dark.

She bent over, put her hand underneath the base of her armchair, rummaged around and pulled out an empty crisp packet.

'The kids! God, they just don't listen!' A glance at the clock: 1500 hours Blakenhall Standard Time. 'Do you mind if I shoot off now? I've got to pick them up from school.'

★

Everyone affected by the illness in the family, even those who didn't realize it was an illness, has, inevitably, like Puli, wondered why. And they have all come up with different answers. For my grandmother, my father fell ill because my mother, for some perverse reason, had dabbled in black magic and put a spell on him. According to an uncle, my grandfather believed my father got ill because a bull had kicked him in the head when he was a child. According to another uncle, my father's 'blood pressure was too high and the doctors reduced it with electricity', i.e. ECT.

As it turns out, these explanations aren't much more preposterous than many of those put forward in the West. At various points through history, mental illness has been blamed on the devil, masturbation, character weakness, and for much of the twentieth century many blamed bad mothering: so-called 'schizophrenogenic' mothers were thought to have so corrupted their child's development that when their offspring entered the real world, they went mad.

Meanwhile, there are real people in the real world today who argue that schizophrenia doesn't actually exist. Thomas Szasz, an American psychoanalyst commonly cited by Scientologists, argues, for instance, that people with schizophrenia have a 'fake disease', that schizophrenia fails to stand up to scientific scrutiny, that psychiatric practice is nothing more than a legitimized form of social control that uses medical terms such as 'treatment', 'illness' and 'diagnosis' to deprive 'sufferers' of their liberty.

Evidently, what Szasz needs is a 'kick' in the 'bollocks', but the reason people like him are able to get away with such ludicrous arguments is that nobody knows why people get schizophrenia. Even if you persevere with the eye strain engendered by reading scientific papers with titles like ORBITOFRONTAL CORTEX VOLUME LINKED TO BEHAVIORAL AND NEUROPSYCHOLOGICAL DYSFUNCTION, the only thing you'll discover is that there is as much agreement about the causes of schizophrenia as there is agreement about the meaning of Shakespeare's plays.

All that can be said is that there are interesting patterns. It has been variously established, for instance, that individuals with schizophrenia are born disproportionately in the winter and spring, are born and/or raised disproportionately in urban areas, that the prevalence of schizophrenia is significantly higher among higher castes than among lower castes in India. Other curious research findings include reports that sufferers have more complications during their mothers' pregnancies and births, the discovery of an inverse association with rheumatoid arthritis – individuals with schizophrenia almost never get it – and the fact that while the majority of individuals with schizophrenia smoke cigarettes, the lung cancer rate among them actually appears be lower than in the general population, not higher, as you might expect. And then, of course, there is the fact that the disease runs in some families.

Which brings me to the subject of Miha Singh, referred to simply as 'Meemal' in documents relating to my father's farmland: my father's grandfather, my grandfather's father, the head of the family, whose farmland my father would have spent his life cultivating if he hadn't come to England, whose farmland I will in part inherit one day. Of course, I had enough on my hands trying to get my head around my parents' story, but Meemal's name kept on cropping up during conversations, and five facts about his life intrigued me: (i) he had only one son, my grandfather (and such a low number is unusual in my family); (ii) he died young (when my grandfather was just ten, apparently); (iii) he was a teacher in Patiala (which is odd given how poorly educated my family are); (iv) my aunt Bero claimed he had 'the ability to listen through walls'; and (v) his wife left him for another man in the village.

My mother fell silent after blurting out this last fact. 'I don't want to be advertising such scandal,' she remarked when I pressed for further information. '*Imagine what people will say.*' Which gives you a sense of just what a big deal this was. Nearly a century may have passed, and Mum is only related by marriage, but she still feels intense shame. I continued to get the tight-lipped gypsy treatment whenever I raised the subject with relatives passing through my parents' house. 'Well, she was a whore,' remarked one elderly and distant relative. 'That's why she left him. She behaved like a white woman.' Another two relatives mentioned that Meemal beat his wife. Why did he beat her? 'His brother worked on the farm and was envious of his life as a teacher,' said one. 'So he fed him stories about how his wife was misbehaving when he was away and that made him angry.' But another came up with an infinitely more intriguing explanation. 'He went mad. He became so educated that he went insane.'

This wasn't the first time I'd come across the notion that education could send you around the bend: my mother spent most of my degree worrying that my reading was going to make me loopy. But it was the first time it had occurred to me that Meemal, the head of Dad's family, may have suffered from schizophrenia, that three generations of my family might have had the disease.

It was a fascinating question, but also a question I couldn't possibly answer. The disease is hard enough to diagnose in the living – let alone in someone who has been dead for almost a century – and given the difficulties of assembling my parents' narrative, I had no chance of finding out what happened two generations ago. Punjabi genealogy is a futile business: no amount of tapping names of relatives into census-return websites, travelling to places of historical significance at visually striking times of year, was going to fill in the gaps.*

But coming back from Puli's, her question why ringing in my ears, I felt I should at least pursue the mystery as far as I could, which, as it happens, wasn't very far at all: all I had to do was walk thirty seconds down my parents' street to visit my Pindor *bua*, aged sixty-nine, and the eldest surviving member of my father's family. Her husband, my uncle Malkit, was there and we ended up spending several hours talking about what happened in the seventies, and eventually, after what must have been my ninth cup of tea that day, I put the question to her.

'Did you ever meet Meemal?'

'No, he died when your Baba was young.'

'Did Baba talk about him?'

'Yes. He told me he was a teacher. And that he died early.'

'What happened to him?'

'Your Baba used to say he had come back from teaching, was in the village on holiday, when he went to talk to a man at the *khuh* who knew black magic. Apparently, he asked the man to be taught it and it was while dabbling in black magic that something happened to his mind. He never went back to teaching. Lost his job, started living on the *khuh*, died quickly.'

'It was black magic that sent him mad?'

'That's what Chacha used to say.'

It was at this point that I made my now well-practised Punjabi speech about schizophrenia: explaining that it was the disease that had made my father violent all those years ago; that it was the

---

* The most a British Punjabi genealogist can hope for is that after months of research, and recurrent visits to the subcontinent, he will discover a small parchment helpfully informing them that his father's father was a farmer, that *his* father's father was a farmer, and that *his* father's father was a farmer too. Doubtless, future generations of Sikh Punjabis in Britain will have a similar experience when they learn that their father's father was an IT consultant, that *his* father was an IT consultant and so on, back for two centuries, until they eventually discover that – shock, horror – one of their original ancestors was a farmer.

disease that had hospitalized my sister twenty years later; and after I let her recover from the revelation, I put it to her directly.

'Do you think Meemal could have had the same illness?'

'I don't know.' She adjusted her *chuni* as her eyes brimmed with tears. I remembered my aunt in Grays, her sister, doing the same. 'I can only tell you what I was told by Chacha. I didn't see it happen, you see. I never met him. It's possible, though. You've got to remember that your Baba didn't have much education. But I suppose he could have had the same illness. Maybe.' She gazed through her double-glazed patio doors, at the perfect vegetable patch beyond. We had tried to grow vegetables in our garden when we first moved down the road, but the plants had failed to thrive in the compacted soil. 'You know what they used to say about him? They used to say they chained him up. When he started going on about how he wanted to beat people up and kill them, they tied him up at the *khuh* . . .'

Not that any of this gets us closer to an answer to why. As E. Fuller Torrey observes, to say a disease is familial is merely to say that it runs in families; it doesn't tell you why it does. Moreover, the genetic picture about schizophrenia is murky. The disease runs in some families, but many people who develop the illness have no family history of it at all. And the fact that a second identical twin has only about a one in four chance of also getting it means that non-genetic factors must be important. Some researchers even suggest that living in a city is a more significant risk factor.

My point is simply this: maybe, if my great-grandfather's (possible) mental illness had been discussed and acknowledged within the family, then maybe, when my father started showing signs of psychosis, he would have got the treatment he needed sooner, and maybe my mother would have been spared the violent attacks she endured, and maybe she wouldn't have been blamed for the illness, and maybe the family would have made more of an effort to ensure my father stopped drinking, which might have meant he had fewer relapses and wouldn't have throttled that poor schoolgirl, and maybe, if these things had been understood

20. If You Don't Know Me By Now

ਵਾਹਿਗੁਰੂ ਜੀ ਕਾ ਖਾਲਸਾ ।
ਵਾਹਿਗੁਰੂ ਜੀ ਕੀ ਫਤਿਹ ।।

My dearest Mother

There's something important and difficult I've been meaning to tell you and because it's easier to be brave on paper than in person, I thought I would do it by writing this, my first ever letter to you. But now I'm sat here, I wonder whether it's such a good idea. The way I write English is different from the way I speak English, the way I speak English is different from the way I speak Punjabi, and like all mothers and sons, we have been conditioned into communicating with a certain degree of intimacy and distance, so it's possible you won't even recognize my voice in this. But with no better options coming to mind, I will try to do what seems so difficult: stop worrying, trust my translator and hope for the best.

Anyway, as I said, I have something important to tell you, and it relates to the book I've been working on for the past eighteen months. There were a great many reasons why I wanted to write it – to make sense of how Dad's and Puli's lives have been affected by their illness, to attempt to rescue their experiences from oblivion – but one of the reasons I persisted even when it became very difficult was my desire to create some kind of tribute to you. I've always thought you were amazing, Mum. I know you must sometimes think I don't listen when you complain about your ailments, but I know it was all those days at your sewing-machine, to make sure we were clothed and fed, that have left your body wracked with aches and pain, and I know I complain you nag, but I understand your phone calls and advice are just your way of saying you wish you saw more of me. But knowing now what you went through with Dad, and then again with Puli, that admiration has deepened.

I was puzzled when I discovered the extent of their illnesses, wondered how I hadn't worked out they were so sick sooner. But now I understand one of the main reasons is that you shielded me from the harshest aspects of the truth, to ensure I had an untroubled childhood. And that's what I had, Mum. Nearly all my memories of growing up are of feeling loved and happy. You have always given me the support I needed, have taught me the value of hard work, and the importance of keeping the show on the road. Without you and Dad, I'd be nowhere. And without you, Dad would have died, killed someone or – I'm just quoting his psychiatrist here – ended up in a home of some kind. I can't say it has been easy hearing your story, and I know I haven't done it the justice it deserves, but I needed to get to the end because I want everyone willing to listen to know what happened and to understand that there isn't a son on this earth who loves and respects his mother as much as I love and respect you.

However, there is another reason I needed to lay out your experience, a reason I have, I'm afraid, deliberately concealed from you. You see, as well as being about you and Dad and Puli, the book is also about me, a letter from me to you, explaining what I want to do with the rest of my life and why. Of course, the only problem with this is that you won't actually be able to read it. Hence this: a letter, digesting the letter. And to digest further, my message to you, Mum, is this: I love you and I appreciate everything you have been through and done for me, but I am not going to marry a Jat Sikh girl just to please you. This isn't because I have someone unsuitable in mind I want to marry. I'm not seeing anyone. It is simply that I want to marry someone I love, rather than someone who fits your criteria.

I know this will come as a disappointment to you. So much so that you might stop reading at this point. Which is why I'm getting my translator to make a tape recording of these words, so

I can force you to listen to my arguments even if you refuse to read them. And the first of my arguments is simply this: I don't believe it is right, morally speaking, even on the terms of the Sikh religion, to pick a spouse on the grounds of caste and religion. Indeed, when Guru Nanak established our faith, one of his motivations was to free people of the burden of caste. 'Caste is worthless and so is its name,' he wrote in the Guru Granth Sahib. 'For everyone there is only one refuge ... Recognize the light, do not ask about caste.' Furthermore, it was one of the founding principles of our religion that people should not discriminate on the basis of religion. 'God is in the Hindu temple as well as in the mosque,' wrote Guru Gobind Singh. 'God is addressed in both the Hindu and the Muslim prayer; all human beings are one though they may appear different ... They are all of one form and one God has made them all.' If this is true, then why should it be wrong to marry someone of another caste and religion?

Maybe you'll reject such reasoning as perverse. Sikhs have had a caste system, in defiance of the founding principles of their religion, for centuries, and have married within their religion for just as long. Why should I be an exception? Well, Mum, with your encouragement and support, but also because of good luck and my own hard work, I have benefited from an education, and that education has taught me how to think for myself. Sometimes I think you think learning is like something you might buy from a shop, like a new washing-machine or refrigerator: something that improves your life without changing you. But that's not the way it works. My education has changed me, and just because everyone else does something, it doesn't mean I have to. And just because you believe something, it doesn't mean I have to agree.

We've had such different lives, Mum. By the time you were thirty, you had been ripped away from the family that had brought you up, married off to a violent, mentally ill man you hadn't met until your wedding day, were providing for four children and an unemployed husband, and for support you had to rely on a family who didn't always respect you. Meanwhile, you didn't speak the language of your adopted country, your view of the world was informed by just four years of education in India, you had never had a conversation with a white person, had never worked alongside a man, everyone you knew was from India, and work was something everyone around you did to survive.

At the same age, I am unmarried, with no children. I am lucky enough to be surrounded by both family and friends I love. I have a job which involves me using the language of the country I live in – a job I do because I love it, not to survive. I've had eighteen years of education – free education, thanks to the great country I've been allowed to grow up in. I work alongside men and women, I have male and female friends and I have a million and one opportunities within my grasp. And yet you still want me to live my life as if I am a Punjabi farmer in the 1950s. Surely you must understand why I might find this difficult?

The world has changed. Even India has changed: people have started marrying outside their caste there. It is only a matter of time before it starts happening in our family: the next generation growing up in this country, your grandchildren, and their children, will marry who they want. But you never acknowledge it. You get upset when a cousin marries a Sikh boy from her own village. I suppose I could just accept it as my destiny not to enjoy such freedom, but I don't want to live a partial life. I want to make the most of the freedoms I've been granted and I want to end up with someone who wants to be with me for who I am, not for what I am.

Having said that, it would be disingenuous of me to suggest my decision is entirely intellectual or moral. I think I believe in God. Or at least I believe we all have to answer for our actions, in one way or another, eventually. And if I had to pick a religion according to its founding principles, I would pick Sikhism. But I'm no saint, and many of my reasons for giving up on the arranged marriage thing are personal. Among them there is the simple fact that in the more than twenty set-ups I've had with Sikh girls over the last decade, I've not come close to finding someone I could spend the rest of my life with. And God, I've tried. There was even a Sikh doctor I spent three months dating, even though it was evident from the beginning we had little in common, that our personalities did not mesh in any way. I told myself I wanted to give you what you wanted, that I could bury my true desires to make you happy. But it slowly became apparent I could never go through with a marriage where I didn't love the other person. I want more from my life than that.

And this is the thing: I have had more from life than that. I've loved and been loved back and now I know what it feels like, it's impossible to settle for less.

I don't think you'll be that surprised to learn I've had a couple of relationships with girls who were not Sikh or Jat. English girls. They didn't work out. They may have ended for other reasons anyway, but one of the problems has been that I was too scared to tell you about them. And even though they failed, the relationships changed the way I see things. I've been racking my brain trying to think of how to convey to you what it is like loving someone and being loved back, mentally thumbing through the thousands of songs and books and poems I've come across on the subject during my life, but on reflection, I don't think I need to try. It is because you have loved me that I know how to love others.

There was one English girl I think you might have really liked. I know she would have liked you. She was always asking about my family and my background and my religion, and though you never met, I told her about you and she thought you were amazing.

And this is another thing, Mum: I think you assume that anyone who is not a Jat or a Sikh cannot understand our culture, that if I married someone who was not Jat or Sikh, you would lose me. But that's not the way things need to be. I would never be with anyone who didn't respect my background and family. And, if anything, if you accept me for who I am, rather than who you want me to be, we could be closer. The reason I haven't come home to Wolverhampton much in recent years, why I don't invite you to London so often, is that I've had to keep my two lives separate, to stop you from finding out about things. But if you accepted me for what I was, there would be no need for secrecy and separation. You could come and stay with me in London whenever you wanted. I would love you to meet my friends and they would love to meet you and maybe stay with me in Wolver-hampton sometimes.

I don't think you understand just how difficult it has been for me. In trying to please you at the same time as trying to have the life I want, I've done things I'm not proud of. I'm particularly ashamed of the arranged marriage meetings I went on to just keep up a pretence. There was the guilt of lying to whoever I was going out with at the time piled on to the guilt of lying to the girl I was being introduced to, piled on to the guilt of lying to you. During some of those meetings I acted obnoxiously on purpose, so the girl would refuse me and save me the difficulty of having to explain it to you.

And then there has been all the help and advice I have sought. I'll put it in monetary terms, because I know it's a good way of getting things across to you. Apart from the tens of thousands of pounds of debt I've got into since quitting my job, to build up to this, for the past few months I've been seeing a therapist once a week, at a cost of £90 an hour, and, in addition, I recently spent £120 on a session with a 'life coach' called John Rushton, whose specialist area of expertise, despite being an Englishman, is emotional blackmail in Asian families. I arranged to meet him at the Ramada Hotel in Ealing Common (the taxi cost £15), bought some drinks (£9), and told him about my predicament.

He listened carefully, made notes and at the end told me my situation wasn't in the least bit unusual: he'd come across hundreds of men and women facing the same dilemma, men and women you'd think were on the top of the world with their successful careers and money and houses and cars, but who were in fact tormented by their parents – mostly their mothers, it has to be said – who wanted them to fulfil a role they felt they couldn't. He said the pressure had led to nervous breakdowns and suicides and I needed to resolve matters before the stress and anxiety enveloped me entirely.

Afterwards he sent a letter reiterating the advice. 'You have a RIGHT to live regardless of ANYONE else, Santham (sic),' he wrote. 'You are 100% entitled to a happy life, Santhan (sic), you live your life for no one else, ever. You are responsible for your life, no one else ever . . . The biggest hurdle you'll ever have to overcome is you. Not your mum . . . You don't have to be rude, but you have to be FIRM, to the point, strong, and ask her, "Do you want me to be happy?" . . . Santham, you have a choice, it's a big choice. You have the potential for a great future with emotional security, happiness, love, joy, passion and harmony, or you will go forward with a mental "toothache" that will strike at any given moment when your guard is down. Don't live in dread. Life is really too short . . . If you want to marry a Zulu girl then OK, go for it, you have to live with her, no one else. And that is that. That is the whole reality of it all.'

As it happens, I don't think that is the 'whole reality of it all' at all. I don't subscribe entirely to the Western view that individual happiness is all that matters, that there is no such thing as duty. I owe you a great deal. I have responsibilities to you and Dad in your old age, and I have to make sure Puli is okay. But I do not owe you my happiness and the happiness of some poor unsuspecting girl whose life I could ruin by marrying her, just to please you.

Sometimes I struggle to understand why you are so insistent on the arranged marriage thing, when you have suffered so much yourself. Maybe it all comes down to pride and *izzat*. You worry about what the Punjabi community in Wolverhampton and the extended family might say about me, about you, if I don't do the expected thing. And doubtless some of them might say bad things. But I don't care. And I don't understand why you do. I know many members of the extended family have been good to you, and I am fond of most of them, but some of them have blamed you for Dad's illness, have accused you and continue to accuse you of dabbling in black magic, and now some cross the road when you walk down the street, and refuse to eat food in our house because they think you will put something in it to curse them. Do you *really* care what they think? I certainly don't want to sacrifice my life and happiness, or live my life in the shadows, to impress them.

Indeed, while there was a time when I thought I could carry on living my secret life in London indefinitely, it has become untenable. The strain of all this deceit has had a cumulative effect on my happiness and relationships and that is why, after a decade of keeping things to myself, this public act seems necessary. And I should be clear here. When I say the book is also about me, I mean it mentions some of my relationships. This letter is going to be a chapter, and your response the final chapter. You can decide how it ends.

If it sounds like I'm blackmailing you, it is because I am. I've always sensed a struggle in you between the Punjabi values of your parents and your natural intelligence, a struggle between your *izzat* and more modern ideas, and my hope is that with this I can drag you out of your Punjabi world into my world.

So this is what I want from you, Mum. I want you to stop insisting I marry a Punjabi Jat. Of course, it is possible after all this pain and agony that I will meet one anyway, but it is not something I will do with a gun held against my head. I want you to meet my friends and accept them. I want you to come and stay with me more in London. I want you to promise you won't try to get any of the family to change my mind – I will refuse to discuss things with them. I want you to accept this decision as my own. And if you have any problems with what

I'm saying, I want us to have a calm discussion, without screaming and tears. For once in our family life I want us to deal with something important without *tamasha*. For once in my life, I need to feel that you love me unconditionally, the way I love you.

ਸਤਿਨਾਮ

21. Postscript: Freedom (Back to Reality Mix)

The plan was to just do it. Discussing the letter with a family member was to risk attempts being made to discourage me, innocent victims being caught up in the crossfire afterwards, and news leaking out in advance. But I found myself blabbing it all out to my brother anyway. We'd met for a drink and a movie in London (he was in town on business, I was having a break from Wolverhampton) and he'd asked if I was seeing anyone – I'd given him an edited version of my relationship history by this stage, but the language of relationships still didn't flow easily between us, and it all came out in a weepy, anxious mess.

When he turned a disconcerting grey colour I tried to lighten the mood by asking: 'So you think Mum's going to kill herself then?'

An answer came after he'd polished off the remainder of his lager in a single mouthful: 'Yeah.'

But a few minutes later, he was saying: 'Actually, I think she'll take it okay. Whatever happens, I'll support you.'

The expression of solidarity was welcome, and the contradictory prediction oddly reassuring too: at least it showed I wasn't being crazy in having absolutely no idea how Mum might react. As part of my preparation, I'd come across a book called *Acts of Disclosure – The Coming-out Process of Contemporary Gay Men*, by Marc E. Vargo – and was struck by how much of it related to my situation. 'As it stands, too many gay people respect other people's feelings more than they respect their own, at times being too selfless for their own good. In some cases, this is because the person was brought up to think primarily in terms of the needs of others . . .' Yes! 'Most sons tell their parents because they want to be honest with them. It is often that simple . . . In fact, not doing so may cause his relationships with them to feel unreal, partial and deceitful . . . Still others come forward because they are tired of living two separate lives.' Yes! 'Camouflaging one's true sexual nature can become increasingly tedious over the course of time.' Yes! But the thing that struck me most in the book was the simple observation that 'parental reactions are not predictable'. I didn't, in truth, think my mother would top herself, but in my darkest moods I did think disowning was a possibility, which was almost as terrifying. At my most optimistic I let myself hope she would be hysterical for a while but eventually accept my decision. *Acts of Disclosure* mentioned a study which said it generally took parents two years to accept a son's homosexuality. Two years seemed to be the most I could hope for.

The conversation with my brother was important in another respect, in that it made me realize I hadn't thought through the practicalities of my plan properly. I was intending to hand the letter to Mum in Wolverhampton, switch off my phone, go for a long drive – Scotland was meant to be lovely at this time of year – stay at a country house hotel where the staff were surly and the chef had ideas above his station, and return to face the music a couple of days later. But it was becoming clear that not only would my time away be drenched with nervous apprehension, it would also be selfish to leave my siblings to deal with the fallout, unfair on my mother not to be around to clarify things that weren't clear, and dangerous to leave her to discuss the matter with people who would only reinforce her view of the world. The better thing to do, I realized, would be to drag her into my world, to be there immediately afterwards, to force her to talk to me directly without anyone else getting involved. If I was finally to become a man, I shouldn't be scampering away like a pre-teen girl teased for having the wrong type of Barbie doll.

So I invited Mum to spend a weekend with me in London: the first whole weekend we'd ever spent together, alone. I told her I needed to run what I'd written about her and Dad past her – which was true; that she needed a break – which was true; and I posted her a return train ticket to London. Unfortunately, there was a large gap between arranging this, getting the letter translated and Mum's arrival, during which time I lost and regained my nerve a thousand times.

The first wobble was instigated by my translator, a young and efficient linguist from Patiala in the Punjab, where my great-grandfather was a teacher, as it happens, who had responded to an advert I put on a website for freelance translators. I had made it clear to him from the beginning that I didn't want advice about the content of the letter – the last thing I needed was to be made to feel guilty by a stranger – and that he was not to discuss the letter with anyone; such is the efficiency of the links between the Punjab and Wolverhampton that it would be the gossip of the Dudley Road in no time. He behaved himself. But when he emailed a question about the source of my religious quotations ('Can you give me the Punjabi (source) for this???'), I panicked. I'd taken the words from the internet and had obviously never actually sat down and read the whole of the Guru Granth Sahib in original text. Maybe something had been lost in translation. Maybe my arguments were more outrageous than I realized.

The teeter threatened to turn into a tumble when the recording of the translation arrived. He'd done a great job: it was technically perfect and clear. But so much of what had seemed passable in English didn't seem so in Punjabi, in someone else's voice. The coy Punjabi vocabulary for relationships – 'girlfriend' became 'friend'; 'love' became 'like' – made me cringe. The Punjabi for 'love' – '*pyar*' – seemed pregnant with unintended sexual implications. The Punjabi for 'English girl' – '*gori*' – seemed implicitly racist. The phrase 'gun against my head' sounded too literal, many of my analogies seemed preposterous and elsewhere, whole sentences – 'I want to end up with someone who wants to be with me for who I am, not for what I am' – sounded like I'd picked random lyrics from love songs and put them through one of those internet translators. Listening to the sound file, what had seemed like a good idea months earlier, next to the Man on the Horse, and later, after the first of those consultations with Dad's psychiatrist, suddenly seemed crass and cruel, like a naff reality TV programme.

I think I might well have given up, if Mum hadn't called to recount a conversation she'd had with a neighbour in which the neighbour had apparently said: 'He is thirty years old and he has never had a girlfriend? I don't believe it.' I managed to change the subject but realized that if I didn't have the conversation soon, things were going to come to a head in a way I wouldn't be able to control. There was never going to be a good time to do it. It was never going to be easy. So I edited the letter, making it shorter and clearer, removed some of the analogies and the stuff about the life coach, altered some of the vocabulary, sent it back for re-translation, and though the recording still made me cringe, I settled for it.

I spent the wide-eyed night before Mum's arrival running through my mind all the things I would rather be doing the next day than confront her. In the morning I woke up and threw up. And I nearly threw up again when I saw her arrive at Euston, with the inevitable two carrier bags of food. Mum is such a strong presence in her world, but out of context she always looks vulnerable. I used to hate it when she visited me at college: I'd feel hyper-protective to the point of almost physically lashing out at anyone who didn't open a door quickly enough, or stared a little too long. And while, in normal circumstances, I'm about as forceful as a hamster, I once even found myself shouting at a member of ground staff at Heathrow Airport who had barked at Mum for not following his English instructions. On the train station concourse, the urge to protect her returned. But I wasn't looking after her, was I? Quite the opposite.

The nausea – it didn't help remembering that Euston was where Mum had been dropped off when, still a teenager, she had run away from Dad in Essex – subsided by the time we sat down on a bench a half-hour walk away. After weeks of trying to think of a way to treat her in London, taking Mum to Regent's Park was the only thing I'd managed to come up with. She really is the hardest person in the world to show a good time. You can't take her to the theatre or the cinema, because you'll annoy the people around you with the running translation. You can't take

her out to eat because of her strict religious observance in relation to food. Furthermore, she can't stand money being spent on
anything that doesn't serve a practical or religious purpose. I once
sent her flowers on Mother's Day, only to receive a long lecture
on the importance of saving money and not wasting it on perish-
able decorations. The next year I sent her dried ones, but she still
didn't approve, saying the only gift she wanted from her children
was their happiness, and, in my case, the additional news that I
was about to marry a good Sikh girl who displayed the traditional
skills of cooking, knitting and sweeping.

But Regent's Park actually turned out to be a good idea. It
was the first properly warm day of the year, but not so warm
that people were lying around semi-naked, offending Mum's
sensibilities, and London was at its international best, sprinkling
the park with families from a dazzling array of nations, including
India – sufficiently different from Wolverhampton, without being
totally alien. We spent two hours sitting on a bench there, as
Mum brought me up to date on the latest family news (Bindi's
family had decided to emigrate to Canada, she and my father
had opted to leave Dr Dutta's care and registered with another
practice, Puli's eldest daughter was being put forward for a place
at a local grammar school – *what I would do for her to get the place*)
and I began the task of running through her story, checking facts
about her arrival in England and her time in Grays. She asked
for a few things to be taken out, for a few identities to be
concealed, insisted I was nice about relatives – she didn't want
anything to ignite any festering feuds or start new ones – and
then, because she wouldn't let me get a taxi, we got the Tube
home.

This time I hadn't prepared my flat for her arrival. I left it as
it was: wine in the fridge; bottles of vodka and sherry on the
sideboard; photographs of me with both male and female friends
on the walls; multiple toothbrushes in the bathroom. All that went
were the men's magazines with their semi-naked women on the
covers, and all I added was a bottle of full-fat milk. I used it to
make Mum some English tea, which she accepted with a wince,

before we moved to the sitting room, where she flinched at the sight of the leather sofa, as she had done when she stayed on the way back from Grays, and sat on the floor, from where she ran through the second bit of her story: her time in Wolverhampton, Dad's hospitalizations, the birth of my siblings. This time she remembered an entire committal that she had not mentioned before, a time when my father, who had taken to walking around the streets with a radio, smashed it in a hospital corridor while waiting to see a hospital consultant, and her first trip back to India after being married, when her own mother didn't recognize her, because she was succumbing to dementia. By early evening, we were spent: it doesn't seem to get any easier running through the story. Mum suggested we have supper.

I stood in front of the microwave in the kitchen, watching a plate of *sabzi* revolve behind the dark glass, and wondering how on earth I was going to bring up the subject of the letter. My chance came when Mum called out for me from the bathroom.

'Come and tell me how much I weigh. I don't think the scales at home are accurate.'

I went and read the numbers that were too small for her to see, even with her glasses.

'Excellent, I've lost half a stone in a day then,' she laughed. 'And what's your weight now? You look so thin.'

She would say this if I was thirty stone and waiting for a triple heart bypass, but I saw a potential opening and took it.

'Yeah, I've lost quite a lot of weight recently.'

'How much?'

'A stone.' This was a slight exaggeration, but I had to use every tool at my disposal, including emotional blackmail.

'Over what time?'

'Month or so . . .'

'*Hai rabba.* I knew you shouldn't have written this story. I told you it was going to be too stressful.'

'Well, there has been that. But there's something else.' I felt like I was going to throw up again, but at least the toilet was

309

only a few feet away. 'Mum, you remember when you started telling me about what happened with Dad, and you said, "I've always wanted to tell you this, but didn't know how?" Well, I've got something like that . . . something I've been meaning to tell you for a long time. I just haven't known how to . . . So I've written you a letter explaining it . . .'

'A letter?'

'I've written a letter and had it translated into Punjabi.'

'Why can't you just tell me?'

'My Punjabi is rubbish.'

'I can understand you perfectly.'

'But there are some things I don't have the . . .' Gulp '. . . words for . . . and . . .' Oh God '. . . find difficult to talk about. Anyway, I've also had a tape recording made of the letter. Which would you prefer?' She was wearing an expression on her face I'd not seen since I was fourteen and asked if she would pay for guitar lessons.

'I'll read it, it's no problem . . .'

In the kitchen, the microwave pinged, indicating that supper was ready. It would go cold.

★

As Mum read the letter on the living room floor, I did the courageous thing and hid under my duvet in the bedroom, shivering and thinking: this is what it must feel like waiting to be executed. I thought Mum would come and get me when she was done, but after three-quarters of an hour she still hadn't emerged. I got up and put an ear to the living room door, a thousand fears – heart attack, suicide – racing through my mind. But eventually there was a sniffle and the sound of a page being turned. Which was encouraging, in a way. I went to my study to shiver on the sofabed, underneath the blank, disintegrating wall where the 1800 x 1200mm professional dry-wipe magnetic whiteboard had once hung. When I tired of that I got up and sat at my desk, clicked on ten or twenty websites whose content I couldn't digest, lay across the floor and stared at the ceiling I was supposed to have painted three years earlier, and the lightbulb I hadn't replaced for a year, got up and stood in front of my bedroom mirror to squeeze a spot, plugged my mobile phone into its recharger, rearranged the books on my bedside cabinet into alphabetical order, noticed and hid a pair of kinky handcuffs sent by a PR company – *how would I have explained those?* – and glanced at my watch to discover that the previous hour had actually amounted to ten minutes.

I was back at my desk in the study, with my head in my hands, when I heard the living room door opening, more than an hour after I'd handed the letter over. I didn't have the courage to look up, turn around and make eye contact, and sat frozen as Mum padded into the bathroom.

She didn't say anything until the door was almost fully closed behind her.

What did she say?

She said: 'You should eat now. It's getting late.'

I knew then I might have something resembling some hope.

*

I was standing next to a bookcase with my hands in my pockets when Mum returned to the living room. She didn't say anything initially: just reached out and pulled me towards her. After the tears had been wiped away, she asked: 'Why didn't you mention this before?' It was one of those questions to which the answer was simultaneously so simple and so complicated that I couldn't articulate a response. Mum continued, regardless. 'Why didn't you tell me before? I kept on asking you . . . "Have you got a friend?" Didn't I ask you?'

I eventually managed to stammer some words out: 'You've never asked me!'

'I said it to you the other week: didn't I tell you what the neighbour was saying? You should have guessed what your mother was trying to ask.'

'Okay, so once, one time, last week, you almost mentioned it, but it wasn't really a question. What about the years of nagging and photos and phone numbers and set-ups?'

There was an interval during which she considered what I said deeply, and then decided to ignore it completely. 'You should have understood what your mother was trying to ask you. For years, whenever people have mentioned you to me, they have said, 'He must have a friend. No one says no to that many girls unless they have a friend.' So then, do you have a friend? Do you have a *gori* you want to get married to?'

I cringed again at the vocabulary. '*No*.'

'But you've written here you have.'

'There was someone . . . a couple actually . . . have you read the letter?'

'Yes, I read it twice. What happened to them?'

'They ended. For various reasons. A couple are married now. With babies. They might not have worked out anyway. But part of the problem was that I could never tell you.'

'So who do you like now then?'

'I "like" no one.'

'You haven't got a friend – what's the pressure then?'

'Because . . .' I remembered what my emotional blackmail coach had said: be firm; stick to your guns. 'Because . . . whenever I meet anyone I start worrying they won't be acceptable to you and the family and before I have even worked out if we get along or not, it's ending. It's up to you: either you can tell me I can do what I want and I can have a life, or I am never going to find anyone and be happy.'

At this point she stepped away from one CD stand, the tower dedicated to the works of Stephen Duffy and Ryan Adams, towards another, dedicated to the works of George Michael and Stevie Wonder (what is it with me and male singer-songwriters?), and moved to the leather sofa. It was a sign of the uncharted territory we had entered that Mum actually sat on it. I took the Habitat armchair at right angles to her and listened as she churned out the objections. She said she disagreed with what I'd said about our religion: Guru Nanak was beyond caste because he was a spirit of God, his rules didn't apply to mortals like us; Guru Gobind Singh went into battle to defend the religion and said it was important to stay true to your culture. It was crucial to know about your caste and to marry within it. What was the point of an education if I didn't understand that? Why did I think I should be an exception? Everyone else seemed to manage it. She went on for some time. But there was something about the relaxed way in which she ran through the arguments – she actually laughed at one point – *laughed* – that gave me the surreal sense she was only going through the motions. And then, finally, they came, the words I thought I would never hear.

'Having said that, I'm not going to pressure you. I don't want you to wreck your life. I didn't work so hard bringing you up so you would be unhappy. What would be the point of that? I've read your letter, and I understand. What time has come has come. You shouldn't struggle to fit into a role you can't fit into . . .'

Even the police sirens perpetually ringing around Brixton seemed to be stunned into silence by the revelation.

'. . . There is only one thing I ask . . .'

Ah, the caveats.

'By all means get married to who you want, as long as she is not a Churi or Chamari.'

'What?'

'The Churas and Chamars are different from us.'

'Huh?'

'In India . . .'

'Mum, what are you on about?' I think she was confusing my incomprehension with objection.

'So if you met a Chamari girl – you wouldn't know how they differed from Jats?'

'I know the Chamars are a type of caste but have no idea of the significance.'

'In India the Chamars are leatherworkers.'

'Right.'

'And Churas are sweepers.'

'And?'

313

'They have a different culture to us.'

'Mum, we live in Britain and we're not farmers any more.'

'But this is your history, your culture.'

'I have few Indian friends, and those Indian friends I do have, I don't know or care what caste they are. And that's not the point anyway. To be honest, if I ever manage to persuade anyone to marry me, they will probably be . . .' It was so weird and so amazing to be able to say the words '. . . English.'

'It would be better if you married a *gori* than a Churi or Chamar.'

I laughed out loud, partly out of overwhelming relief, partly at the ludicrousness of the distinctions.

'A Takan, someone of the carpenter caste, would be better too, or a Hindu, but it would be difficult with a Chamar. Not because they are inferior, I have lots of friends who are Churas and Chamars, they are good people, they are just different. They don't like to marry outside their caste either. I mean if you want to do it, if you really want to marry a Chamar, go ahead and marry one, but . . .'

'*Mum* . . .'

'. . . there are so many lovely Jat Sikh girls out there . . .'

'I know. But if it doesn't happen you have to accept who I end up with.'

'You should try to find a Jat Sikh girl but don't screw up your life for us. If you have no love, there is no life. I have passed my days with your father, and he is unwell, but he has always loved you kids, he has never wanted to leave me and it's my duty now to look after him. Maybe I will have a better life next time. But you have to be true to yourself. I want to see you happy. From the youngest age you have not caused us any trouble. Your brother has sorted his life out, now you should. You are very old now.'

'*Mum.*'

'What will be will be. It's neither in your control nor in my control, and even though I say don't get married to a Churi or Chamari, if that is who it will be with, then that is who it will be with. You have a holiday from me. I did put pressure on you,

I know, but you were a child, and I was worried you would get divorced.'

'Divorced?'

'One of the reasons I didn't want you going around with girls, was that I had your fortune told and he said, if you got married before twenty-eight you would get divorced. I almost made myself ill with worry.' None of this was going in: I still had the Punjabi for 'You have a holiday from me' going around my head, and had suddenly remembered that I hadn't watered the plant next to the telly for a month. 'But now it's okay. I had your fortune told again and he said everything is okay for you now. You'll get married in a year or two. We will see what happens.' She was smiling, as if she knew something I didn't. 'You think I don't know what's going on, but I listen to the British news on the Punjabi radio station and I talk to people and I have changed. I have my values, I am religious, but I don't live like I'm in India. There is only one thing I ask of you . . .'

'Yes, I understand, no landless labourers.'

'No, the one thing I ask is . . .'

'Mum, you already said you only want one thing.'

'The second thing I ask is that if you are going to hang out with *goris* and *goras*, just don't drink too much with them.'

'Mum. No one drinks more than Punjabis.'

'You see *goras* on TV sometimes, drinking . . .'

'Mum. No one drinks more than Punjabis.'

'. . . acting crazy, jumping around like baboons.'

'Mum. No one drinks more than Punjabis.'

'I know, I know, your brother-in-law tells me the stories of picking up people in his taxi, of how even Indian boys and even Indian girls behave these days.' She shook her head in despair. I was shaking my head in disbelief. 'Anyway, I want you to write in your book that I told you you were free.' She picked up the letter, folded it up and put it into one of her carrier bags. 'Now tell me, how much did the translation cost you?'

'Two hundred dollars.'

She clutched her chest.

'But he did such a good job I ended up giving him three hundred.'

'*Hai rabba*. For that much money, I would have written it for you.'

★

Curiously – but then, as I said when we began, none of this was expected – there was no euphoria in the weeks that followed. There was relief. Incredible relief: my heartbeat slowed down to below 180 b.p.m.; I stopped wanting to throw up; and I slept well for the first time in months. But there was no celebratory bhangra, no bopping around to Curtis Mayfield's 'Move On Up', no sudden desire to start campaigning for greater understanding of schizophrenia, or against the imprisonment of the mentally ill.

Maybe it was because when I went home with Mum to Wolverhampton – I wanted to spend some time at home, to make sure she wasn't putting on an act – we immediately returned to our usual bickering, spending the train journey back arguing about everything from my refusal to wear a jacket in the twenty-four degrees of sunshine ('You'll catch a cold!'); my purchasing of a book ('Can't you borrow them from a library? You waste so much money'); to the fact that I had two coffees ('You'll send yourself around the twist with all that intoxication').

Maybe the urge to whoop was instinctively checked out of sensitivity for my siblings. After all, their lives had been defined by similar anxieties, and some of them were still suffering the repercussions of trying to please Mum – I had to be careful about how I told them. Or maybe I couldn't make sense of Mum's reaction. Had she been persuaded by the arguments in the letter? If so, which ones? Meanwhile, the stuff about the fortune-teller was flummoxing. If he'd predicted I'd be divorced if I got married before the age of twenty-eight, and if that was why Mum didn't want me to have any relationships, then why did she try to set me up with so many Punjabi girls during that time?

Indeed, it is only now, sitting at a table in a West End restaurant renowned for its service and its seven-hour lamb, a list of forty-six questions inscribed on an A4 pad sitting on my lap, a moderately famous businessman sitting opposite, explaining that there's no such thing as a typical day in his life, or giving me his views on climate change – to be honest I'm not really listening – that something resembling if not euphoria, then satisfaction, is kicking in. And it is kicking in because my mobile phone, sitting on the table between us, is blinking at me, telling me I have an incoming call, and the incoming call is from my mother, and seeing the letters 'HOME WOLVES' flashing, I realize that the jolt of fear I used to experience whenever my two lives short-circuited like this, the worry that my family had found me out and that my mother was calling to disown me, has gone; and though I don't entirely understand *why* Mum was so cool about the letter, I understand it doesn't matter, I just need to accept she has changed, and the thing is, it has taken me so long, a lifetime, to understand the basic fact that people and things can and do change, that Wolverhampton has changed, my father has changed, Puli has changed, Bindi has changed, Rajah has changed, that even I have changed, though not as much as my mother – the distance she has travelled, from collecting cow manure in baskets for fuel in the fields of the Punjab to my leather sofa in Brixton, is a greater distance than I have travelled from Prosser Street to this restaurant – and not completely either, because I'm not suddenly going to give up George Michael for Bob Dylan, or stop worrying or change my life by beginning a campaign for greater understanding of schizophrenia, because another thing I have learnt about myself, or rather, had confirmed about myself, is that dwelling on misery makes me unhappy, that I prefer flitting around lighter subjects, and, you know, even though I suspect this executive has little to say, it's *such a pleasure and a privilege to be here*, to have a new job on a new newspaper that pays me to listen, or not listen to him, to know I'm not going to need a bottle of vodka to get through writing about the encounter, but I have changed, most importantly in the respect that I'm no longer running away from my family, I talk to Puli all the time, I'm taking my parents to visit Bindi in Canada next year, my best friends, a boy and a GIRL, are coming to spend time with me in Wolverhampton soon, and now my interviewee has noticed I'm not really listening, and is asking whether I need to take the call, I'm not going to say, 'It's just my mother,' and let it go to voicemail, like I used to, I'm going to take it, and talk to her, even though I know she is only calling to ask whether I've eaten my lunch, or tell me what she has been up to, or possibly give me the mobile number of a potential bride, because she hasn't changed completely either, and still wants me to marry a Punjabi girl, and, you know what, I might even meet the girl, because I'm looking for love, and another thing I have learnt is that you can find it anywhere, and if we get on, we get on, but if we don't, or if I find someone else who is a Zulu or a leatherworker, I'm not going to beat myself up about it, because I know now my family will love me regardless of what I do or do not do, and that is a feeling I never expected to feel and this is a moment I wouldn't change for anything.

Acknowledgements

It's an understatement, but I am grateful to my family for their love and encouragement. In relation to this book, I would like to thank them in particular for allowing me to subject them to lengthy interviews on painful subjects, and for giving me permission to write our story. Which is not to say they necessarily agree with my views or version of events – and, of course, any errors are entirely my own. I am also indebted to those members of my extended family who generously provided background information – Balbir Sangha, Phuman Sangha, Malkit Sohi and Mohinder Sohi – and to the family of my late Chacha, Kashmir Singh.

These words would never have been written if Mary Mount, my remarkable editor at Viking, had not got in touch, listened, and convinced me that books aren't always written by other people. Meanwhile, I would not have had the courage to follow things through without the support of my brilliant agent, Kate Jones, and my precious friends Robin Roberts, Lachlan Goudie, Lottie Moggach, Preetha McCann, Joanna Manning-Cooper and Lucy Ellison.

Further back, I would like to thank Tony Burgess and Keith Ball, formerly at Woden Junior School, for cajoling my family into submitting me for a place at Wolverhampton Grammar School, and at WGS I was fortunate that David Radburn and James Lockley were there when things got dark. I would also like to thank Peter Rhodes at the *Express & Star* for giving me my first break in journalism, and James Harding for attempting to rehabilitate my career more recently.

Love, thanks and, in some cases, apologies also to: Richard Adams, Waheed Alli, Harleen Anand, Kamalpreet Badasha, Hartosh Bal, Lionel Barber, Alan Beattie, David Bell, Venetia Butterfield,

Tom Catan, Helen Chapman, Peter Cheek, Andrew Davis, Mike Duff, Steve Gandar, Matthew Gwyther, Jennifer Harris, Emma Jacobs, Kate Johnson, Lucy Kellaway, Annie Lee, Jagtar Malhi, Gautam Malkani, Deborah Moggach, Cathy Newman, Alex O'Connell, John O'Connell, Laura Sampson, Gurharpal Singh, Raminder Singh, Bernard Trafford, Emma Tucker and Adam White.

To the staff at the Croft Resource Centre in Bilston, I would like to express my enduring gratitude for the unrecognized and under-funded work they do; and finally, here's to the next generation, my adorable and adored nephews and nieces: Harminder, Jaspal, Jasveen, Simran, Manraj and Kiran. Know where you come from, but don't let it stop you becoming who you want to be.

List of Illustrations

All photographs taken from the author's personal collection, with the exception of the photograph on p. 263, reproduced by permission of Wolverhampton Archives & Local Studies.

He just wanted a decent book to read ...

Not too much to ask, is it? It was in 1935 when Allen Lane, Managing Director of Bodley Head Publishers, stood on a platform at Exeter railway station looking for something good to read on his journey back to London. His choice was limited to popular magazines and poor-quality paperbacks – the same choice faced every day by the vast majority of readers, few of whom could afford hardbacks. Lane's disappointment and subsequent anger at the range of books generally available led him to found a company – and change the world.

'We believed in the existence in this country of a vast reading public for intelligent books at a low price, and staked everything on it'
Sir Allen Lane, 1902–1970, founder of Penguin Books

The quality paperback had arrived – and not just in bookshops. Lane was adamant that his Penguins should appear in chain stores and tobacconists, and should cost no more than a packet of cigarettes.

Reading habits (and cigarette prices) have changed since 1935, but Penguin still believes in publishing the best books for everybody to enjoy. We still believe that good design costs no more than bad design, and we still believe that quality books published passionately and responsibly make the world a better place.

So wherever you see the little bird – whether it's on a piece of prize-winning literary fiction or a celebrity autobiography, political tour de force or historical masterpiece, a serial-killer thriller, reference book, world classic or a piece of pure escapism – you can bet that it represents the very best that the genre has to offer.

Whatever you like to read – trust Penguin.